# GETTING INTO THE ACT

During the last quarter of the eighteenth century in London there was a remarkable surge in the number of produced plays written by women. In fact, it was the largest showing since women had entered playwriting for the first time over one hundred years before. *Getting Into the Act* argues that this infusion was intimately connected to developments in theatre management, and particularly to the career of David Garrick. Garrick's management of the Drury Lane Theatre made it possible for a number of female playwrights to secure a foothold in the profession. But as these women rapidly emerged from contingency status into full-fledged professional membership, their very success began to undermine the prevailing expectations around gender. By 1829, the momentum of this earlier period was broken, and in critical discourse and public memory, these female playwrights had all but disappeared.

Ellen Donkin explores the careers of seven such women playwrights. This tiny cohort created a formidable pressure and presence in the profession, in spite of contemporary obstacles. However, it is disturbing to discover that women today still make up only about 10 percent of the playwriting profession. Donkin argues that old patterns of male approval and control over women's drama have persisted into the late twentieth century, with undermining results. But she also believes that by paying close attention to these histories, we can identify the insidious repetitions of the past in order to break through them, and imagine a fuller and more resolute presence for women in the profession.

**Ellen Donkin** teaches theatre at Hampshire College in Amherst, Massachusetts. She is the co-editor with Susan Clement of *Upstaging Big Daddy: Directing Theater as if Gender and Race Matter* and has written widely on issues of gender in theatre history and practice.

# GETTING INTO THE ACT

## Women Playwrights in London
## 1776–1829

*Ellen Donkin*

London and New York

First published 1995
by Routledge
11 New Fetter Lane, London EC4P 4EE

Simultaneously published in the USA and Canada
by Routledge
29 West 35th Street, New York, NY 10001

© 1994 Ellen Donkin

Typeset in Baskerville by
J&L Composition Ltd, Filey, North Yorkshire
Printed and bound in Great Britain by
Biddles Ltd, Guildford and King's Lynn

*British Library Cataloguing in Publication Data*
A catalogue record for this book is available from the British Library

*Library of Congress Cataloguing in Publication Data*
Donkin, Ellen
Getting Into the Act: Women Playwrights in London, 1776–1829/
Ellen Donkin.
p.     cm.—(Gender in performance)
Includes bibliographical references (p.     ) and index.
1. English drama—19th century—History and criticism.   2. Women
and literature—England—London—History—19th
century.   3. Women and literature—England—London—History—
18th century.   4. English drama—Women authors—History and
criticism.   5. English drama—18th century—History and
criticism.   6. Women dramatists, English—19th century—
Biography.   7. Women dramatists, English—18th
century—Biography.   8. Theater—England—London—History—
19th century.   9. Theater—England—London—History—18th
century.   I. Title.   II. Series.
PR734.W6D66   1995
822'.6099287—dc20        94–48735

ISBN 0-415-08249-8 (hbk)
ISBN 0-415-08250-1 (pbk)

*for Larry*

# CONTENTS

# LIST OF PLATES

# LIST OF FIGURES

# ACKNOWLEDGEMENTS

The people who made a difference: Tracy Davis and Nina Payne.

Special thanks for help of all kinds to Talia Rodgers of Routledge, Serena Weaver of the Hampshire College Library; Deborah Payne, Jack Wolcott, Mercedes Lawry, Helen Bacon, Joe Donohue, Doris Abramson, Margaret Cerullo, Susan Bassnett, Ciji Ware, Joe Keller, Miriam Slater, Jill Lewis and Penina Glazer. Thanks also to Cerena Ash, secretary to Lord Harrowby; Cathy Cherbosque of the Huntington Library, Kathy Innes of Pembroke Street Daycare, David Jesson-Dibley, Michael Wilson, Ellie Prosser, Alan Read, John Lutterbie, Kathleen Donkin, Audrey Bibby Donkin, Heidi Holder, Stephen Archer, Margaret Fielders and Kathy and Walter Rose.

I would like to acknowledge the following institutions for generous financial support: Hampshire College through the Hewlett-Mellon Foundation, the William Andrews Clark Memorial Library in Los Angeles, the Folger Shakespeare Library, and the American Council of Learned Societies. For permission to reproduce prints and letters, my thanks to the Public Archives of Canada, Ottawa; the Huntington Library in San Marino, California; the National Library of Scotland; the Folger Shakespeare Library, Washington D.C.; the Society of Antiquaries, London; the National Portrait Gallery, London; the Donald Hyde Collection, Somerville, New Jersey; the Harvard Theatre Collection, Cambridge; the Princeton University Library; and the Harrowby Manuscript Trust at Sandon Hall, Stafford. For intellectual and moral support, my thanks, year after year, to the members of the Women in Theatre Program of the Association for Theatre in Higher Education.

My essay "The Paper War of Hannah Cowley and Hannah More," is reprinted courtesy of the Ohio University Press, publishers of *Curtain Calls*, edited by Marianne Schofield and Cecilia Macheski (1991).

Finally the family: this book honors the memory of my great-grandmother Mary Sheridan of Ireland and New York; my grandfather, George William McKay Donkin of Nova Scotia and New York; my godmothers Julia Park and Dorothy Fiske Claxton, and Margaret Soltis. Special tribute to my parents, Audrey and Willis Donkin, my husband Larry Winship for unflagging generosity and support, and my daughters, Molly Donkin Winship and Grace Cobb Winship.

# 1

# OCCUPATIONAL HAZARDS
## Women Playwrights in London, 1660–1800

In 1660, Charles II issued permission for actresses to join the legitimate theatre.[1] It has been a common error in theatre history to assume by extrapolation that women were thereby also welcomed into other areas of theatre practice, particularly playwriting. They were not. Cultural and economic resistance to women *creating* meaning by becoming playwrights continued long after it became acceptable for women to *carry* meaning onstage as performers.

Of all playwrights whose plays were being produced in London from 1660 to 1800 only about seven percent were women. At certain points the percentage was higher, and at others it was lower. But taken as an average, there were ninety-three male playwrights for every seven female playwrights. Perhaps this should not astonish us. There were mitigating factors in the culture, some of which I hope to make plain in this chapter, which made entering the theatre, especially for the daughters of the emerging middle class, which all of our playwrights were, a risky proposition.[2] But two things have astonished me. The first is that for years, it never occurred to me to question why the numbers were so low. The information, such as I had in those days, constituted an unconscious judgment on women's capabilities and interests, rather than an entry point for inquiry and investigation. In the absence of information, I reflexively constructed for myself a history of defeat.

The second thing that has astonished me, now that I have actually undertaken those investigations, is that there were any women playwrights at all. Given the constraints – economic, educational, social, and legal – the fact that a handful of women made their way to the top of the profession has changed not only

1

how I assess that history of women in playwriting, but also how I assess the historians who erased it. The constraints on women as playwrights did not stop with death or retirement. There was a powerful tendency in historians and critics to minimize or dismiss a woman's work in the theatre if she were not an actress; to assume after the fact that women's contributions to most artistic enterprises were a form of pastime, rather like the way young eighteenth-century women of a certain class learned music, drawing, and dancing.[3] The feminist historian is constantly battling an uneasy sense that she is recovering marginal histories and second-rate art, and to what purpose? Setting the record straight? Complicating the dull master narratives? Yes, she is setting the record straight and complicating the dull master narratives. But at the heart of this operation, she is peeling back the protective layers to expose the mechanics of a system that worked with remarkable efficiency to keep women voiceless, propertyless, and acquiescent.

Playwriting as an art form holds a particular fascination for me because it is a collaborative art form. As such, it is distinctly different from the writing of novels or poetry, which can take place in relative peace and privacy. Writing for the theatre puts a playwright into immediate physical contact with a host of people and tangible objects connected to the fact of production. My operating assumption in this book will be that the work of any playwright is strengthened immeasurably by that contact, and by concrete first-hand exposure to that backstage production process. But my other operating assumption will be that gender expectations in the eighteenth century complicated that contact in ways that need careful clarification. The prevailing wisdom has been that theatre was somehow a more "public" form of writing, that it exposed women (actresses and playwrights alike) to wicked company,[4] and that a woman's reputation was at risk of contamination on contact. All of these things were true to some extent, but they leave certain questions begging, and in any case they have little resonance for a twentieth-century reader; they seem quaint and distant, of another period and another set of mores. My hope is that in the specificity of the cases I have chosen, this comfortable sense of "quaintness" will give way to something a good deal more disturbing and recognizable.

The seven playwrights who are the primary focus of this study, Hannah Cowley, Hannah More, Frances Brooke, Sophia Lee,

2

Elizabeth Inchbald, Frances Burney and Joanna Baillie, represent about one quarter of the total number of women whose plays were produced in London between 1775 and 1800.[5] They experienced widely different degrees of success, but the fact that they were produced at all meant that they had already negotiated a range of social prohibitions successfully before the fact of production. In fact, because the system was so tightly controlled, it is probably more accurate to think of these women as the *designated* survivors of the system, the ones chosen to succeed. Ironically, their presence – which ostensibly demonstrated the openness of the field to all comers – had the effect of showing that in spite of the open doors, only a small fraction would succeed anyway, reinforcing a general notion that women were inherently unsuited or unequal to the task. This kind of demonstration had the effect of preserving the status quo: even as it foregrounded the exceptions, it restated and underscored the principle.

The secondary focus of this study is the theatre managers. When I speak of the "system" being tightly controlled, and of these women being the designated survivors of that system, I do not speak metaphorically. The eighteenth-century theatre managers occupied positions of enormous discretionary power with respect to theatrical production in London. In the three theatres which concern this study, Drury Lane, Covent Garden, and the Haymarket, all the managers were male, white, and middle-class. As individual personalities, they were as distinct from one another as any group of people could be, but as middle-class men of the period they partipated in certain social expectations around gender that indelibly marked their working relationships with women playwrights. They are a useful focal point because they give a human dimension and voice to the otherwise rather nuts-and-bolts process of theatre production. In other words, by tracking a woman's experience of theatre production through her work with one of the theatre managers, we are better able to assess just how that process was inflected by gender.

However, in any analysis of this kind, it is important to contextualize the struggles of women playwrights within the larger economic operations of theatre production. In fact, the obstacles facing any playwright, male or female, were formidable. At the very point when women were finally permitted to perform onstage, Charles II simultaneously restricted the number of theatres that could operate legally in London, from the diverse multitude that characterized Elizabethan and Jacobean London, to only two houses. The process was called "patenting," and the Crown was the sole giver of patent rights. This maneuver by the Crown was originally rationalized as an economic contingency (the would-be patent holders complained of competition outstripping the market, and the Crown benefitted from payments from the patent holders), but more recent scholarship has suggested that limiting dramatic representation in London facilitated political surveillance and control.[6] As the eighteenth century unfolded, the number of legitimate houses eventually inched its way up from two to three and stabilized there (Drury Lane, Covent Garden, and finally the Haymarket for summer shows on a year-to-year renewable license). Houses for other related kinds of entertainment (music, opera, and animal acts) came and went. But the number of legitimate houses to which a playwright could apply in London was astonishingly small, compared to what it had been in the days before the Commonwealth, and the situation was made worse by the fact of London's late-eighteenth-century population boom. Frances Brooke, in her novel *The Excursion,* summed up the state of things from the perspective of a worldly-wise character named Mr. Hammond. It is his painful task to inform a bright and gifted young woman that her play has been dismissed out of hand by a key London theatre manager, who has just made a series of elaborate excuses to Mr. Hammond:

> Would it not have been wiser, as well as more manly, [said Mr. Hammond to Maria] to have said in the clearest and most unambiguous terms, "Sir, we have no occasion for new pieces while there are only two English theatres in a city so extensive and opulent as London; a city which, in the time of Elizabeth, when the frequenters of the theatre were not a tenth part of the present, supported seventeen. We will therefore never receive any new production but when we are compelled to it by recommendations which we dare not refuse: nor will I read the tragedy you bring, lest its merit should make me ashamed to reject it."[7]

In addition to the limited number of places to which a playwright could apply, the material a playwright could draw upon

4

became increasingly restricted. By 1737, the Licensing Act legalized blanket restrictions on any kind of political or religious content in plays. This overt censorship had drastic consequences for the kinds of plays allowed into production for the next two centuries. It was particularly true of the last quarter of the eighteenth century, the period on which this study focuses, that the French Revolution created widespread paranoia in England, and that the Licensing Act made it possible to eliminate at the source plays making any reference to social struggle. Most politically volatile plays never made it past the manager and consequently were not even submitted to the censor. Later in the century, the office of the censor also became extremely squeamish about any references to things sexual. For most of the eighteenth century, because the number of legitimate theatres was so tiny, it was possible for the Lord Chamberlain's office to maintain rather careful control over what they produced.

Censorship could take other forms as well. The eighteenth-century audience was extremely verbal and responsive by today's standards. A new show could be shut down completely by being "damn'd" by an audience on opening night. Mrs. Inchbald experienced audience response as a form of mob rule. She wrote this oft-quoted statement about the difficulties of being a playwright:

> The Novelist [by comparison] is a free agent. He lives in a land of liberty, whilst the Dramatic Writer exists but under a despotic government. Passing over the subjection in which an author of plays is held by the Lord Chamberlain's office [the Censor responsible for enforcing the 1737 Licensing Act above], and the degree of dependence which he has on his actors – he is the very slave of the audience. He must have their tastes and prejudices in view, not to correct, but to humour them . . . the will of such critics is the law, and execution instantly follows judgement.[8]

However, the most immediate problem facing a playwright was where and how to get a script produced. The power of those two or three managers was absolute in the matter of considering scripts: even before a script was submitted to the censorship of the Lord Chamberlain's office, it had to be read, approved and scheduled by the manager. Managers were deluged with scripts. Playwrights described coming into a manager's office and

5

discovering stacks of untouched manuscripts numbering in the hundreds. Making one's way up to the top of that pile required attracting special notice or having some leverage, unless one already had a track record as a successful playwright. In this, oddly enough, women may have had a small advantage, since being female tended to mark them as a curiosity.

One additional complication for new playwrights, male or female, was how to get a good working knowledge of production and stage mechanics. The introduction on the public stage of moveable scenery around 1660 had a profound effect on the *writing* of plays. Practical considerations for a playwright might include the following: how quickly and in what sequences could the scenery be made to shift? How long did a line of dialogue need to be in order for an exiting actor to get offstage? How many layers of activity could be simultaneously facilitated by scenic elements to create situations of multiple eavesdropping? What constituted audience expectations for elapsed time between scenes?[9] If a novice playwright was not a working actor, or at least a company hanger-on, and had not learned the craft through performance itself, the only other avenue of entry into a working knowledge of theatre craft was to watch a great number of plays or to be carefully edited by a manager willing to take the time. But in the first case, attending plays regularly, there were certain logistical difficulties. Seats in the London theatre were not reserved except in the case of people who owned boxes or could send servants ahead to wait in line and hold their places. For everyone else, there was a considerable wait before the doors opened under conditions that were always inconvenient, and often unsavory. It was a situation that probably discouraged a number of would-be theatregoers, particularly women without an escort or without means.[10]

Conversely, if a novice playwright was lucky enough to receive the editorial attentions of the manager himself,[11] there was yet another level of complication. Those managers who were the most astute and capable editors of drama were themselves also playwrights. David Garrick (1717–1779), Richard Brinsley Sheridan (1751–1816) and both the George Colmans (the Elder 1732–1794, and the Younger 1762–1836), are conspicuous examples. Their playwriting experience at once conferred upon them a special competence for dealing with novice playwrights, but it simultaneously put them in the awkward position of being in competition with those novices. During the eighteenth century, a manager's annual salary was generally fixed for a given year. Additional income could come from several sources, one of which was producing his own dramas. As a general rule, playwrights received a benefit on the third, sixth and ninth evening, if they were lucky enough to have a play last that long. A benefit meant that once a certain specified amount of overhead had been cleared at the box office, the remaining box-office take went to the playwright. The play's copyright could be purchased either by the theatre or by a publisher, although once it was printed, it was in the public domain. As a whole, playwrights made their money on their benefit nights, or by negotiating a flat fee with the manager before the run, which necessarily put the risk back onto the manager, since the playwright was supposed to get paid whether the show failed or succeeded. This kind of arrangement, however, seems to have been reserved primarily for playwrights with a proven track record.[12] As a general rule, in any given season it was economically prudent for management to use as many "old" plays as possible, that is, plays already in the public domain. This way he maximized the amount of income for the house and minimized the amount going out in playwrights' benefits.[13]

However, the public understandably expected a certain amount of novelty. Deciding who would be placed in one of the limited available slots and how many slots there would be for new plays was an important part of the manager's job. If the manager himself also happened to be a playwright, it was clearly to his personal advantage to reserve some of these openings for himself. This was never called a conflict of interests; it simply was the way things worked. The unchallenged prerogative of the manager was to designate how many open slots there would be and who would get them. It made the prospects for a beginning playwright very narrow indeed.

For the time being, however, let us imagine that our playwright, female or male, has maneuvered past these obstacles and miraculously (or otherwise) had a script read and accepted by one of the theatre managers. A fair copy together with a letter of application signed by the manager has been submitted to the Lord Chamberlain's office, and (with a handful of negligible changes) has been returned to the manager with permission to perform. There were still a host of contingencies connected to production which could materially affect a playwright's chances for success. There was the cast. The actors could protest a script, learn its lines incorrectly, or simply fail to show up for an opening performance. Two examples from the experience of the women will illustrate, although this was by no means a problem experienced by women playwrights alone: Aphra Behn's *The Dutch Lover* (1672) was allegedly sunk by an actor who never learned his lines and ad-libbed his way through the entire performance. Later, Susanna Centlivre's comic classic *The Busy Body* (1709) was rejected by the actors, who were at some pains to sabotage rehearsals and create bad publicity for its opening. Needless to say, it rarely mattered to an audience whether problems like these were the fault of the playwright or not. If a show was poorly performed and damned by an audience, it could be closed on the same night it opened. There would be no further performances at all, and no benefit night for the playwright. The play had to survive into a third night for the playwright to see any financial return. By the second half of the eighteenth century, a successful play could generate as much as five or six hundred pounds for its playwright, which was a very substantial sum for the period, certainly enough to keep the playwright comfortably provided for until the next script was forthcoming. So a great deal rode on production itself, the area in which playwrights frequently had very little control, especially on opening night.

There were other dangers connected more directly to the discretionary power of the manager. If a manager was unscrupulous and wanted to use a play without paying a large sum to the playwright through legitimate benefit nights, he could delay its opening to a period of the season in which normal box-office receipts were low anyway, or when end-of-season actors' benefits made it difficult for anything else to play successfully. Even if the play was a success, it meant that he paid out a lower amount of cash overall than he would have if it had played at the height of the season. After the ninth night, if it lasted that long, he could purchase the copyright cheaply and milk it for as long as it brought money into the theatre over the next fourteen years. Maneuvers of this kind were always difficult to prove, but the evidence of Hannah Cowley's experience with Richard Sheridan (see Chapter 3) strongly suggests that Sheridan's legendary delays and graceful excuses to playwrights with accepted scripts almost certainly had an underlying economic motive.

We come now to a more difficult and elusive area, which is the way women faced obstacles to becoming playwrights that were a consequence of gender. I have broken these down into two rough areas: education and conduct.[14] Both areas were indirectly but deeply connected to theatre. They constituted the preparation that would have preceded a woman's actual entry into a manager's office with a manuscript in hand, and also a template for behavior once the play had moved into production.

Education was a potent means for imposing separate sets of expectations on female and male children. One of the things that characterizes the backgrounds of male playwrights is some access to formal education. There were schools for boys and colleges for men. The schools often encouraged theatricals as a part of routine training at the secondary level, and so a young man heading off to university was already familiar with Terence and Seneca, and had perhaps memorized and performed hundreds of their lines. By contrast, schools for young women at the secondary level were comparatively rare in the early part of the eighteenth century. They proliferated during the century (Sophia Lee's school in Bath and Hannah More's in Bristol are two examples among many) but there were frequent debates in journals and other publications about whether young women were getting any substantial training, or if these institutions were really in place to instil airs and graces. I have found no evidence to indicate that young women during this period were trained in declamation or oratory; the emphasis seems to have been on music and drawing. College education for women in any formal sense did not exist. There is an apocryphal story that as a very young woman, Susanna Centlivre cross-dressed and followed a male friend into his rooms at Cambridge, where she stayed and studied in disguise for several months before finally getting caught. The incident is usually offered to illustrate Centlivre's youthful high spirits or the illicit love lives of women in theatre, but it has struck me that its real subtext is that in order to obtain education, a woman had to enter the university in drag.[15]

Typically a girl's primary education was handled privately at home on a probationary basis, often by an indulgent father or male relative. If there was a tutor, it was because he had been hired to teach a brother, so access to tutoring was contingent upon how long the brother studied at home. This form of teaching ran the twofold risk of alienating an ambitious young woman from her mother, who was often without formal training, and of laying the groundwork for a later sense of dependency on a primary male figure to give her access to intellectual life. The system, such as it was, conspired to underscore her sense that agency in the world of letters was only hers through the auspices of the male mentor or guardian. As Vivien Jones sums up, the overwhelming effect of available education for young middle-class women "was to reinforce rather than undermine obtaining gender definitions."[16]

In the absence of extensive education, role-modelling could provide certain compensations. For example, the playwright Edward Moore (1712–1757), whose formal education was actually quite limited, began life as a linen draper and wound up a playwright (his most successful plays, *The Foundling*, 1748, and *The Gamester*, 1758, were a standard part of the repertory well into the nineteenth century). He appears to have suffered none of the anxieties one might have expected in making the transition. As his biographer points out, "it was quite natural that the son of a minister who had written at least one small book, the grandson of another who had written a controversial pamphlet or two, and the nephew of a schoolmaster who had a book to his credit, should turn to letters as a means of livelihood."[17]

The career of the playwright Richard Cumberland (1732–1811) offers a useful insight into the way women within the family often were positioned in the course of a young man's educational development. Cumberland's maternal grandfather was the noted literary critic Dr. Richard Bentley (1662–1742). It is clear from Cumberland's memoirs that the presence of this grandfather was a powerful one, but his early training in literature was actually managed by his mother, Bentley's daughter Joanna. Cumberland wrote:

> She had a vivacity of fancy and a strength of intellect in which few were her superiors: she read much, remembered well, and discerned acutely: I never knew the person who could better embellish any subject she was upon . . . All that son can owe to parent, or disciple to his teacher, I owe to her.[18]

The complexity of Joanna's contribution to Cumberland's development is that she established an intellectual *conduit* from the grandfather, but did not attempt to establish herself autonomously as a woman writer or to move in intellectual circles outside of the family. Cumberland's expectations of himself (to fulfil a Bentley tradition in letters) and of women (to service *his* professional development but not their own) are paradigmatic for a man of the age. In the chapters that follow, there are two documented incidents of his overt hostility to two other would-be women playwrights: Charlotte Lennox in 1769 and Frances Burney in 1779. These incidents suggest that Cumberland's sense of world order did not include tolerating women either as colleagues or as competitors.

Formal schooling also led to connections outside the academy that were to offer important professional introductions and develop into a network later on. Cumberland, for example, was educated at Trinity College, Cambridge, and was subsequently employed by Lord Halifax as a secretary. Halifax, by chance, owned the country estate next door to David Garrick's. Upon hearing that young Cumberland had written a play, Halifax marched over to see Garrick, play in hand, and insisted that Garrick read it in hopes that he would approve it for production at Drury Lane. This at least got Cumberland to the top of the manuscript pile. After two days, Garrick returned the piece with the requisite apologies, but the connection had been made, and Cumberland was to follow it up to advantage in later years. His story contrasts vividly with Hannah Cowley's, who submitted her first play to Garrick and then waited humbly for a year before daring to approach him for some kind of response.[19]

Moore's networking was rather more circuitous. In the 1740s he became a friend to Henry Brooke, a distinguished literary and political figure, who subsequently introduced him to George, Lord Lyttelton, himself member of a literary circle into which Moore was invited. Brooke is probably responsible for having introduced Moore to Thomas Arne, a composer at Drury Lane, and the brother of the well-known actress (and sometime playwright) Susanna Cibber, who in 1748 helped to make Moore's first play a major success. It was in fact Arne who encouraged Moore to be a dramatic writer, and who probably introduced Moore to David Garrick.

The significance of these convoluted paths to success is not

11

that women were barred outright from literary circles *per se* (Hannah More was a familiar figure among the *literati*), nor that they were prevented from making acquaintances in the theatre. But a young woman whose background was genteel enough to have included education was unlikely to be as mobile in public as this kind of networking made necessary. No matter how educated, she could never have become a secretary to anybody. Nor was it possible for her simply to be a hanger-on at coffee houses or the theatre itself, picking up ideas and gossip and a sense of the way theatre worked, without seriously compromising her reputation. Education was difficult, role-modelling was very difficult, but informal opportunistic networking was almost impossible if respectability and reputation were to be maintained.

By contrast, middle- and upper-class males in the seventeenth and eighteenth centuries belonged to an educational tradition and had literary ancestors with whom they could identify. They felt themselves mobile within a network of possibilities. This is not to imply that they did not meet with their share of setbacks, but it does suggest that they had more equipment at their disposal for surviving those setbacks. They operated from a sense of entitlement and mobility that was a gendered legacy.

The second area that had important consequences for a woman's decision to be a playwright was the area of conduct. Barring formal prohibitions against women being playwrights, what kinds of messages were women getting about appropriate female conduct that might have prevented them from putting themselves forward, as professionals, as writers, as playwrights? In other words, even if the theatre had not presented itself as a place of dubious morality, were there deeper constraints which mitigated against "committing art" (to use Joanna Russ's term) of any kind, and particularly an art form like theatre which required collaboration?[20]

I am imagining now a young woman with a modest education who has seen some plays, and realizes that she is starting to spin scenes in her head. She wants to commit them to paper. She does. She conceives of taking them into London and submitting them to a manager. She does. The play is accepted. It is approved by the censor. She is given some suggestions for revision by the manager. She listens to it being read informally by actors in the green room, and discovers she has some revisions

12

of her own. She is anxious to know how the scenery will look, how the piece will be cast, and what production date is assigned. She watches rehearsals, makes further cuts, strengthens and focuses a character in response to an actress's inspired interpretation. She consults with the manager about a scene that feels dead, no matter how it is played. She cuts the scene. The actor whose scene it was is upset. She inserts more lines for him in another section of the play, and he is mollifed. It is opening night. One of the actors turns up drunk, but he sobers up in time to get his costume on and make his entrance. She sits with her family in the manager's box; there is a ripple around the house as the news spreads that she is the author. She feels faces in the crowd turning in her direction. The play meets with approval. After the epilogue, there are shouts of approbation. The audience now turns *en masse* to applaud her in her box. Electrified, she nods her acknowledgement.

The obvious place to begin is with the conduct books. There is one extended passage which I will quote in full because it imaginatively counters opposition from young women with thwarted ambitions. The writer is Thomas Gisborne, M.A., and the year is 1797:

> The sphere of domestic life, the sphere in which female exertion is chiefly occupied, and female excellence is best displayed, admits far less diversity of action, and consequently of temptations, than is to be found in the widely differing professions and employments into which private advantage and public good require that men should be distributed . . .[21]
>
> Young women endowed with good understandings but . . . disappointed at not perceiving a way open by which they, like their brothers, may distinguish themselves and rise to eminence; are occasionally heard to declare their opinion; that the sphere in which women are destined to move is so humble and so limited, as neither to require nor to reward assiduity; and under this impression, either do not discern, or will not be persuaded to consider, the real and deeply interesting effects which the conduct of their sex will always have on the happiness of society.[22]

Gisborne goes on to name the three "particulars in which the effect of the female character is most important:"

First, in contributing daily and hourly to the comfort of husbands, of parents, of brothers and sisters, and of other relations, connections and friends, in the intercourse of domestic life, under the vicissitudes of sickness and health, of joy and affliction. Secondly, in forming and improving the general manners, dispositions, and conduct of the other sex, by society and example. Thirdly, in modelling the human mind during the early stages of its growth, and fixing, while it is yet ductile, its growing principles of action; children of each sex being, in general, under maternal tuition during their childhood, and girls until they become women.

Are these objects insufficient to excite virtuous exertion? Let it then be remembered that there is another of supreme importance set before each individual; and one which she cannot accomplish without faithfully attending, according to her situation and ability, to those already enumerated; namely, the attainment of everlasting felicity, by her conduct during her present probationary state of existence.[23]

The conduct books of the eighteenth century have been carefully considered by feminist historians elsewhere; my particular contribution to this larger discussion is only to remark that if we imagine a young woman growing up with these kinds of expectations – stated or unstated – circulating around her, it is difficult to conceive of the circumstances that would allow her to leapfrog over this long line of people who, according to Gisborne, have a prior claim to her care and attention, and plunge into a deeply absorbing activity that not only demanded all of her resources but also required that she be away from home. It is interesting in this context how many women who do take the plunge are careful to frame their artistic activities in terms of family duty, providing for children, and so forth. Charlotte Lennox wrote Garrick in 1775: "I am not indifferent to theatrical rewards; could I obtain them, they would assist me to bring up my little boy and my girl . . ."[24] Strained family finances were a central motivating factor for many women who ventured into theatre (why else would anyone take on the risks involved?), but given the expectations around conduct for the period, it is small wonder that family emergency was a necessary precondition for many women to justify their venturing outside of the home in the first place. In any case, their determination to provide for their families constituted them as cultural males, but in the context of family survival, their willingness to undertake professional exposure was deemed to be an unfortunate and necessary sacrifice, more deserving of sympathy than of censure.

There is another area of discussion in Gisborne's conduct book which gives us some clues about middle-class daughters and prevailing attitudes towards the theatre. It comes as something of a surprise to learn that although he is disturbed by what a young woman might hear by attending a public performance, he is even more concerned about the impact on her of doing amateur theatricals in a private home:

> Among the usual causes by which female modesty is worn away, I know not one more efficacious, than the indelicate scenes and language to which women are familiarised at the [public] theatre . . .
>
> For some years past, the custom of acting plays in private theatres, fitted up by individuals of fortune, has occasionally prevailed. It is a custom liable to this objection among others; that it is almost certain to prove, in its effects, injurious to the female performers.

He then lists the kinds of injury that this experience is likely to inflict on females:

> To encourage vanity; to excite a thirst of applause and admiration on account of attainments which, if they are to be thus exhibited, it would commonly have been far better for the individual not to possess; to destroy diffidence, by the unrestrained familiarity with persons of the other sex, which inevitably results from being joined with them in the drama; to create a general fondness for the perusal of plays, of which so many are unfit to be read; and for attending dramatic representations, of which so many are unfit to be witnessed.[25]

Gisborne's list of the undesirable appetites which home theatricals might generate is precisely the same list we would have to draw up if a young woman planned to work effectively as a playwright in a theatre environment. She had to dispense with diffidence in order to communicate effectively with managers and actors; she had to circulate freely backstage so that she could take in rehearsals and anticipate problems with actors; she had to read and see plays routinely in order to understand better the complexities and potentials of her craft. And last but not least, she had to be ambitious and want the applause and admiration that came with a successful production. "Vanity" is Gisborne's word because it suggests the sinfulness of such needs. But it is difficult to imagine why anyone, especially a woman, would undertake playwriting if they did not have powerful incentives, financial or otherwise. It was a gruelling process, and the risks were high.

One of the other areas which comes up repeatedly in the conduct-book literature is the issue of obedience and compliance. This passage is taken from a conduct book about married life, and unlike most conduct books, is written by a woman.[26] The date is 1798:

> Men have naturally great Obstinacy; the best of them have some of it: They all have Pride too; and the best of them some times the most of it. They do not love to be forced, nor even to be persuaded out of their Customs. They cannot bear to be led by a Woman to any Thing. They have a settled Opinion of us, as Inferior in Natural Authority and in Understanding; and it will have an Appearance of Meanness to themselves, to be guided by those whom they should direct; or to be governed by those whom they should command. Endeavour not to get the better of this Opinion: I believe it is justly founded; but, if it was not, 'tis not your Business to reform the World; nor can it be your Interest to hazard your own Happiness upon a dangerous Experiment.
>
> It is not enough that a Wife in all Things does what her Husband requests that is at the best, in the Language of the greatest Judge in the World, being but an unprofitable Servant. I have recommended to you, my Dear, a Conformity of Mind, Temper and Sentiment; that you may be able to execute all that a Husband can request, without the making it a matter of Obedience . . . You will resemble him in all his Sentiments; his opinions, his Determinations will all be yours; and you will act as he would wish it without his naming it. The Wife, on my Principles, should be in all her Thoughts, in all her Actions, the Attendant and true Resemblance of her Husband; *she should no more depart from*

*him than the Shadow from the substance*; nor should she any more than that can be, unlike to him. [my italics][27]

The image of the woman, the wife, as *Shadow* is a powerful one because it activates two very contradictory lines of reasoning. On the one hand, the woman as shadow has the opportunity for the kind of close observation and empathy which are essential for insightful and detailed character development in any form of writing. On the other hand, the woman as shadow has no separate identity from the dominant male, be he husband, father or brother, and so it is difficult to imagine all of this close observation resolving itself into an artistic point of view, a defined authorial subjectivity, unless there had been a concomitant separation from the shadow self that made writing possible. It is scarcely necessary to observe that any woman going into playwriting as a profession would have to have undergone some kind of separation from the shadow self in order to survive the process. If she was the generator of the script and the scenario, if she had intentions for her characters which needed to be made clear to the actors, if she was to survive the necessary pain of having to cut lines and scenes appropriately, and if she was going to hold her manager to the terms of their financial agreement, she needed a model for self-assertion and consultative collaboration which was the antithesis of this prevailing model of submissive selflessness.

This concept of the shadow self is by no means limited to the pages of conduct books. It was reinforced most palpably in the law. A married woman as a *feme covert*[28] (*sic*) virtually disappeared as a legal entity, and relinquished to her husband all control over her children, her property and her earnings. Susan Staves writes that even though the laws appeared to change significantly in the years between the Restoration and the mid-nineteenth century, in fact what she sees is a recurring pattern by which, through legal means which vary ingeniously from one period to another, "patriarchal society rules concerning married women's property have always functioned to facilitate the transmission of significant property from male to male; entitlements of women have been to provide them with subsistence for themselves and minor children dependent upon them."[29] By contrast, women who stayed unmarried, while they maintained a certain legal autonomy, were extraordinarily constrained in the ways in which they might earn even a subsistence living.[30] Writing, in fact, was one of the very few ways in which a woman could earn money, and writing for theatre had the potential, at least, of earning for the playwright a windfall of money in a relatively short space of time. For women like Hannah Cowley, Elizabeth Inchbald, Frances Brooke, Sophia Lee, and Frances Burney, there is clear evidence that the prime motivating factor for undertaking playwriting in the first place was a struggle for economic survival, for themselves and for their dependent families. The struggles this book records must be understood not just in the context of playwriting as a form of artistic expression, but playwriting as one of the handful of ways a woman might earn a living.

Women grew up learning the rules of dependence upon men. These rules were not a form of charming lip service to convention, but a necessary means of justifying and coping with economic bondage on a day-to-day basis. Without "significant" property or political weight, they were powerless to substantively influence the way their society had positioned them. The conduct books, in a variety of ways, give women instruction on how to submit gracefully and even purposefully, to a life of secondary dependent status, married or unmarried.

Playwriting, as a profession, violated all the rules of conduct. It conferred on women a public voice. It gave them some control over how women were represented on stage. It required that they mingle freely with people of both sexes in a place of work that was not the home. It made ambition a prerequisite, and, perhaps most importantly, it offered the possibility of acquiring capital. In other words, playwriting was something of a loophole; it allowed women to push the system considerably further than it was prepared to go.

There was one circumstance that mitigated in women's favor. Rebecca Gould Gibson's research has shown that from the Restoration forward, there had been a slow, steady increase in the number of women publishing poetry. The numbers escalated gradually until about 1769, when there was suddenly a surge in numbers, with another major surge in 1785.[31] Judith Phillips Stanton's figures for a variety of genres concur, although her figures show the major increase in published poetry, fiction, letters, religion and autobiography by women taking place between 1760–1769, a decade before the same increase takes place in drama. Her findings show big increases for women publishing in drama from 1770–1779.[32] These increases in all forms of writing undoubtedly had a domino effect. I am intrigued particularly by the fact that the increase in drama appears to be later. Why would drama be the "copycat" genre, the one to follow all others? It may mean that writing for the theatre continued to pose the most problems, perhaps because it was so closely connected to the idea of production, and that any involvement in production necessitated rethinking eighteenth-century rules of female conduct.

\* \* \*

The long view of this 140-year period of women in playwriting reveals two rather distinct clusters of activity and a hiatus in between. The first active period runs from about 1670 (Aphra Behn's first professional production) to 1717. Other active women during this period were Mary Pix, Delarivière Manley, Catherine Trotter, Jane Wiseman, and Susanna Centlivre. Then follows a period in which the number of new women writing plays diminishes quite drastically, and the momentum appears to be broken. During this period, which lasts from about 1717, the date of Susanna Centlivre's last new production, to 1750, there are productions by Eliza Haywood, Charlotte Charke, and Elizabeth Cooper, but these productions are spread quite thinly over a thirty-five-year period. The precise beginning of the second period of activity is a little more difficult to determine. In 1750 we pick up a pulse: Catherine Clive wrote and performed in a piece for her benefit night. She was followed by more productions of women's plays in 1755, 1763, and again in 1765. After 1765, there was a slow but steady rise in new productions by women playwrights, which accelerated noticeably in 1779, and continued through to the end of the century. Then beginning in 1800, there was a rapid tapering off, both of new women playwrights, and of produced plays by women playwrights.

These alternating periods of increased and decreased activity for women playwrights were structurally related. When women entered the field in the 1670s, the idea of a female playwright was a novelty, and it generated a good deal of testing. A gender boundary had been broken, that is, a job which had always been the province of men was now open to invasion by women. The collective response of the culture was to seek ways of labelling

these women that would stigmatize them and limit their economic and artistic mobility. Not everyone was disposed to be
hostile; one of the benign figures of this period was the manager
Thomas Betterton, to whom several women playwrights wrote
very flattering and grateful prefaces. But as a whole, the culture
gave its angriest and most hostile members permission to speak
their minds. There were no cultural inhibitions or prohibitions
in place to counter those voices, whether they came from the pit
on opening night, or in the press the day after. It was a free-for-
all. Women playwrights were labelled libertine, whore, hussy,
harlot, amazon, and sappho. Virtually no woman whose work
was produced professionally during this initial period escaped
this kind of calumny. The name-calling did not stop after their
deaths; eighteenth- and nineteenth-century theatre historians,
particularly on the subject of Aphra Behn, routinely lost all
control. This loss of reputation was an occupational hazard for
the period, a kind of "professional expense." For a number of
women interested in writing for the theatre in the period after
1717, this cost may simply have been too high, which would help
to account for the drop in numbers.

After this dry spell, women started to re-emerge as playwrights
in the last half of the eighteenth century. This time, however,
something was substantively different. There were incidents of
hostility, to be sure, and expressions of contempt in various
venues (usually from men inside the profession), but taken as a
whole, women playwrights occupied a space of relative security
and respectability by comparison to their seventeenth- and early-
eighteenth-century sisters. Many of the same old arguments that
had appeared in the conduct books since the seventeenth century persisted (that a woman's first duty was to her home, that
women were to avoid public life at all costs), but the attacks on
women were increasingly isolated events, and were often countered in public media with equally strong voices claiming that
women were capable of "genius" and that attacks on them were
"illiberal." In other words, it was no longer a foregone conclusion that women had no place in playwriting. It was a subject for
spirited debate.

The underlying reasons for this shift in the way women playwrights were positioned are at the core of this study. There was a
new element of protectiveness in the air that had not been in
place sixty or seventy years before. My hypothesis is that the

relationship between the woman playwright and her theatre manager had undergone an important transformation that was a peculiar compromise between the ideology of womanhood, as it is evidenced in the conduct books, and a growing pressure from competent, literate women of a growing middle class that they be allowed into this profession. It is no accident, surely, that this cultural compromise was struck in the midst of a ground-swell of women publishing in other genres. One wonders if there was some anxiety in the theatre community that either one had to follow suit or risk being labelled resistant and illiberal.

I have described the theatre manager earlier as being a very powerful figure. Historically, his relationship with male and female playwrights had been largely a matter of personal style. Some managers were neglectful, some abusive, and some bene-volent. But during the second half of the century, a certain ethos began to emerge which formalized the relationship between manager and playwright into something resembling patronage. This new version of the theatre manager was also a mentor. He took on the job of editing, encouragement, guidance, protection, and even financial advising. There is no evidence of this kind of relationship in the first half of the eighteenth century, nor in the last part of the seventeenth. The new manager's assistance and attention was by no means limited to women playwrights, but it was to have crucial implications for their work and their sense of professional acceptance, much more so than for men.

Evidence for the beginning of this evolution towards the manager-as-mentor is largely anecdotal but fairly consistent. As far back as 1660, stories about the actor-manager Thomas Betterton reveal a pattern of benign neglect where the develop-ing work of new playwrights is concerned. He was warmly praised by Mrs. Manley on at least two occasions:

> I have since often heard Rivella laugh and wonder that a Man of Mr. *Betterton's* grave Sense and Judgement should think well enough of the Productions of a Woman of Eigh-teen, to bring it upon the Stage in so handsome a manner as he did, when her self could hardly now bear the reading of it.[33]

And again, in the preface to her *Almyna*: "[It was] admirably Acted . . . owing to Mr. Betterton's unwearied care, (who is desired to accept the Author's acknowledgements for so faithfully discharging the Trust that was repos'd in him)."[34] But the encomiums have to do with mounting the plays rather than with developing them as texts. Her use of the phrase "Trust that was repos'd in him" is suggestive of a transaction in which the playwright handed over her work to the manager, *fait accompli*. I have found nothing in the memoirs and histories of the period to suggest the kind of relationship whereby a fledgling playwright might have advanced a draft to the manager and then under that manager's supervision developed the script into production. Produced playwrights were allowed to either sink or swim. The scholarly consensus is that new playwrights were treated poorly, both at the Duke's Company (Betterton) and at the King's Company (Christopher Rich).[35] Mrs. Pix had a play stolen outright from her by the King's Company, and Mrs. Manley's experience of rehearsals at King's was so abrasive that she migrated over to the Duke's Company. Women playwrights seem to have gravitated to Betterton, perhaps because he was, officially at least, co-managing the Duke's Company with the actresses Elizabeth Barry and Anne Bracegirdle, and it was a potentially more congenial atmosphere. But in any event, women playwrights did not flock to Betterton because there was any training to be had in playwriting: there was no training ground for *untried* playwrights at either company.

Did this *laissez-faire* treatment of novice playwrights have particular implications for women? I think it did, some of them positive. When a woman during the Restoration decided to be a playwright, regardless of class, she had to abandon conventional notions of female propriety.[36] The problem was not so much becoming a *literary* woman, but a literary woman *in the theatre*, for as Mendelson argues:

> Perhaps the most enduring legacy of the Civil War was women's entrée into the male domain of publication. The huge flood of printed works by women of the Interregnum did not cease at the Restoration; instead there was a further incursion into masculine preserves as women like Aphra Behn turned to secular subjects. This trend marks the beginning of a long process of evolution whereby literature lost its 'male' status as a professional discipline and became neutral intellectual territory, accessible to both sexes. So long as a woman avoided immodest subject matter and disguised

her literary ambitions through anonymous or pseud-
onymous publication, she could write and even print her
works without jeopardizing her personal reputation.[37]

For a literary woman in theatre, avoiding "immodest subject
matter" and disguising her literary ambitions were well nigh
impossible if she sought successful production in the main-
stream, particularly during the Restoration. Luckily, Betterton's
*laissez-faire* attitude made it possible for a woman interested in
writing plays to destroy her reputation of her own free will. He
did not set himself up as a father figure, and try to "protect"
women from themselves by disallowing their presence in the
theatre as playwrights. Women could, under Betterton, join
the club and mix freely with male counterparts in order to
learn about theatre. How else were they to familiarize themselves with the actors for whom they wrote, with the stage
machinery that would dictate the rhythm and speed of scene
changes, with the tastes of the audience, except by mingling,
talking, observing, and asking questions? Unlike their literary
sisters writing poetry and novels, they did not have the luxury of
retreating to a garrett room with paper and pen: that was a
component of the work, but only one among several.

The other positive aspect to this laissez-faire policy was that
women apparently could become quite centrally involved with
production. For example, Aphra Behn, when she worked under
Thomas Betterton, had some control over how her plays moved
from the page into production. When the actor Edward Angel
ruined *The Dutch Lover* by ad-libbing his lines, she wrote afterwards that she had known he was a risk beforehand: "which
though I knew *before I gave him yet the part*, because I knew him so
acceptable to most o' th' higher Periwigs about the town." [my
italics][38] This fragment indicates that she had been involved in
casting the play. She shows herself a seasoned professional,
someone whose knowledge of the actors and her audience is
intimate, and whose regret over the incident is tempered by her
consciousness of having weighed an unavoidable risk as best she
could. We have scant information about whether or not Behn's
production work also extended into the territory we now designate as directing, but her biographer comments further that *The
Widow Ranter*, produced after her death in 1689, "was a failure

partly because Behn wasn't there to cast it and oversee the production."[39]

The picture of Behn that emerges during her twenty years of work for Betterton sums up the complexity of the situation in which women playwrights found themselves in the late seventeenth and early eighteenth centuries. On the one hand, the internal structure of management, at least under Betterton, appears to have been one in which a woman playwright might integrate herself successfully into the production process, increase her knowledge of stagecraft, and exercise some control over her productions. On the other hand, the mobility and power which that integration implied laid her open for inflated and vicious criticism, from men and women both, and from countless theatre historians and chroniclers afterwards. This early period was a trade-off between reputation and professional mobility. Playwriting by its very nature did not allow for the kind of privacy that was culturally linked in the conduct books to chastity and virtue.[40]

This unpredictable combination of generosity, benign neglect and outright abuse of new playwrights continued well into the first half of the eighteenth century. Little or no systematic help was offered to beginning playwrights, nor was there any need seen to institute such help. Many important playwrights survived and matured without it, but these playwrights were all men: William Congreve, John Dryden, George Farquhar, Nathaniel Lee, Thomas Otway, Edward Ravenscroft, Elkanah Settle, Nahum Tate, George Villiers and William Wycherley in the late seventeenth century, and Joseph Addison, Colley Cibber, Henry Fielding, George Lillo, Nicholas Rowe, Richard Steele, and Sir John Vanbrugh in the early eighteenth are some of the most familiar names. The list of female playwrights during this same period is a small fraction of the list of men, and the relative number of plays they wrote even smaller.

That so few women could have destabilized the prevailing cultural norms is surprising, but they did. Centlivre's career in particular raised powerful questions about how the culture was to acknowledge its women playwrights. One strategy had been to ignore them entirely. In all of Jeremy Collier's 1697 tirade against the stage, for example, the presence of women as playwrights is completely erased. Women play an important role in his argument as actresses, but as playwrights they simply never appear.[41] However, after Centlivre, it became increasingly awkward to ignore them; the enduring success of plays like *The Busy Body*, *A Bold Stroke for a Wife*, and *The Wonder! A Woman Keeps a Secret* was incontrovertible evidence that women could write for the stage successfully. But if women were becoming a permanent presence in the theatre, both as actresses *and* as playwrights, might it be possible to incorporate and regulate that presence, instead of attempting to dismiss or defeat it?

The problem was intrinsically a more difficult one to solve than it had been with the introduction of actresses, because actresses, by virtue of appearing on stage every night, were constantly under surveillance, subject to the approbation or disapprobation of that very vocal audience. Women writing plays operated a little outside of that circle of light. What was needed was a combined form of surveillance and sanction, one that made it possible finally for women to enter playwriting but within certain culturally approved boundaries. As sometimes happens, this need for sanction and surveillance coincided perfectly with another agenda, which was the long overdue need to offer beginning playwrights some systematic guidance as they learned their craft. It was a perfect intersection of two distinct agendas. Developing a script in response to the practical inner workings of the theatre was the area in which respectable young women wanting to be playwrights were most at risk, in terms of personal reputation and competent craftsmanship. The manager as a combined chaperone and mentor, *in loco parentis*, must have presented a very timely solution. If the daughters and wives and mothers of the middle class were determined to abandon home and venture forth into this disreputable area, it was some measure of comfort that this new venue would replicate home by putting the manager into place as mentor, father, "*patronus*."

At this historical juncture, sometime between Centlivre's death in 1723 and the midpoint of the century, David Garrick appeared. He worked for some years as an actor, and then took over the management of Drury Lane in 1747, where he stayed until his retirement in 1776. For the managers who worked alongside him and those who succeeded him, he redefined theatre management. He had none of the rapacious commercialism of Christopher Rich or the overtly hostile tendencies of Colley Cibber.[42] His career, from beginning to end, was marked by an extraordinary consciousness of himself as a public figure, and eventually as a public icon. This kind of high profile was unprecedented in the history of theatre management. He did not just produce for British middle-class culture; in a sense he *represented* that culture. He worked all his life at constructing a public presence for himself and his theatre that combined urbane wit with moral respectability and fiscal responsibility. He ran a conspicuously clean shop. Among his theatre-manager contemporaries, there were unconscious efforts to imitate him: in both George Colman the Elder and the Younger, in John Philip Kemble, in Richard Brinsley Sheridan, and even in the flatfooted person of Thomas Harris. Even when the manager was not himself a playwright, like Harris or Kemble, or unwilling to extend himself to new playwrights, like Sheridan, the patronal quality of Garrick's management continued as a *style*. Above all, Garrick was a man with whom one could trust one's daughter, and families of the middle class did, both literally and figuratively.

Garrick took pride in his reputation for helping new playwrights, but he took particular pride in having helped new female playwrights. He took pleasure in their public demonstrations of gratitude, usually in prefaces, and occasionally indulged himself by reflecting on the women he had helped in letters to friends.[43] But his mentoring, as I hope to show, also contained certain invisible hazards for women playwrights. At its core, it functioned to establish monitoring and control of the influx of these women, even as it gave a select few professional access. The benevolent model he set up for mentoring obscured the fact that by taking some initiative where women were concerned, he also was in a prime position to determine which women, and how many, would be selected.

As one of Garrick's chosen, a female playwright risked being positioned as a "literary daughter," someone who had been singled out for special attention by the literary "father."[44] Her identity as a writer for theatre depended upon the approving presence of that "father." This pairing of the male mentor and the chosen daughter invoked parallel formations in the education and conduct literature. Women were trained to please; this coupling of the daughter and the father was at once a part of that training and a testament to its success.

In fact, the approval of the manager was essential for getting a play produced by any playwright, male or female. But among women, the sense of debt appears to have extended well beyond the practicalities of editing and producing, and to have worked its way into the creative mechanism itself. For Cumberland and Moore, writing was the natural inheritance of men of a certain class and educational background. But when the literary father chose to cross gender lines and offer a place of privilege to the literary daughter, to invite her into a community of dramatists, a cultural expectation was breached: the woman became a producer of culture rather than its conduit. Hence the necessity for positioning her as literary *daughter*, no matter what her age or stage of development. If she was the grateful recipient of discreetly publicized editorial advice and protection from the manager, her creativity and autonomy could always be called into question. She could always be returned to conduit status again.

One feminist historian calls this the "imposter syndrome," suggesting that the manager's help and protection became so important that the woman's sense of herself as a writer became wholly dependent upon his ongoing support and approval.[45] In its most extreme forms, a woman's pride and pleasure in her own success was diminished by an uneasy sense that without him she could not have written her plays, never mind have seen them into production. She began to wonder if somehow he had written plays *through* her. She felt like a fake.

The only escape for a woman in this situation was to survive this first stage of mandatory mentoring by having a play produced successfully, and then to begin building a more independent career based on her own reputation. However, that meant a psychological separation from the mentoring manager. The transition was not always easy. The women in this study who were long-term survivors, like Hannah Cowley, Elizabeth Inchbald and Frances Brooke, have histories that are marked by conflict, disobedience, or adversarial behavior. These were the prerequisites for separation and survival. By contrast, Sophia Lee bowed out early, Joanna Baillie foundered, and Frances Burney – although she discovered the necessity for the break and was finally able to make it – did so too late for a playwriting career. Of these seven playwrights, Inchbald seems to have sensed most acutely how the protection offered by managers colluded to construct the correspondingly docile and grateful presence of the female playwright. Inchbald kept a careful

27

distance: the prefaces of her plays are conspicuous for the absence of encomiums to managers and the sustained refusal to thank anybody.

Were these conflicts different in kind from those Garrick had with male playwrights? Could it not be argued that Garrick's power – and indeed the power of any theatre manager – was so enormous that this kind of anxiety to please would have been equally a problem for incoming male playwrights? The difference, I think, is an important one. Male playwrights who found themselves in an adversarial relationship with Garrick over the editing or producing of a script – Arthur Murphy, Joseph Reed, and Samuel Crisp, to name only a few – were dependent upon Garrick for production. They were not dependent upon Garrick for *legitimizing their right to apply for production.* The consequence of this difference is that the women, with no exception, buried their negative feelings about Garrick, if indeed they had any, in private correspondence[46] or deeper still, in the unconscious. The men did not operate from the same sense of endangerment. Their entitlement to the profession of playwright had historical precedent and security. As a result, they were much more likely to take Garrick on directly, either in correspondence, as Joseph Reed does, or in prefaces like Murphy's, which take Garrick to task in full view of the reading public.[47]

The women's conflicts, conscious or unconscious, are important for us not because the women had named dominant ideology as the enemy or because they had an articulated feminist postion. They had not. In fact, Inchbald found Mary Wollstonecraft objectionable, and Lee was outspoken in her dismay at the prospect of equality between the sexes. But there was opposition being staged, not so much in the plays, as I read them, but submerged in the day-to-day details of their production and pre-production experiences.[48] These were, to use Jameson's term, "*muffled* oppositional voices," [my italics][49] in the sense that the formulations of feminism which were to follow in the late nineteenth century were not yet sufficiently established to lend any conscious structure to their experiences. But I am irresistibly compelled by how these women operated in their prefaces, their rehearsals, and their dealings with managers, to create pressure for a voice and a presence in their culture, a *subject* position, the power to represent self. Whether they named the struggle or not, they knew they were entering a system which historically had demonstrated overt hostility towards women. Their stories show all the conflicted signs of women artists caught between the cultural constructs of femininity, and a driving need from within to achieve artistic recognition and financial autonomy. But because their legitimacy within the profession did not have the same degree of historical precedent as it did for the men, their conflicts have to be interpreted and extrapolated rather differently.

One wonders how and why Garrick's support of women playwrights got started in the first place. His actual record of support for women playwrights, upon close examination, is somewhat less risky and innovative than my convenient historical narrative might lead one to suppose. It is absolutely true that Garrick was operating more consciously with respect to gender than any other manager of his period. But it is important to keep the actual size of his contribution in perspective, because, like everything else about Garrick, his reputation starts to become larger than life. In point of fact, it could be argued that Garrick's contribution was as much a matter of setting a trend in motion as it was of actual intervention.

In 1750, just three years after Garrick had assumed the management of Drury Lane, his leading comic actress, Catherine Clive, wrote an experimental one-act for her benefit night. It was a brilliant success. The play was called *The Rehearsal, or, Bays in Petticoats*, and it was weirdly prophetic. It featured a female playwright, pointedly named "Mrs. Hazard," who has had a play accepted for production at Drury Lane. But in her desperate efforts to get her play rehearsed, she becomes the laughing stock of her friends, and is left to the tender mercies of the apathetic Drury Lane stage manager and a recalcitrant cast. The manager of the theatre is conspicuously absent, as is the leading actress (an ill-behaved hussy, also named "Catherine Clive," who doesn't even bother to show up for rehearsal). Mrs. Hazard finally storms out of the theatre in a rage, determined never to write for the stage again, and both her rehearsal and the play itself come to an abrupt halt.

I have often wondered if this play didn't pose a challenge for Garrick that lingered in the back of his mind until he decided to act upon it. The challenge, as I imagine it, was this: what if Mrs. Hazard had *not* been abandoned to the cynical laughter of her friends and the contempt of the cast? What if the manager had

29

decided to take a more active role on behalf of women play-wrights, instead of letting them become laughing stocks? I have no way to prove that this was either in Garrick's head or in (the real) Catherine Clive's when she wrote her play, but it was as if a gauntlet had been thrown down. *Who, the play seemed to say, is going to bring Mrs. Hazard back into the theatre?*

Clive (not the character, but the actress/playwright) followed this play up with another play a decade later in 1760, one in 1761, another in 1763, and a fifth in 1765. Each new play was bracketed by the fact that Mrs. Clive had written solely for her own benefit night, and in that sense was not to be considered with the same seriousness as a playwright who takes the chance of a full run. I wonder at what point actresses writing plays crossed a certain line and became playwrights. In any case, I think her success with *Bays in Petticoats*, and perhaps even the story of the play, may have put a slow-growing idea into Gar-rick's head. In 1755 he produced *The Oracle* by Susanna Cibber (also a lead actress in his company). In 1763 he produced Frances Sheridan's *The Discovery* and later in 1763 a second play by Sheridan, entitled *The Dupe*. He then produced Eliza-beth Griffith's *The Platonic Wife* in 1765, and *The School for Rakes* in 1769.[50] In 1771 he produced Dorothy Celisia's *Almida*, which had a decent run, and Henrietta Pye's *The Capricious Lady*, which did not. In 1775 he produced Charlotte Lennox's *Old City Manners*, and then, just months before his retirement in 1776, Hannah Cowley's *The Runaway*, which was probably the biggest success of them all. As a retirement project, after leaving Drury Lane, he shepherded Hannah More's play *Percy* into production, and began editing More's *The Fatal Falsehood*.

Sometime during that decade of 1750 and 1760, between Mrs. Clive's first and second play, Garrick must have decided that it was Mrs. Hazard's turn to get into the act. He began slowly and carefully. The early model of the woman playwright in this period is the actress who, like Clive and Cibber, has decided to dabble, or, like Frances Sheridan and Dorothy Celi-sia, is the wife or daughter of a colleague.[51] I think Garrick wanted to ease himself in, keeping the risks to a minimum. But later, with Griffith, Lennox, Cowley and More, he took on women who were outside the London theatre community and willing to commit to an entire run. Taken as a whole, Garrick's record comes to fifteen productions (including one of Hannah

More's) by women during twenty-nine years of theatrical management. About six of these productions were one-night benefits, leaving nine productions by women that had full runs. These nine productions constitute a slender record, spread out over twenty-nine years, but they mark an important departure from what had preceded Garrick and had a long-term influence on what was to come.

\* \* \*

Around the turn of the century, beginning in about 1800, I see a fairly rapid deterioration of the momentum that had characterized the last quarter of the century. There are occasional plays produced by women, but no one emerges to replace Elizabeth Inchbald or Hannah Cowley as a long-term professional until Catherine Gore in the 1830s.[52] The concept of the manager as mentor to the playwright had atrophied. Playwrights could not expect even minimal editing assistance. There are some women writing and producing plays in London during the early nineteenth century, but they appear only sporadically, in a way that is reminiscent of the dry spell in the early eighteenth century. Furthermore, most of the women writing and producing in this early part of the century, with only a couple of exceptions (notably Mary Russell Mitford), were theatre "insiders," people who already had strong family or professional connections. The Drury Lane actress Maria Theresa DeCamp, to take one example, wrote and produced four plays between 1805 and 1815. But these were, for the most part, written to be benefits, either for herself, or for her husband, the actor and manager Charles Kemble. In other words, there was a retrenchment back to the earlier model set by actresses like Catherine Clive and Susanna Cibber in the 1750s and 1760s.

It is a surprising turn of events because the number of theatres was increasing significantly, both in London and in the provinces, and there were presumably more opportunities for playwrights, especially in alternative genres. The grip of the patent system had started to loosen a little: a host of "minor" theatres, like the Lyceum and the Olympic, were cropping up all over London, and a reinterpretation in 1804 by the Lord Chamberlain of the regulations protecting patent houses accelerated the process. In 1800 there were six theatre companies in London; by 1843 there were twenty-one. This expansion should have worked to women's advantage, but there were problems. The new theatres were stigmatized with a reputation for not being genteel. In 1817, for example, Joanna Baillie attended her comedy entitled *The Election* at the Lyceum. But after a tumultuous evening in which the activity on the floor (which included a stamping, roaring audience and a madman howling imprecations at the Duke of Wellington from a side box) completely overwhelmed the activity on stage, Baillie commented: "This new theatre is struggling with many difficulties, above all the terrible misfortune of not being reckoned *genteel*, and Mr. Arnold [the manager] has not had such good houses as he & his actors deserved."[53] For many middle-class women, the reputations of the smaller houses precluded their serious consideration as places in which to produce.

The change can also be blamed on the turmoil within Covent Garden and Drury Lane. Audience tastes were changing, partly as a consequence of the theatres themselves, which had increased vastly in size during the 1790s but lost both visibility and audibility. The result was a tremendous increase in the popularity of spectacles. The evolution of the star system and the enormous debts incurred by oversized theatres and elaborate scenery destabilized a machinery of which the playwright had been one part. By 1801, Drury Lane was in such a state of financial chaos that a trustee was appointed by the Lord Chancellor to monitor the theatre's accounts. This gradual decentralization of managerial power, from one decision-maker to several, had serious consequences from the point of view of the playwright. The manager was no longer the sole point of access for a playwright; the playwright now had to negotiate the whims not only of the manager and members of an administrative committee, but also often of the star performer. There were inevitable struggles for power in and among these various constituencies, and sometimes the playwright got caught in the middle. To take two examples, Jane Porter's playwriting debut (*Switzerland*) at Drury Lane in 1818 was deliberately sabotaged by its star, Edmund Kean, for whom the play had been written, because he was battling with the management committee for control over the repertory. This committee had initially agreed that Kean might choose his own plays, but after a season of failures, they had strongly urged him to try Porter's play, among others. Kean was determined to show the committee that he would tolerate no interference or even suggestions from them. There were a series of very promising rehearsals. On a particularly sadistic impulse, Kean invited Porter to attend these rehearsals and made a point of soliciting her opinion of his interpretation. On one occasion he even received spontaneous applause from the other actors. On opening night, Miss Porter's expectations were devastated. Kean deliberately played in a flat, mumbled monotone, speaking like an "Automaton," dropping lines and throwing all the other actors off, while Porter watched in horror from her box seat. The fact that even the audience blamed Kean for the failure did nothing to save the play. The show closed the same night; Porter never wrote again for the London stage.[54] Joanna Baillie wrote a friend that she had just been to see Miss Porter's play: "She was led to suppose that Drury Lane wished to have it and would do all they could for it . . . What will become of that ill-fated theatre I cannot guess, for there is nothing but discord and division, I am told, amongst all who have anything to do with it."[55] There is no evidence that Kean had any grudge against Porter personally, but rather against what her play stood for, which was the power of management over the power of the star performer. Barbarina Wilmot's *Ina*, also performed by Kean, had been shouted down its first night at Drury Lane in 1815. Baillie concludes in the same letter, now four years after Mrs. Wilmot's failed debut: "I have not seen Mrs. Wilmot all the Winter, but I have heard from her and she is well. Still hankering after the Drama, *but fearful and diffident of herself*." [my italics][56] This scenario would have been inconceivable under David Garrick. Garrick ran Drury Lane with an iron hand; star performers rose up to challenge his authority periodically, but there was no question about who was really in control. The lesson to be drawn from Porter's and Wilmot's experiences is that while the unilateral power of the manager in the mid- to late-eighteenth century imposed certain compromises on a female dramatist's career, the changes in power structure in the early nineteenth century did nothing to improve the situation.

In addition to the internal theatre turmoil, there were also external sociopolitical forces which may have conspired to deplete the ranks of women playwrights. Leonore Davidoff and Catherine Hall, in their study of the period 1780 to 1850, describe a trend in which the place of women increasingly was separated from the place of work. They suggest that as the middle class in industrial England began to prosper and to express a cultural identity during the eighteenth century, distinctively structured roles emerged for men and women. They write: "gender and class always operate together; consciousness of class has always taken a gendered form."[57] This structuring resulted in new divisions of labor and the establishment of a domestic world for women quite separate from the world of commerce and enterprise, where before there had been family cooperatives. In one section of their study, they look at the Cadburys, a family of drapers, who in the senior generation (from 1797) all lived above the shop, the mother sharing responsibility for running the shop as well as the home. By 1824, in the second generation of the same family, the married daughters lived quite separately from the place of business, in an early version of a British suburb. Married life for women in the eighteenth century might start over the shop, but "the physical separation between workplace and home which affected all of them at some point in their lives symbolized the more rigid demarcation of male and female spheres that was taking place" in the early nineteenth century.[58] This physical separation between workplace and home was partly the result of accumulated wealth that now made it possible to run a business without unpaid family labor. But it was also importantly connected to industrialization itself: families which once produced woollen cloth at home in the late eighteenth century, for example, by the mid-nineteenth century were forced into large-scale factory production in order to stay competitively priced.[59] These changes created an inevitable "separation between work and home, between the production of things and the reproduction of people."[60] One of the effects of this separation was that spheres of public and private activity were now also seen to be separate, and gendered. The world of the home was the place of privacy and women's work; the world of business and affairs was designated male and public.

This sexual division of labor had some interesting implications for women writers. It did not, as Mendelson has pointed out, necessarily prevent a woman from being a writer, if she could write at home and if she conducted her efforts with appropriate modesty, anonymously or pseudonymously. For the woman playwright, however, things were more complex. Theatre was a public medium, not just in the moment of performance, but even in the development of scripts, and it necessitated a considerable degree of personal mobility. Garrick had solved some of the problems connected with that mobility by invoking the precepts of protection and obedience implicit in the father-daughter relationship, and recreating a place of "family" work, for which there was ample precedent elsewhere.[61] As the nineteenth century unfolded, however, even this kind of compromised arrangement was no longer tenable. Not only was there increasing social pressure for middle-class women to remove themselves from the workplace, but also there were pointed attempts to name playwriting as something that women were intrinsically *not equipped to do*, in spite of considerable evidence to the contrary.

The conspicuous financial and artistic success of a handful of eighteenth-century women playwrights probably contributed to this claim that playwriting was something best left to the men. Davidoff and Hall offer an economic explanation:

> men felt the need to systematically contain women and limit their potential. A society increasingly based on new forms of property, on liquid capital, could no longer depend upon traditional forms of male dominance . . . New forms of capital required novel methods of restraining women. It was never the laws of property alone which prevented the myriad middle-class women who owned property from using it actively. Rather it was the way in which the laws . . . intersected with definitions of femininity. The active generation of lasting wealth was virtually impossible for women.[62]

In addition to the pressures generated by an emerging middle class, another powerful external factor played a role in this retrenchment of professional women. The last quarter of the eighteenth century was profoundly influenced by two major political revolutions. Recent scholarship has argued that both the American and the French Revolutions shared their philosophical and theoretical roots with the origins of feminism. Hobbes, Hume and Locke, whose thinking had brought into question the entire system of privilege on which the *ancien régime* was based, had implicitly called into question the assumptions by which women were judged inferior to men.[63] During the 1790s in France, this thinking crystallized in the writings and speeches of the Marquis de Condorcet, who "suggested that women participate in all aspects of public life with the exception of military service," and contended that women should enjoy with men the rights and responsibilities of full citizenship, including the franchise.[64] The historian Jane Rendall comments:

> Although earlier women writers . . . had written effectively and movingly of the condition of women, and suggested that educational reforms, in particular, might improve their situation, it was only in the context of a world in which revolutions in America and in France opened up the possibilities of reshaping the social as well as the political order that radical changes between the sexes began to seem feasible.[65]

In England during the same decade, the work of Condorcet and others was instrumental in the development of British feminism. British feminism constituted both a challenge and a transformation to the legacy of the Enlightenment. At the center of the debate was a group of intellectuals which included Mary Wollstonecraft, William Godwin, the playwright Thomas Holcroft, and Elizabeth Inchbald. Rendall observes:

> The conservative reaction to the feminist arguments of the 1780s and 1790s was, in England, France and America, a powerful one. With the conservative victory, following the federalist and constitutionalist success in the United States, Thermidor in France, and Pitt's repression in England, and the polarisation of opinions on social as well as political issues, those arguments were to be brutally suppressed . . . reaction to further claims for female autonomy was swift and vicious.[66]

In effect, the sexual division of labor and the sequestration of female life into domestic isolation was part of a reactionary response to feminism and all that it implied. The women dramatists of the late eighteenth century participated in the final flurry of professional activity for women on any serious scale before conservative reaction devastated liberal momentum, at least until the 1840s.

By 1814, if we can judge from Jane Austen's *Mansfield Park*, theatre activity of any kind signalled trouble for the daughters of the middle class. Even private theatricals, which we recall were counselled against in Gisborne's 1797 conduct book, were now seen to be a more serious liability. The little home rehearsal in

Austen's story is sharply and unequivocally terminated by a furious father who orders the scenery dismantled and all copies of the play *burned*. Mr. Bertram, we are informed, is acting in the best interests of his daughter Maria, who by participating in private theatricals may have irreparably damaged her chances of making an advantageous marriage. In other words, home theatricals are causing Maria's value as property to decline, and she risks becoming a financial burden to her father, who may now be faced with her continued support.

The play responsible for all this potential damage to property and marriage was Mrs. Inchbald's translation of Kotzebue's *Lovers' Vows*. Austen never names Mrs. Inchbald, but I wonder if she was intentionally invoking her presence to underscore the irony of the situation. Certainly as modern readers we are sharply reminded in this novel of just how alien the theatre world had become to the nineteenth-century middle class. It is inconceivable that any one of Austen's female characters could have undertaken the reckless adventures of Frances Brooke's heroine in *The Excursion*, or of Elizabeth Inchbald herself, who at age seventeen went to London for the first time, penniless and unaccompanied, to seek her fortune as a writer. Just thirty years before *Mansfield Park* was published, in 1784, theatre had been Inchbald's ticket to national reputation and personal fortune. In stark contrast to Maria Bertram, theatre had enabled Elizabeth Inchbald to think of herself *as owning property*, rather than as *being* property.

\* \* \*

In 1780, the year that she started acting at Covent Garden for the manager Thomas Harris, Elizabeth Inchbald began carrying her scripts back and forth from one manager to another, determined to find someone to produce them. It would be four years of relentless effort before she got her chance. Her diaries, of which 900 pages survive, are terse and undemonstrative. They rarely tell us what she was thinking or how she felt. In a minute, crabbed hand, they record events and cash transactions with little inflection or affect. In the course of reading those diaries, I came across an entry for 1780 that was as moving as it was uncharacteristic. It begins in her usual flat, terse style:

To the House [Covent Garden theatre] to fit my dress [costume] but was disappointed – very uneasy – came home put on my hat and after saw Mr. Harris [Thomas Harris, manager of Covent Garden] and spoke to him about it – he made me amasing [*sic*] happy as to my Farce [probably *The Mogul Tale*] and raising my salary.[67]

Nowhere else in the diaries does the term "amazing happy" appear. For anyone who has written a play, seen it performed, and earned money in the process, Mrs. Inchbald's moment of being "amazing happy" is a poignant and powerful reminder of what it means when we talk theoretically about claiming a subject position. Women wanted, continue to want. In the case of these women playwrights, they wanted money and they wanted to see characters they had created speaking dialogue that they had written. They wanted to watch audience members rapt, weeping, convulsed with laughter, or thundering their applause. They wanted to be noticed, to be counted among the people who are taken seriously in the world as writers and thinkers and shapers of human action. They wanted power, agency, self-respect, historical consequence. They wanted to earn a living.

The irony of this excerpt from Elizabeth Inchbald's diary is that what was needed to make her "amazing happy" was so modest and plain. She needed encouragement, the possibility of production, and a little more money, none of which was forthcoming from Thomas Harris in 1780. But even these modest needs, for herself and for other women playwrights, proved extraordinarily threatening to the culture. Perhaps it was what they *represented* that was so troublesome.

When women started writing for the theatre, no matter how innocuous the material, male critics were quick to sense that something was slipping out of their control. Not only did this writing put men into the object position, because a woman's eye and hand were controlling the pen, but additionally it took control of the authorship of human action. It was only a symbolic loss to be sure: there were only characters moving about on a stage. Certainly no woman was setting policy in top government jobs. But the authoring of action, and the authority to do so, whether in the context of a short comic afterpiece or a full-scale tragedy, created a ripple of anxiety. What kind of precedent did this set? Michelene Wandor writes exactly to the point:

She is providing words, emotions, and an imaginative structure for others to inhabit and create anew onstage. A playwright – in this theoretical sense – thus makes other people speak and act –. No wonder then, that even the woman playwright with the mildest of messages is bound to be seen as an anomaly, if not an actual threat. Who knows what she will say once she gives voice?[68]

From a distance of two hundred years, it becomes clear that women wanting power, wanting money, wanting anything, was profoundly disruptive to a culture that had been built upon the idea of women being the thing wanted (or not wanted). The prospect of women *doing the wanting* implicitly called into question the codes of feminine conduct, and by extension the inequities of an economic system which had depended upon those codes to procreate itself. When eighteenth- and nineteenth-century critics of women's drama used terms like "whore" or "hussy," it was as if the boundaries between sex and playwriting, conduct and art, had dissolved, and the critics themselves had lost control of the categories. Promiscuous sexuality was perhaps the closest analog they had for a woman desiring power. They experienced her imaginatively as rapacious, insatiable, devouring.

In retrospect, we know that these critics were describing what as yet had no name or concept: the possibility of a woman speaking for herself, without the grey fear of slander or censure, exerting control over the way she was represented, a subject rather than an object in culture. This was a dilemma faced by all women, but it was a particularly acute issue for women working in the arts, because fear had the potential for nullifying their work at the source. Frances Burney once said in her girlhood journal, "why, permit me to ask, must a *female* be made Nobody?"[69] Her question hovers over the six cases that follow.

It should not come as any surprise that this 140-year period is marked by struggle and eventual defeat. Mrs. Hazard wanted to get back into the theatre. Garrick's mentoring signalled cautious permission to do so. But then, as often happens in history, something happened that no one, least of all Garrick, could have foreseen. Two women, one of them his protégée, emerged into the front ranks of playwriting. Even though the representation of women playwrights as a whole was vastly below that of men, they showed themselves not only able to hold their own, but able to take the field. Women were not only getting into the act; they were accumulating capital, shaping the canon, and creating role models for other women. The kindly, paternal figure of the mentor was rapidly becoming an embarrassing anachronism. If the cultural imperatives of femininity and masculinity were to survive, something would have to be done.

# 2

# FRANCES BROOKE
## The Female Playwright as Critic

In 1753 or early 1754, Frances Brooke's first play, entitled *Virginia*, was rejected by David Garrick for production at Drury Lane.[1] Certainly this was to be expected in some sense; who can hope to get their first script accepted and produced? But the rejection had some peculiar and interesting aspects. Two plays based on the same story by Livy were written and produced, one also called *Virginia* by Samuel Crisp at Drury Lane on 25 February 1754,[2] about the time of Brooke's rejection, and the second by John Moncrieff, entitled *Appius*, at Covent Garden on 6 March 1755.[3] Brooke states in the preface to the published version of her play in 1756 that Garrick had received Crisp's and Moncrieff's before hers, and had refused to read hers until Crisp's was published. None of this seems to me particularly noteworthy; Garrick appears to have operated in this instance on a first-come, first-served basis, and to have been very careful about protecting himself and both playwrights from possible charges of plagiarism. What does interest me, however, is a letter he wrote on 28 September 1754, later in the same year that Drury Lane produced Crisp's play, and after Crisp's play was published. He wrote this time in reference to the second play on the same subject, John Moncrieff's, to an unnamed correspondent:

Dear Sir: I am engag'd already to more plays than I can possibly perform in the two next seasons – I have seen Mr. Moncrief [*sic*] since yr letter and told how my engagements stood, but have promised him all ye service in my power, provided he can get it acted at ye other house. When I see you I shall explain farther to you; in ye mean time be assur'd that yr recommendation will always have great weight with, dear sir,

yr most obedt servant, D. Garrick.[4]

41

*Plate 1*
David Garrick
1717–1779
Occuptations: Theatre Manager, Actor, Playwright

One of Garrick's oldest friends was the actress and playwright Catherine Clive. In 1778, shortly before his death, she wrote him: "I must needs say I admire you (with the rest of the world) for your goodness to Miss [Hannah] More; the protection you gave her play, I dare say, she was sensible was of the greatest service to her; she was sure every thing you touched would turn into gold; and though she had great merit in the writing, still your affection for tragedy children was a very great happiness to *her*, for you dandled it, and fondled it, and then carried it in your own arms to the *town* to nurse; who behaved so kindly to it, that it run alone in the month." Mrs. Clive's 1750 farce, *Bays in Petticoats*, may have challenged Garrick to an awareness of the plight of women playwrights. Perhaps this was her way of acknowledging his contribution and thanking him for it. She signed this letter "affectionate and forgiving." (Quoted from *The Private Correspondence of David Garrick*, ed. James Boaden, London, Henry Colburn and Richard Bentley, 1832, vol.2, p. 295.)

*Plate 2*
Frances Brooke
1724(?)–1789
Occupations: Playwright, Theatre Manager, Novelist, Translator

So far as we can tell from the surviving portraits, the women who were most successful at finding mentors among the theatre managers were also strikingly handsome. Mrs. Brooke was not strikingly handsome; in addition, she was someone who tended to speak her mind. These descriptions of her have come down to us courtesy of Frances Burney, who met Mrs. Brooke when she (Burney) was twenty-two years old, and was greatly impressed by Brooke's considerable reputation as a novelist: "Mrs. Brooke is very short & fat, & squints, but has the art of shewing Agreeable Ugliness. She is very well bred, & expresses herself with much modesty, upon all subjects – which in an *Authoress*, a Woman of *Known* understanding, is extremely pleasing." At a gathering with a particularly obnoxious guest named Dr. John Shebbeare, Burney recorded Shebbeare's offer to make another guest, a woman artist, "immortal" by writing her biography. Brooke retorted quietly: "She'll make *herself* immortal, by her Works." (Recorded by Burney in 1774, published in *The Early Journals and Letters of Fanny Burney* (1768–1773), ed. Lars Troide, Kingston and Montreal, McGill-Queen's University Press, 1988, vol. 2, pp. 4 and 9.)

And indeed, Moncrieff's play on the same subject was produced at the other house (Covent Garden) in the following season, 1755.[5] Mrs. Brooke had no way of knowing about this letter, but I wonder now why her play didn't get the same consideration and the same encouragement. Why send Moncrieff over to Covent Garden with a strong recommendation, and not also Brooke, since he no longer had any investment in either one of them? The letter to "Sir" seems to me to speak of a network of influence and connections that did not include Frances Brooke. There was no political payoff for supporting her script over Moncrieff's, and so her script fell by the wayside. Brooke had as yet no connections powerful enough to ease the transition from unproduced to produced playwright. It is a feminist issue on the larger scale of things, but there is no evidence here to suggest any discriminatory practices that directly targeted women *per se*. The failure to have powerful connections could have been anyone's misfortune.

Later, however, the picture began to change. Brooke, instead of retreating from the field after her play was rejected (both by Garrick and by Rich at Covent Garden), undertook the editing of a periodical she called *The Old Maid*.[6] Her editorial pseudonym was "Mary Singleton," and between 15 November 1755 and 4 July 1756, she published thirty-seven issues. In the 13 March 1756 issue, she observed:

> It has always been a matter of great astonishment to me, that both the houses have given Tate's alteration of King Lear the preference to Shakespear's excellent original, which Mr. Addison, the most candid, as well as judicious of critics, thinks so infinitely preferable, as to bear no degree of comparison; and one cannot help remarking particularly, and with some surprise, that Mr. Garrick, who professes himself so warm an idolater of this inimitable poet, and who is determined, if I may use his own words, in the prologue to Winter's Tale, "To lose no drop of this immortal man," should yet prefer the adulterated cup of Tate to the pure genuine draught offered him by the master he avows to serve with such fervency of devotion . . . As to Mr. Barry[7] [Spranger Barry, Garrick's main rival among actors of the period, especially as Lear] I think he was perfectly right to take the Lear which is commonly play'd that the competition between him and Mr. Garrick in this

trying part may be exhibited to the public upon a fair footing; I have not yet been so fortunate as to see the latter in it whose performance, I doubt not, is no less justly than generally celebrated and admired; but the advantage Mr. Barry has from his person, the variety of his voice, and its particular aptitude to express the differing tones which sorrow, pity, or rage, naturally produce, are of such service to him in this character, that he could not fail of pleasing, though he did not play it with all the judgement which in my opinion he does [*sic*].[8]

We may never know which critique, the one about using Tate's *King Lear*[9] or the one about Barry's attractive presence onstage as Lear, most infuriated Garrick, but there is no question that he was infuriated. He didn't tolerate criticism well under the best of circumstances. To my ear, Brooke's comments seem conspicuously even-handed and fair. She strikes a careful balance between stating an admiration for Barry's physique and voice and expressing certain reservations about his acting choices; she is careful to acknowledge (with no negative innuendoes) that she has not seen Garrick's performance, and she makes a remarkably prescient case for preserving Shakespeare's original texts. There is nothing here that sounds like sniping. In any case, criticisms of Garrick's voice and physique cropped up routinely in other publications. As for the debate about which version of *King Lear* was the right one, Brooke features as one voice among many. Samuel Foote, as early as 1747, had said of Garrick's Lear:

Why will you do so great an injury to Shakespeare as to perform Tate's execrable alteration of him? Read and consider the two plays seriously, and then make the public and the memory of the author some amends by giving us Lear in the original, fool and all.[10]

This is the identical message in much stronger language. Garrick, however, continued on cordial, even warm terms with Foote until Foote's death in 1777.[11] In 1756, Theophilus Cibber published his *Two Dissertations on the Theatres*, adding his voice to the debate about the Tate version, and in 1754 there were essays on *Lear* in *Gray's Inn Journal* and *The Adventurer*. George Winchester Stone has speculated that these pieces collectively represented certain shifts in the eighteenth-century response to

Shakespeare's tragedy, and that Garrick seems to have responded to those shifts by producing Lear again in October of 1756 with many of Shakespeare's original lines restored, although he never did restore the tragic ending or the Fool.[12] Gwendolyn Needham argues that Brooke's piece in the *Old Maid* may have been an additional spur to that new production.[13] If it was the spur, Garrick did not thank her for it.

Garrick's anger at Brooke was still festering seven years later, when by a series of odd coincidences he found himself in a position to do some damage to her career as a translator of French novels. In 1763, Garrick and his wife decided to take a tour of the continent, during which time he made friends with a French author named Madame Marie-Jeanne Riccoboni (1714–1792).[14] This was a period in which the epistolary novel was at the zenith of its popularity: *Les Liaisons Dangereuses* had just been published, and Madame Riccoboni's novel, *Les Lettres de Juliette Catesby*, had been published in Paris in 1759, and been translated into English the following year by Frances Brooke.[15] Brooke's translation was an immediate success in England, and went through three editions in the first year, and three shortly thereafter. Brooke subsequently undertook to write her own epistolary novel, which she entitled *The Letters of Julia Mandeville*, and which was published in 1763. This novel received excellent critical acclaim, was translated into French, and was mentioned favorably by Voltaire in a review essay he wrote in 1764.[16] By the time Frances Brooke left London for an extended stay in Canada with her husband in 1763, she was a minor literary celebrity, and was given a send-off dinner with a distinguished list of guests that included Samuel Johnson, James Boswell, and Hannah More.[17]

Mrs. Brooke came back from Canada for about a year's visit during November of 1764 through 1765, and it is during this period that Madame Riccoboni's surviving correspondence with Garrick commences. On 15 May 1765 Riccoboni wrote:

J'ai reçu hier par un libraire de Paris, des complimens très-honnêtes d'une Madame Broock, ou Brock, je ne m'en souviens plus. C'est la traductrice de *Milady Catesby*. Elle écrit qu'elle en est à la quatrième édition. Cela est fort différent de Monsieur Becket, qui s'est ruiné avec *Miss Jenny*. Cette dame me fait demander *la permission* de m'envoyer ses ouvrages. J'avois dessein de lui faire tenir les miens mais Monsieur Hume ne la connoissoit point, et s'avisa de donner cette malheureuse *Jenny* à Monsieur Becket, qui en a fait un garde-boutique; un fond de magazin pour ses arrières neveux. J'ai encore de la rancune, comme vous voyez.[18]

[*Through a bookseller in Paris I received yesterday best wishes from a Mme. Broock or Brock – I don't recall. She is the translator of* Milady Catesby. *She writes it is in the fourth edition. Quite a difference from Mon. Becket who had a disaster with* Miss Jenny. *This lady asks my permission to send me her works. I had thought to send her mine but Mon. Hume doesn't know her and advised I give the unhappy* Jenny *to Mon. Becket who has it now in a storehouse for his grand-nephews. I still feel rancorous, as you see.*]

It is difficult to believe that Riccoboni hardly remembered Brooke's name, but I know of no reason at this point why she might have pretended to forget. Brooke's letter to Riccoboni may have been an effort to establish direct contact with a possible future translator for Brooke's own novel, *Julia Mandeville*, into French. Riccoboni evidently has also thought about sending more of her work to Brooke, because Brooke's translation of *Catesby* has been so remarkably successful, unlike the disappointing job commissioned by Becket on another of Riccoboni's novels, *Miss Jenny* (1764), now moldering in the overstock section of Becket's bookstore.

Garrick's reply to Riccoboni is dated 13 June 1765. Seeing his opportunity, he made his move:

> I am not acquainted with Mrs Brooke: she once wrote a play, which I did not like, & would not act, for which heinous offence she vented her female Spite upon Me, in a paper she publish'ed call'd ye Old Maid, but I forgive her as thoroughly, as her Work is forgotten – I am told she has merit & is very capable of a good translation, tho [*sic*] not of an Original – *five hundred* of her will not make half a Riccoboni. You will be civil to her & no more, all this is Entre Nous. Becket is your Don Quixote . . .[19]

Garrick's letter is a masterpiece of diplomatic vengeance. He describes having rejected Frances Brooke's play (*Virginia*) because he didn't like it, which flatly contradicts the information provided by her preface and by his own letter to the unnamed correspondent above, both of which indicate that quality had very little to do with his decision. He also constructs the *Old Maid* editorials (which had just been reissued the year before and were probably quite fresh in his mind) as a form of vengeance, and sets Mrs. Brooke up as a woman scorned. He implicitly compares the two women ("*five hundred* of her will not make half a Riccoboni") as if to undermine the possibility of a collaborative relationship between the two women. He says Brooke's work is "forgotten" and that she is not capable of a good original, when in fact at this date her own epistolary novel, *Julia Mandeville* (1763), was still very popular,[20] and she was mingling with a literary set among whom Garrick himself had friends.

These maneuvers put Madame Riccoboni in the unenviable position of having to choose between his advice and protection on the one hand (whether she wanted them or not), and Frances Brooke on the other. Although it is abundantly clear that Brooke's translation of *Juliette Catesby* had made Madame Riccoboni's name in England, and that Becket had fumbled the *Miss Jenny* translation badly, these facts played no part in Mme. Riccoboni's decision to abandon Brooke and go back to Becket again, this time with Garrick as her emissary. But even as he offered Madame Riccoboni his assistance and his advice, he also made it implicitly clear that spurning his offer might have certain consequences. "You will be civil to her & no more" has the cool sound of command. Madame Riccoboni had to demonstrate her loyalty to Garrick or face the consequences.[21]

Against logic and good business sense, Madame Riccoboni replied to Garrick on 29 July 1765:

> Eût-elle tous les talens du monde Mistress Brooke n'aura jamais mes ouvrages; pour moi je hais l'esprit vindicatif et les satiriques me sont en horreur.[22]
>
> [*Had she every talent under the sun, Mistress Brooke would never receive my works; for myself I detest a vindictive spirit and find satirists abhorrent.*]

Riccoboni had very little choice but to proclaim her passionate loyalty to Garrick and to abandon Brooke as a collaborator. The consequences of doing anything else were slightly menacing. She wrote Garrick again on 31 August, and having described in indignant detail instances of incompetent translation in *Miss Jenny* and another of her works called *Ernestine*, she wistfully remarked:

Mistriss [*sic*] Brooke s'est trompée lourdement en cinquante endroits de *Catesby*, mais il faut lui rendre un justice due, ce qu'elle entend elle l'exprime très bien.

[*Mistress Brooke is grossly in error in fifty places in* Catesby – *but to do her justice what she understands she expresses very well.*]

Riccoboni may have been putting out feelers to see if Garrick might relent. But he would have none of it. At one point she made the mistake of calling Becket's competence into question,[23] and Garrick was offended. His rebuke to her has not survived, but her letter to him, dated 2 August, is abject, almost terrified, and she babbles in alternating French and English:

Your pardon my dear, dear friend, I writ[e] to you upon my knees. Vous méritiez mille et mille remerciemens, je vous ai querellé, traité comme un chien: il faudroit m'assommer, mais, you are so good, j'espère ma grâce, forgive this fault.[24]

[*Your pardon, my dear, dear friend. I writ[e] to you upon my knees. You are deserving of endless gratitude; I quarreled with you, behaved like a dog: I should be beaten – but you are so good, I hope for my forgiveness. Forgive this fault.*]

Her evident terror of offending this man who has as yet done nothing for her career, and certainly was never to do anything as substantial as Brooke had, is almost as disturbing as the way Garrick manipulates and interferes in what he must have known would be a financially and artistically useful collaboration for both women.

The postscript to this episode is that Garrick's friend Becket continued to publish the translations of Madame Riccoboni's novels, although none of them ever came close to the popularity of Frances Brooke's translation of *Catesby*. On 24 December 1771, Garrick wrote Madame Riccoboni about her new novel, *Lettres de Sophie de Vallière*, saying "I have procur'd a good Man to translate it . . . We will do our utmost for your Reputation, & (What You less regard;) Your interest. Our friend Becket will Obey your Commands directly. . . ."[25] But the translator was not a good man. His name was Maceuen, and *The Monthly Review* commented: "Of her Translator we cannot speak in any terms of commendation. He does not always comprehend the meaning of his original; and he no where conveys it with propriety or force."[26]

Nevertheless, Garrick's manipulations, which undoubtedly

cost both Brooke and Riccoboni substantially in terms of remuneration and, in Brooke's case, career momentum, have come down to us as generous assistance and support. James C. Nicholls (1976) continues the tradition of Garrick's unchallenged generosity:

> He took time from his busy schedule to do her numerous favours. The most important of these was acting as her intermediary with the publisher Thomas Becket who published the English translations of many of her novels. Since Becket was also his publisher, Garrick found many ways to assist mme Riccoboni without her suspecting charity and he helped spread her literary reputation in England by helping to sell her works.[27]

In the enthusiastic prose about Garrick's generosity, Frances Brooke, whose original translation had brought Madame Riccoboni to England's attention in the first place, drops quietly out of the picture.

In 1772, Brooke began approaching theatre managers with a little opera entitled *Rosina*. Samuel Foote, who was managing the Haymarket, urged her not to attempt a summer production. She wrote her good friend Richard Gifford:

> Foote has persuaded me not have my opera done at his house in summer, but to ask the chamberlain's leave for a few nights in winter, & I believe I shall take his advice: I had no reason for wishing to have it done in summer, but happen'd to want the money more than I hope I shall a twelvemonth hence; but I must do as well as I can.[28]

She must then have approached Colman, who was at this point managing at Covent Garden with Harris; the correspondence doesn't survive, but he apparently turned her down too. She again wrote her friend Gifford:

> There is nothing to me so astonishing as that Colman should be another Garrick, which I am told he is: I yearn to know how to believe it & hope I shall not be <u>convinced</u>. My design is, if he refuses, to apply to G. [Garrick], and if he refuses, to apply to the Ld Ch [Lord Chamberlain] for leave to act it at my own hazard, for weekly nights at Foote's; which . . . will probably pave the way for a third theatre, which is in agitation. I know the Ld. Ch. is very angry at some

instances of theatrical tyranny, & think I can roll my story up and back it with friends that will carry my point; and the best female singer we have, Miss Catley, is in town, & not engaged at either house, is ready to take such a revenge as I can be, but if I hint my design, they will engage her & prevent it. I cannot do this until I have tried both houses, because till then I have no right to complain. There is no saying what hurt such a scheme would do them, and I have spirit enough & friends enough, to carry it thro' if anybody could. Do you approve? . . . If it chanced to be, it might be more profitable than it's being received of the other theatres. You see I ought to be secret as to this scheme.[29]

Finally, as a last resort, Brooke wrote Garrick a letter requesting that he read her opera and consider it for production at Drury Lane. The letter, which is almost comic in its efforts to appease and placate, leads one to wonder if her good friend Mary Ann Yates, a leading actress in Garrick's company, was coaching from the sidelines.[30] In any case, it was all to no purpose; Garrick rejected the opera, as Brooke probably knew he would, and *Rosina* went unproduced for twelve years. However, Brooke's comment to Gifford that Colman is turning out to be "another Garrick" is intriguing. She intimates that Colman and Garrick are working hand in glove to exclude certain people for reasons of their own, herself and Miss Catley being two, and she further states that she is willing to undertake an organized effort to challenge the power of these two patent houses so that she and others have more choice about where they can work. Although it is unlikely that Brooke could have known anything about Garrick's manipulations regarding Madame Riccoboni, she had apparently sized him up not only as hostile to her personally, but as representative of a system that was getting in the way of her work. She sees Colman as someone who is content simply to follow suit. She recognized, as I think other women playwrights did not, that the fundamental battle was not with any one particular manager, but with the patent system itself, which had created a handful of interlocking fiefdoms that absolutely controlled theatre activity.

The planned opposition to the patent houses must have fizzled out. Instead, this rejection of *Rosina* by both main houses fuelled Brooke's move into theatre management with her friend Mrs.

Yates at the King's Opera House in 1773. It was her bid for autonomy, an effort to rid herself of the managers altogether and finally see her work produced. But although she and Yates produced operas at King's with conspicuous success from 1773 to 1777, her hopes of securing a license to produce plays there were never realized. Richard Brinsley Sheridan and Thomas Harris bought King's in 1778 with the same ambitions to secure a license, and met with the same frustration. The patent system did not undergo any serious changes until about thirty years later.

Garrick retired in 1776, the same year Yates and Brooke made an effort to secure a license for a theatre in Birmingham. They apparently solicited Garrick's help in lobbying Edmund Burke in Parliament; Garrick wrote to Burke on their behalf, probably as a favor to the Yateses, but the license was not granted due to political pressure within Birmingham itself.[31]

After Garrick's death in 1779, Brooke turned her efforts back to the two patent houses in London, and at long last found an ally in Thomas Harris, the new manager of Covent Garden, who produced her tragedy *The Siege of Sinope*[32] in early 1781, and a year later, her opera *Rosina*.[33] *Rosina* went on to become the second most popular afterpiece in the entire last quarter of the century, playing over 200 times.[34] In 1788, another opera by Brooke was produced at Covent Garden, entitled *Marian*.[35] The following year, in 1789, Frances Brooke died. One cannot help but notice how rapidly her fortunes in the theatre shifted after Garrick's death.

One final epilogue to this story: in 1777, a year after Garrick's retirement, Frances Brooke published a novel called *The Excursion*.[36] In *The Excursion*, Brooke leaves us her thoughts about the situation in which women playwrights found themselves. The heroine of her story is a young woman named Maria who has ambitions to become a playwright. Her dear friend and mentor Mr. Hammond, a literary man of consequence, takes her play to Mr. Garrick at Drury Lane, who promises to read it and offer his comments. Our heroine has high hopes. At the appointed time, Mr. Hammond goes forth to meet with Mr. Garrick, but he comes back with bad news. Mr. Garrick had evidently not read the play; he had it confused with someone else's script, he paged through it while Mr. Hammond sat in the office watching in disbelief, and pontificated about fledgling playwrights not knowing their business:

But these authors – and after all, what do they do? They bring the meat indeed, but who instructs them how to cook it? Who points out the proper seasoning for the dramatic ragoût? Who furnishes the savoury ingredients to make the dish palatable? Who brings the Attic salt? – The Cayenne pepper? – the – the – a – 'Tis amazing the pains I am forced to take with these people, in order to give relish to their insipid productions –[37]

Mr. Hammond attempts to pin Garrick down to a possible date for production:

The next season, my dear sir? – why – a – it is absolutely impossible – I have now six-and-twenty new tragedies on my promise-list – besides, have I not read it? – That is – if – if – a – your friend will send it me in July – if I approve it in July, I will endeavour – let me see – what year is this? O, I remember – 'tis seventy-five – Yes – if I think it will do, I will endeavour to bring it out in the winter of – the winter of – eighty-two.[38]

Mr. Hammond finally gives up and returns home to report to our heroine:

The incoherent jumble of words without ideas which I have been repeating to you Madam is, I am told, the general answer to dramatic writers, who are intended to be disgusted by this unworthy treatment, which the managers honour with the name of policy, from thinking of any future applications . . .

Mr. Hammond goes on to name the patent system as a culprit, arguing that there are too many plays and playwrights and not enough theatres to produce them in. He praises Garrick as an actor and as an author. But in her disappointment and frustration, Maria's concentration is dwindling. She speculates that if only Mr. Hammond had argued her case differently, she might have had a better chance:

He should have urged that the piece in question was the production of a woman, and that the part of the heroine was exquisitely adapted to display in full light the brilliant powers of the actress who filled the first characters at his theatre. The truth is [comments the narrator], he declined using those arguments because he thought them both extremely unfavourable to the cause.[39]

This was Brooke's final shot at David Garrick, and at the system over which he had reigned for thirty-five years.

These passages from Brooke's novel are interesting for a number of reasons. On the one hand, they deftly demonstrate Brooke's considerable skills with dialog, character, and comic situation, as if to suggest that a writer of talent will find a way to use her skills whether she is given her opportunity in theatre or not. I have no doubt that Brooke knew of Garrick's extreme sensitivity to criticism, and that a comic satire, laced with lip service to his talents, was guaranteed to upset him. In this respect, Brooke was a tenacious and resilient adversary. She also had the good sense not to publish this satire until after his retirement.

Most compelling, however, is Brooke's claim in *The Excursion* that being female actually mitigated against Maria's chances of having her play produced. This, evidently, is the reason that Mr. Hammond makes all the visits to Mr. Garrick; not just to use his influence on Maria's behalf, but to delay the revelation of her gender. Our evidence, from the experience of Hannah Cowley, Hannah More, Charlotte Lennox, Dorothy Cilesia, Elizabeth Griffith and a few others, is that Garrick actually was an ally to women playwrights. How are we to resolve these conflicting perspectives? Does Brooke mean that there was a small quota of chosen women each year, and that if you were not one of the anointed, you had no chance? Does she mean that if a play strongly favored its female characters he would be less interested because he was scouting characters for himself to play? This is undoubtedly an indirect reference to her own tragedy *Virginia*, and to the talents of Mrs. Yates, who had been a member of Garrick's acting company for years. Is Brooke simply registering her own experience of having had both her tragedy and her opera rejected by him? Or does she know it to be untrue, and say it just to make him angry?

Even though Brooke's satire is intentionally comic, I take her comments about Garrick with great seriousness. She is, after all, someone whom Garrick's system of patronage had not served; in fact, we can say with certainty that he had neutralized her literary efforts on several fronts. Her experience tells us that we would do well not to inflate Garrick's reputation for helping women. His choices of which women to assist were based, it seems, not on principle or on talent so much as on personal taste. The implicit contract he made with them was a form of narcissism. Certain women, like Hannah Cowley, Dorothy Cilesia, and especially Hannah More, created precisely the right combination of respect, gratitude, and compliance to underscore his own need for unchallenged power and leadership. Mrs. Griffith ultimately proved to be a less successful choice. Frances Brooke was anathema. From the earliest days, she had demonstrated her critical independence. She had called into question, legitimately as it turned out, his choices for *Lear*, and implied a preference for someone else's physical presence onstage. These wounds to Garrick's ego made a working relationship with her impossible. His letters to her over the years, about loaned scripts or conflicting schedules for performers, are curt to the point of rudeness. This final satire of him, as a manager who did not willingly entertain scripts from women, was intended not so much to injure his reputation, which was virtually unassailable anyway, or to reveal a truth about him, but to jab him in precisely the area where she knew him to be most vulnerable.

When *The Excursion* was published in the summer of 1777, Garrick's fury was unbounded. This time he did not make even a pretence of forgiveness or judicial restraint. He received a copy in mid-July and within a week he had fired off letters to several close friends, including Charles Burney, Henrietta Pye, Madame Riccoboni, and Frances Cadogan, in an attempt to justify himself and vent his rage. His letter to Cadogan was especially revealing:

> I hope You have seen how much I am abus'd in yr. Friend Mrs. Brooke's new Novel? – she is pleas'd to insinuate that [I am] an Excellent Actor, a so so author, an Execrable Manager & a Worse Man – Thank you good Madam Brookes – If my heart was not better than my head, I would not give a farthing for the Carcass, but let it dangle, as it would deserve, with It's brethren at ye End of Oxford Road. She has invented a Tale about a Tragedy, which is all a Lie, from beginning to ye End – she Even says, that I should reject a Play, if it should be a Woman's – there's brutal Malignity for You –[40]

Garrick's own brutal malignity towards Brooke exposes the

bones and teeth of a system which included women playwrights, but only at the pleasure of the presiding manager. When Brooke emerged in 1755 as "Mary Singleton," critic, she breached an unspoken contract between Garrick and his women, that their part of the bargain was to extol him. Brooke would not, and it cost her dearly. It was her self-appointed position as critic and peer to Garrick that sealed her fate, since the substance of her critique had been raised previously by other people. She made it subsequently impossible for herself to enter Garrick's theatre in the submissive posture he required from women playwrights. There was no retreating once she had violated his sense of the woman's place. If she was not going to be part of his literary harem, she faced a certain kind of exile from the world of London theatre, at least until Garrick was dead. Her resourceful solution was to set up shop at King's, but that venture still kept her on the margins of London activity, and didn't last as long or serve as well as she probably had hoped.

I cannot help but reflect briefly on Nahum Tate's *King Lear*, the one in which the fool is absent, and in which Cordelia marries and she and Lear are reconciled. There is some parallel here to Garrick's own image of himself, with all the implicit ironies of kingship, the viper daughters and the loyal daughter, and the penalties for failing to make public one's undying devotion to the king. Both Brooke and Garrick should have read the original play more carefully, Garrick because it might have reminded him of the consequences of absolute power and a failure to know oneself, and Brooke because of the way Cordelia's refusal to pay public homage created an insensate fury in her father and resulted in exile. But I think Brooke knew. She took a calculated risk and lost.

Garrick's choice of the sentimentalized version of *Lear* is a telling one, not just because, as Stone argues, he had his fingers on the pulse of the public, but also because it provided a roseate vision of forgiveness and redemption that had no basis in reality, either in Shakespeare's original text or in the way events unfolded between him and Brooke. If indeed the wisdom of the original play ever revealed itself to Garrick, it was too late. By the time *The Excursion* was published, Garrick was retired and near death, and Brooke herself was almost at the close of a stalemated career. There was no happy end.

# 3

# THE PAPER WAR OF HANNAH COWLEY AND HANNAH MORE

When David Garrick died in January of 1779, he left in his wake a group of women playwrights who suddenly found themselves without a mentor. In the vacuum created by his death, a brief but violent controversy erupted between the two most prominent of these playwrights, Hannah Cowley (1743–1809) and Hannah More (1745–1833), both of whom had made successful theatre debuts as the result of Garrick's careful sponsorship. In the summer of 1779, Hannah Cowley accused Hannah More of having plagiarized. She stated in the press that More's production of *The Fatal Falsehood*, which had opened in May of 1779, had borrowed substantially from Cowley's play *Albina*, which opened in July of 1779 but allegedly had been written some three years before.

The debate was much publicized, both in the London papers and in the preface to Cowley's printed edition of *Albina*. There were charges and counter-charges. Eventually the controversy died down, largely because a new theatre season was under way, but it was never satisfactorily resolved. Hannah More subsequently quit playwriting altogether; by contrast Hannah Cowley continued a successful and productive career as a professional playwright until 1794, when she retired of her own volition. More's biographers have tended to treat Mrs. Cowley as a crank, and the entire sequence of events as the accusations of a desperate and failing playwright. Cowley allegedly stood up in the theatre on the second night of *The Fatal Falsehood* and shouted "That's mine! That's mine!" before fainting dead away.[1] But Mrs. Cowley was neither failing nor desperate, and the profile which emerges of her long and successful career does not suggest a paranoid crank, but points toward a larger and

*Plate 3*
Hannah More
1745–1833
Occupations: Educator, Essayist, Poet, Playwright

Hannah More was a protégée of David Garrick's and a close personal friend to both him and Mrs. Garrick, consulting with both of them on revisions to her plays. In July 1777, word reached Miss More that the Garricks might be coming to visit. She wrote: "I am almost out of my wits for joy! Is it possible that you and Mrs. Garrick can come so far out of the way to see such poor miserable animals? Your promise has made us happy past all expression, and proud past all enduring. What we want in wit and wealth, we will make up in love and gratititude . . . Please to give my affectionate respects to that dear lady, and tell her I rejoice I am in so good hands: I beg she will reduce me to the precise point of dramatic slenderness . . . Seriously, there is no person on earth by whose opinion I shall more implicitly abide; – 'Except mine,' methinks I hear you exclaim. I cannot help making my scenes too long, but care not how much of the rubbish is cut out." The Garricks' visit to Bristol never materialized. (Quoted from *The Private Correspondence of David Garrick*, ed. James Boaden, London, Henry Colburn and Richard Bentley, 1833, vol. 2, pp. 242–243).

*Plate 4*
Hannah Cowley
1743–1809
Occupation: Playwright, Poet

Patronage continued to play an important but often invisible role in the development of a playwright's career and reputation. Mrs. Cowley's early success with *The Runaway* (1776) did nothing to ensure her entrée to the other managers after Garrick's retirement, so she was forced to make use of her father's political connections to Lord and Lady Harrowby, whose estate bordered Tiverton where she grew up. Mrs. Cowley's father, Philip Parkhouse (1712–1787), a bookseller of Tiverton, gave his daughter's career his undivided support, as did Mrs. Cowley's husband Thomas. This kind of support was rare. In December of 1780, Parkhouse wrote Lord Harrowby a letter appealing to him for financial subsidy for his daughter and her family (a husband and four children) so that she could continue writing plays. Harrowby decided that the best course of action was to pursue a promotion for Mrs. Cowley's husband, who worked in the Stamp Office, instead of an annuity for Mrs. Cowley herelf. To this end, he wrote a well-placed friend in 1782 (in secret code) detailing Thomas Cowley's skills and personal merits. He also commented on Cowley's wife: "His wife, Mrs. Hannah Cowley, has distinguished herself much in the dramatic line having been the author of a comedy called *The Belle's Stratagem* and several other pieces which have been very well received, and what is rather extraordinary in a female play-writer, is a most excellent wife and mother." (The Harrowby-Tiverton Manuscripts, Vol. IV, f 101 b, Sandon Hall, Staffordshire. Quoted by kind permission of the Earl of Harrowby.)

more grave explanation. In large part, Mrs. Cowley's accusations must be understood as a barometer registering degree to which women playwrights suddenly felt endangered and powerless in the absence of Garrick's mentoring.[2]

But Garrick's mentoring was itself a part of the problem. We have seen in Mrs. Brooke's story the consequence of Garrick's malevolence. It now appears that even Garrick's benevolence carried with it certain costs. In the case of Hannah Cowley and Hannah More, one important consequence of his mentoring was that the literary daughters found themselves in competition with one another for the attentions of the father.[3] The pattern was reminiscent of the famous opening scene in *King Lear*, in which each daughter is called upon publicly to name her love and loyalty for Lear as greater than that of her sisters. As in *Lear*, the legacy of this dynamic did not show itself fully until the retirement of the patriarch, at which time incipient hositilities became manifest among the sisters.[4] In the case of this paper war, Cowley identified the source of the trouble as another woman playwright, instead of Garrick's mentoring, and the relationship of that mentoring to theatre in eighteenth-century England.

When Garrick chose to be kind, it would be hard to imagine a more energizing and energetic presence. From the letters, prefaces, prologues and epilogues, he emerges as a benevolent and canny mentor to a number of playwrights; however, for a significant number of women playwrights, this kind of assistance constituted a critical point of access into the profession. Garrick's particular contribution to women was in giving their work the painstaking care in the difficult middle process from rewrites to actual production. In this he stands alone in his generation, with the possible exception of his close friend and colleague, George Colman the Elder. The statistics are revealing here: between 1747 and 1776 (the duration of his tenure as manager of Drury Lane), Garrick produced nine contemporary women playwrights (not counting Hannah More whose first play opened the year after he retired), for a total of 128 performances, as compared to Covent Garden, which produced three contemporary women playwrights in the same span of time for a total of twenty performances.[5] The ratio of performances of plays by women, Drury Lane to Covent Garden, is approximately five to one. One of the three women produced at Covent Garden, Elizabeth Griffith, had already been produced by Garrick, and thus constituted a lesser risk. If we include plays by women of earlier periods, specifically Behn, Centlivre and Pix, the ratio of performances of plays by women playwrights from 1747 to 1776 is 292 for Drury Lane as compared to 111 for Covent Garden, which narrows the ratio to three to one, and suggests that Covent Garden was more likely to produce women playwrights once they were tried and true, but was unlikely to take a chance on an unknown. Garrick, by contrast, took chances on unknown women playwrights, sponsoring one woman who was to become a career professional (Hannah Cowley) and engineering short-term successes for a number of others.

It is intriguing to speculate why Garrick made efforts on behalf of women in an age that was often ruthlessly critical of their literary efforts. One explanation is altruism, but the larger picture suggests something more practical. Given the size of the collective theatre audience in London, it was to the manager's advantage to have at least several new scripts within a season's repertory, so as to keep audience interest alive and repeat attendance high. By this encouragement and receptivity to the work of women, Garrick was not only enhancing his reputation as a benevolent man of letters; he was also encouraging the submission of new scripts and increasing his chances of finding good ones. It is also true that the women he took under his wing were grateful for the opportunity to be produced by him, and anxious to please him, to be molded by his tastes and wisdom. It was a kind of patronage that exactly suited Garrick, whose long experience in playwriting, performing and producing made him an excellent judge of what would succeed with his audiences. The relationship that developed between him and these women gave him access to a maximum amount of new material with a minimum amount of resistance to his editorial advice and guidance.

Garrick's advice and guidance emerge in a variety of ways from letters and other records. Dorothy Celisia, in her advertisement for *Almida*, referred to the "the judicious and friendly hand of Mr. Garrick," and reported that "he spared neither pains nor expense to please the public in the respect of decoration,"[6] by which she meant not only new scenery and stage decor but also new costumes. Garrick wrote for his new playwrights: for Hannah More's maiden production of *Percy* he wrote the prologue, and for Hannah Cowley's *The Runaway* he wrote the epilogue. He was concerned financially: for Hannah More he carefully invested her profit of £600 after *Percy* closed; to Elizabeth Griffith, who was in financial straits, he wrote that he would personally seek a bookseller for her play, since publication depended largely upon a guarantee of production from him.[7] Another letter from him to Mrs. Griffith indicates that she had anxiously tried to dictate casting for her upcoming production of *The School for Rakes*, and that here Garrick had gently but firmly insisted that she trust his judgement in the matter.[8] She relented, and the result was a major success. In this case, Mrs. Griffith also was indebted to Garrick for the very subject matter of her play; it was he who had suggested a script by Beaumarchais as the basis for her English adaptation. A similar kind of solicitude emerged in his development of More's *Percy* after his retirement from Drury Lane; his assistance to her included getting her an introduction to Thomas Harris at Covent Garden, since Garrick's own producing days were over.

One of the most subtle and important kinds of help that Garrick was able to offer was in the fine art of timing a production's opening advantageously. For this reason he wisely delayed Griffith's opening of her version of *Père de Famille*, despite her anxious protests,[9] and allowed More's *Percy* to go up relatively early in the 1777–1778 season. In spite of More's dire predictions, the play had an extremely successful run of nineteen nights; similarly Cowley's *The Runaway* played for seventeen nights when it opened in the 1775–1776 season, an outstanding run for a new play by a novice playwright.

But it was in the areas of editing and shaping dramatic texts that Garrick made his most significant contributions. Neither Cowley nor More was an actress, so their practical experience of the production and rehearsal process was limited, experience which might have played an important part in developing playwriting skills. Garrick's wide experience as manager, director, playwright, and actor constituted a crucial missing link in their transition from writer to playwright. His alterations and suggestions consistently point in the direction of performability, that is, of creating roles for actors that offer possibilities for vigorous characterization and action, instead of endless speechifying. One particularly valuable piece of evidence is the manuscript to Hannah Cowley's first play, *The Runaway*, which bears approximately sixty different additions, deletions and alterations in

Garrick's handwriting to the fair copy submitted to Larpent on 5 February 1776. For example, the opening lines of the play are a speech by George, who has just come home from university on vacation, and says: "Oh, for the luxury of Night Gown and Slippers! No poor jaded Hack of Parnassus can be more tired than I am. The Roads so dusty and the sun so hot – 'two'd be less tolerable riding post in Africa."[10] Garrick's rewrite of the same line reads simply: "Oh, for the luxury of Night Gown and Slippers! No poor jaded Hack of Parnassus can be more tired than I am." Here Garrick cut away unnecessary exposition and reduced the length of the speech to a size manageable for someone who is too hot and tired to talk. Later, in the climactic moment of the play, it is revealed that old Mr. Hargrave, George's father, intends Lady Dinah, a woman of fortune in her fifties, not for himself but for poor George. George and his friends have all been laboring under the misconception that old Hargrave has intended to marry Lady Dinah himself. In a scene between George and his father, the stage directions at the moment of revelation read: "A long pause, staring at each other." George's line as it is originally written by Cowley, reads: "Then I hope we shall soon be awakened. I was never in so horrible a dream in my life." Garrick cuts the entire line and replaces it with "Wife! Lady Dinah my wife!" Again, Garrick insisted on less text and more subtext; his line for George heightened the moment of shock and disbelief in a way that Cowley's had inadvertently flattened it.

What is most striking overall about Garrick's work on *The Runaway* is the way he tightened the text without damaging the charm and ingenuousness of the characters and situations, and helped her structure into the text moments that are clearly *performable*. One very early letter (probably 1775) from Cowley to Garrick suggests the strain of trying to adjust her script to his expectations, but her effort and willingness paid off.[11] Later Cowley would learn from adapting the work of earlier playwrights like Aphra Behn (*The Lucky Chance*) and Susanna Centlivre (*The Salamanca Doctor Outwitted*), but it was David Garrick who initially taught her how to craft a dramatic moment.

Garrick's work on More's *Percy* and *The Fatal Falsehood* appears to have been more broadly structural in nature. The work on Cowley's script left the larger plot intact and concentrated on restructuring small comic moments; in More's plays Garrick characteristically challenged the basic structure of the plot itself. Unlike Cowley's work, the fair copies of More's *Percy* and *The Fatal Falsehood* are virtually untouched, so we have to rely on the letters that passed between them to understand Garrick's work on these two manuscripts, and, significantly, Mrs. Garrick's as well (the revisions on More's play were to become a family affair). As usual, Garrick's letters indicate a finely tuned sense of his audiences. Of *Percy*, which revolves around the meeting of two estranged lovers, he wrote More that her first draft of the third act

> raises such Expectation from the Circumstances, that a great deal more must be done, to content ye Spectators and Readers – I am rather vex'd that Nothing More is produc'd by that Meeting, which is the Groundwork of the Tragedy, & from which so much will be required, because such an Alarm is given to the heart & the Mind –[12]

The final version ended with Percy throwing Elwina to the ground, suggesting that More took Garrick's advice to heart and worked the scene up to a climactic ending. To judge from the correspondence, More tended to round off the ends of her acts instead of bringing them to a fine pitch of excitement and creating a natural appetite for the next act. A good deal of More's other writing, like *Sir Eldred and the Bower*, was in verse, some of it taken from ballads, and most of it less concerned with dramatic situation than with language and narrative. Garrick's suggestions countered her tendency to create cantos with a downward inflection rather than acts and scenes with a rising inflection.

As a whole, one is repeatedly struck by the sagacity and generosity of Garrick's editorial efforts for these women, and at the same time by a certain paternal concern which extended well past the normal call of duty. Nor was Garrick unaware of his impact upon women playwrights. Towards the end of his career, he wrote a letter to his friend Frances Cadogan, in which he said with evident satisfaction: "– have not ye Ladies – Mesdames Griffith, Cowley & Cilesia spoke of me before their Plays with an Over-Enthusiastick Encomium? What says the divine Hannah More?"[13] There are even faint resonances with *Lear* : "What says our second daughter, our dearest Regan?"[14]

Whatever the ambiguities, the extent to which these women had been nourished and promoted by Garrick would make itself clear in the period following his retirement and death. In all areas the playwrights experienced setbacks.[15] Editorial assistance was non-existent. In the production and timing of openings it is difficult to distinguish between flagrant carelessness and deliberate sabotage. For example, Cowley's first produced play after Garrick's retirement, a small gem called *Who's the Dupe?*, was promised a good mid-season opening by Sheridan, but instead was allowed to languish, opening late in the season (mid-April) by which time it could not have a regular run because of end-of-season benefits. Mrs. Cowley was then to pay 100 guineas to the management "(Thirty of which had been added by the present Managers) for the chance of a Benefit, at a time when the current business of the Theatre would not produce that Sum."[16] In other words, far from making money on *Who's the Dupe?*, she actually stood to lose substantially. In another instance, her tragedy *Albina* went unperformed for three years after its original completion in 1776 while it was passed from Sheridan to Harris with spurious promises of production. When George Colman the Elder finally agreed to produce it at the Haymarket in July of 1779, the timing was so conspicuously bad that even the prologue made jest of it: "Hang these authors and their airs! . . . What right has She upon our *Summer* stage?"[17]

In addition to being badly timed, *Albina* suffered from serious miscasting. Robert Palmer, an actor noted for large stature, was cast as Gondibert, the dwarf lover. The novice Miss Montagu made a hash of the villainous Editha, and after the reviews went against her, burst into tears on stage in mid-performance, and made a moving plea for audience sympathy (a performance ludicrously inconsistent with the behavior of the character she was supposed to be playing). Ultimately she was replaced by a Miss Sherry, who did admirable work, but not in time to save the show from closing. Colman apparently had a conscience; he scheduled Cowley's third benefit night for the seventh instead of the normal ninth evening of the run, perhaps to make sure she received some compensation in case the show closed prematurely.

Hannah More's fate at the hands of Thomas Harris with *The Fatal Falsehood* in 1779 was no better. She and Garrick had worked hard on the play in its early stages, and the two of them believed that another summer of work on it would make it a good prospect for the fall of 1779. Unfortunately, Garrick's death in January made these revisions impossible. Shortly after Garrick's death, Harris

> no sooner understood that the play was in readiness, than he solicited her with so much earnestness to let him bring it out the very next month, that she yielded to his persuasions, against the better judgement of herself and her friends, and suffered it to appear at an unfavourable season.[18]

So *The Fatal Falsehood* opened in May of 1779, a very late date for a new mainpiece to be introduced into a season. It was harshly reviewed, in spite of a fine performance by Miss Younge as Emmelina, and lasted only three nights, just long enough for a single benefit night, instead of the three More must have hoped for.

Nor were the difficulties for women playwrights limited to mismanagement. The literary climate for women playwrights, which had been tempered by Garrick's efforts on their behalf, became uncertain again after his death. In 1779, there was no way to tell which way things might go. Would women playwrights be allowed to continue, or would they be returned to the kind of unprotected status they had endured prior to Garrick's tenure?

The early signs were not particularly promising. Several satirical treatments of women playwrights appeared in rapid succession on the London stage. We could interpret this positively, as a measure of just how much presence women now had in the profession. But one cannot help but notice that the satires themselves were being written by the very theatre managers to whom these women had to apply for production. For example, in August of 1779, George Colman the Elder took the opportunity of lampooning women playwrights in a comedy called *The Separate Maintenance*, which was produced at the Haymarket simultaneously with *Albina*. His play featured a lady playwright named Mrs. Fustian, a "strange, ranting, crazy being,"[19] and an indignant reader wrote to demand if the satire was pointed directly either at Mrs. Cowley or at Miss More.[20] In a later play called *The Female Dramatist* (1782) by his son, George Colman the Younger, the central character was a Madam Melpomene Metaphor, whose young nephew Beverley determines that her passion for scribbling needs to be cured: "You shall see me transform her into a downright housewife – and by a Single

Stroke of my Art, turn her pen into a Needle, and her Tragedies into thread papers." Interestingly, this early effort was roundly disapproved of by the audience, and was immediately cancelled.[21] Then there was Richard Brinsley Sheridan's epilogue to More's *The Fatal Falsehood,* which reinforced the same familiar theme of the lady scribbler, surrounded by evidence of domestic irresponsibility and unfulfilled literary pretensions. Although it was by no means unusual for an epilogue to denigrate humorously the play preceding it in order to solicit warm compensatory applause from the audience, this epilogue was so astringent that one critic reported: "The audience evidently did not relish the jest, for it certainly wore a strong appearance of a severe and illiberal attack on female genius."[22] During this crucial period after Garrick's death, when the prospects for women playwrights appear to have been uncertain, the public played a significant role in voicing support for the idea of women playwrights, or conversely voicing disapproval for satirical treatments of them, even when the playwriting managers were giving off decidedly negative signals in plays and epilogues.

Attacks on women playwrights were by no means limited to plays and epilogues, but appeared also in the press. In 1779, taking a direct shot at Garrick's patronage of women playwrights, the *St. James Chronicle* complained:

> We are tired of indulging Authours because they are Females. The Success of these Amazonian leaders brought forward a Mrs. Griffith, a Mrs. Cowley, and a Miss More. Some well-timed flattery to a late Manager and Actor brought on the Tragedy of *Percy,* the most interesting parts of which were borrowed from a French Play, without the common good manners of acknowledging it.[23]

It was an old and familiar theme: if a woman playwright had a conspicuous success such as *Percy,* it could only be explained by her having lifted her material from some other (male) source. The epilogue for More's *Percy,* written by Garrick himself in 1777, constituted a striking contrast to the spiteful irritability of his contemporaries:

> Tho' I'm female . . .
> I come, the <u>friend</u> and <u>champion</u> of my sex;

I'll prove, ye fair, that let us have our swing,
We can, as well as men, do any thing.

Certainly there were satires of male playwrights: there is
Sheridan's savage and very funny portrait of Richard Cumberland as Sir Fretful Plagiary in *The Critic*. But Cumberland, who
was one of the most successful playwrights of the late eighteenth
and early nineteenth centuries, was a robust and worthy target.
Furthermore, the attack on Cumberland was specific to the man
himself, rather than to the *idea* of men being playwrights. However, when Sheridan satirized women playwrights in his epilogue
to *Percy*, he was not satirizing any particular woman playwright;
he was satirizing the *idea* of a woman playwright. Consciously or
unconsciously, he had chosen to call into question women's
continuity in the profession.

It was in this charged atmosphere that Hannah Cowley and
Hannah More came to grief in the summer of 1779, just six
months after Garrick's death, in the wake of both women's
productions having been severely mismanaged. The term
"paper war" is an interesting overstatement. In fact, only two
relatively polite volleys were fired off by the protagonists; the
battle was in large part fought and promoted by other parties
and by the newspapers themselves. At some point during the
summer, the voyeuristic thrill of this altercation surpassed the
excitement of what was being offered onstage, and the paper war
became a substitute for theatre. The flavor of the exchanges in
the newspapers suggests a kind of meta-theatre, a mud hen
wrestling match into which Cowley and More had been reluctantly pressed. Dibdin best expressed the unhealthy pleasure a
bored and restless London found in watching two women go at
it: "Had these foolish ladies no friend to prevent their making
themselves a town talk? What were they cavilling about after
all?"[24]

The paper war actually began as early as 7 May, when a
review of More's *The Fatal Falsehood* stated that the play was
"astonishingly similar" to a manuscript as yet unpublished by
Mrs. Cowley.[25] This same reviewer on 2 August (in the review
for Cowley's *Albina* which had opened 31 July) stated that the
reader would discern a strong resemblance to *The Fatal Falsehood*,
but suggested that in fairness to Mrs. Cowley, "we feel ourselves
bound to declare that we read the play of *Albina* four years ago,

and that it was essentially the same piece that it is now." In the 5–7 August edition of the *St. James Chronicle*, the position shifted subtly from a defense of Mrs. Cowley's originality to an accusation of plagiarism directed at More. An open letter to the paper (which may have been a plant by Cowley's husband, who was himself the theatre critic for the *Gazetteer*), relates that the writer overheard a conversation at Haymarket in which it was hotly debated whether More stole from Cowley or Cowley from More, and implies that Garrick himself may have been implicated in assisting More to steal from Cowley.[26] Hannah More, in a letter to the *Morning Post*, responded directly for the first and last time in language which clearly indicates her anxiety about voyeurism:

> It is with the deepest regret I find myself compelled to take a step repugnant to my own Feelings, and to the delicacy of my Sex; a Step as *new* to me as it is disagreeable; for I never, till this moment, directly or indirectly, was concerned in any paragraph in any London paper . . . I am under the necessity of solemnly declaring, that I never saw, heard, or read, a single line of Mrs. Cowley's tragedy.[27]

To which Mrs. Cowley replied, in language that indicates similar anxieties about voyeurism: "I wish Miss More had been still more sensible of the indelicacy of a newspaper altercation between women, and the ideas of ridicule which the world are apt to attach to such unsexual hardiness."[28] She promised to explain herself more fully in the forthcoming preface to *Albina*.

This preface, which was published later that August, gives our best account of Cowley's version of the dispute. She began by recounting her early success with *The Runaway* in 1776 as a novice playwright working under Garrick, "but this success closed with the unfortunate period in which Mr. Garrick resigned the management of Drury Lane."[29] Following his retirement, Cowley sought Sheridan's help in producing *The Runaway* for a second season at Drury Lane, but discovered, after a demoralizing series of broken appointments, delays, and reports of mislaid manuscripts, that she had been "shelf'd."[30] *Albina*, which by this time had already been returned by Garrick and by Harris, was then offered to Sheridan, who deflected it back to Harris, but promised to produce her third play, the aforementioned *Who's the Dupe?*, which as we know also was badly delayed until it became a financial liability. In the meantime, More's *Percy* had come out in 1777, bearing some likeness to *Albina* but nothing provable. The *Albina* manuscript at this point was still circulating among managers.

The final disaster was the opening of *The Fatal Falsehood* in May of 1779. This time, stated Cowley, the similarities were so striking that they were impossible to ignore, because by the time *Albina* finally straggled to a late July opening the same year, the public impression was that Cowley had borrowed from More instead of the reverse. Cowley was careful not to accuse More outright of having plagiarized, but she left the reader little doubt about her own opinion, that "by some *wonderful* coincidence, Miss More and I have but one common stock of ideas between us."[31] She states that while the play was in Mr. Garrick's possession at Hampton (his country home), "Miss More was a visitant at Hampton," but softens the implications by adding that the managers may have inadvertently communicated the ideas of Cowley's script in the process of editing and advising More. However the information travelled, directly or indirectly, Cowley felt robbed of ideas, reputation, and remuneration.

Cowley and More never directly confronted one another again, although the debate continued in the newspapers through various editorials and letters. On 19 August 1779, the *Gazetteer* took the solemn step of initiating a public inquiry by committee, which came down (predictably, because of Captain Cowley's affiliation with the paper) on the side of Mrs. Cowley. With the advent of the new September season, the controversy finally died out completely. But the questions raised by the allegations were never completely resolved. The question of whether or not More deliberately borrowed from Cowley is a complex one and deserves careful examination.

Briefly, the similarities between the two plays, *The Fatal Falsehood* and *Albina*, can be summarized as follows. The most striking one, which so upset Cowley, was that in both plays, a villain/villainess (Bertrand/Editha), plots to destroy a romance (Rivers and Julia, Edward and Albina) in order to better his/her own position. This plotting takes the form of convincing a gullible character (Orlando/Gondibert) that his affections are returned by the lady in question (Julia/Albina), when in fact nothing could be further from the truth. It is the hope of each villain that the duped suitor (Orlando/Gondibert) will kill or defeat his 'rival'

(Rivers/Edward). In a startling plot reversal at the end, Orlando accidentally kills Bertrand whom he mistakes for Rivers, and Gondibert accidentally stabs Editha, mistaking her for Albina. The resolution in *The Fatal Falsehood* is somewhat contrived and unsuccessful: Orlando's betrothed, now abandoned and thinking that Orlando has killed her brother Rivers, enters the stage "distracted" and dies for no accountable reason; in remorse, Orlando kills himself. The original romantic pair, Julia and Rivers, are thereby left intact and unencumbered. In *Albina*, Gondibert, upon killing the woman he thinks to be Albina, kills himself before realizing that Albina lives, and that it is Editha he has killed. Again, the central couple, Albina and Edward, are left intact.

In my reading of the plays, it is easy to see why Cowley was angered. In her preface, she claims no source for her play, that it was entirely original (although she had obviously borrowed a character name from Davenant). More makes no such claims, but the surviving letters between her and Garrick make no mention of outside sources and show evidence of the plot having evolved and changed over a period of many months.[32] So in spite of startling similarities, the evidence points towards More's innocence, although there is nothing conclusive.

Other evidence is equally circumstantial. The only common link between Cowley and More which might have constituted a leak during the writing of *The Fatal Falsehood* (which took place from July 1778 through January of 1779), was Garrick himself. According to Cowley's preface, her script of *Albina* went first to Garrick, with the title *Edwina*, early in the summer of 1776, and then to Mr. Harris in the summer of 1777, after which it bounced back and forth between Harris and Sheridan to no effect until the summer of 1779, when it was at long last picked up by Colman for the Haymarket. We know with certainty that Hannah More received no editing or advice from either Sheridan or Harris; in fact, she is quoted as saying that Harris was so anxious to get his hands on *The Fatal Falsehood* that he would hardly give her time to finish it. The logical conclusion is that when Garrick and More were working on *The Fatal Falsehood*, it had already been two years since he had seen the early version of *Albina*, if indeed he ever read it at all (since by the time she submitted it to him, he had already retired from management). No letters survive to prove that Garrick ever read *Edwina/Albina* or that he made any editorial suggestions to Cowley. On the contrary, the letters from this period indicate that his work with playwrights as a whole radically diminished, with the striking exception of Hannah More, who really must be seen as a personal family friend rather than as a developing commercial playwright. If Garrick did indeed "leak" any of Cowley's ideas for *Albina* to More, it would probably have been unconscious; as Cowley herself says, "Amidst the croud of Plots, and Stage Contrivances in which a Manager is involv'd, *recollection* is too frequently mistaken for the suggestions of the *imagination.*"[33]

In an alternative scenario, Cowley said in her preface that she had been informed that Hannah More was a "visitant" at Hampton during the period in which Garrick was holding Cowley's play, the clear implication being that More might herself have happened upon the manuscript and helped herself to its contents. But here Cowley appears to have been misinformed; More did not visit the Garricks for about a year after his final performance on 10 June 1776, and the correspondence bears this out.[34] So we may conclude that More could not have seen the script on her own, because by the time she was visiting the Garricks again in the summer of 1777, the script had already been forwarded to Thomas Harris.

Another important bit of evidence is a letter about *Fatal Falsehood* written by More to Garrick on 10 October 1778, which reads: "Be so good as to treat me with your usual candour, and tell me how I have failed or succeeded in unfolding the story and characters; and above all, *if you can recollect any other tragedy that it is like, as I shall be most careful of that*" [my emphasis].[35] More was making implicit reference to her earlier failure to adequately acknowledge her sources for *Percy*, which had gotten her in some minor difficulties with the press in 1777 and which later were resolved. What is striking about her letters from this earlier period is the care with which she discusses and weighs each source with Garrick, from a French play by Belloy to Percy's *Reliques.* The overall impression is of a rather academic and scholarly process, rather than the furtive gleanings one might expect from a career plagiarist. Garrick, in a much earlier letter to Mrs. Griffith, wrote on the subject of borrowing:

> that there can be no Objection to the introducing Circumstances, Incidents, Characters, and Even Scenes, that may

bear some resemblance to other Plays; Authors should only take care that Such incidents, Characters & Scenes are not too nearly imitated or ill-chosen.[36]

But Garrick was speaking in the context of a play that had long since had its run and was in the public domain; the ethics of dipping into an unproduced and unpublished script whose author still hoped for remuneration were another matter entirely.

The final piece of evidence is the most circumstantial and indeed the most subjective of all. The overall impression which emerges out of the cumulative correspondence that More's real reason for involving herself in commercial playwriting was because it created a structure within which she could legitimate and prolong her contact with David Garrick. As her later work was to bear out, she did not really approve either of theatre or of theatre people (with the singular exception of Garrick himself) except in the service of religion. The writing of *Percy* and *The Fatal Falsehood* were a kind of slum adventure for her, not the foundations of a playwriting career. For Garrick's part, playwriting and producing, the two things he most needed to get away from after his retirement, were his gift to her as an adopted literary daughter, a Cordelia to his old age. They were a way of structuring the relationship, which fell into a strangely gray area and required the legitimating presence of Mrs. Garrick in the form of an additional editor. This scenario is consistent with More's strikingly indifferent attitude towards the success or failure of *The Fatal Falsehood* after Garrick's death. In an early letter to one of her sisters written sometime in 1776, she wrote: "I find my dislike of what are called public diversions greater than ever, except a play; and when Garrick has left the stage, I could be very well contented to relinquish plays also."[37]

The evidence on the whole, although largely circumstantial, tends to suggest several things: first, that plagiarism had probably not occurred. The logistics of manuscript access, combined with More's lack of ambition in commercial playwriting, make the case for plagiarism a thin one. The logic of Hannah More's having borrowed from Mrs. Cowley, when she already had a strong literary advisor and critic in Garrick, is strained. Second, if Garrick did unconsciously leak Hannah Cowley's ideas to Hannah More, it is a slippage that is consistent with the way he handled women playwrights as a *separate category* from male

73

playwrights. There is nothing whatever to suggest that his mind was slipping in these final years; it is far more likely that he unconsciously had conflated the two Hannahs within this category of female playwright. Third, whatever else the evidence suggests, it does prove conclusively that Mrs. Cowley was not the crackpot that More's biographers have tended to portray. Her grievances, both artistic and financial, are in all cases rational and legitimate ones. But if there in fact was no plagiarism, and Mrs. Cowley was not a crank, how then may we account for these charges?

Two documents resonate throughout this narrative and may point to an explanation. The first is a letter to Garrick written by Mrs. Cowley in 1777, the year after his retirement, and one year after their successful collaboration on *The Runaway*. Mrs. Cowley, after a fruitless effort to re-establish contact with him in which her husband was rebuffed by Garrick's servants, says with heart-rending simplicity: "I have lost your friendship!"[38] Subsequently, Garrick replies to her with great solicitude, explaining that he has been desperately ill, and that she and Captain Cowley are still welcome guests.[39] One final letter survives to Mrs. Garrick, in which mention is made of an unnamed Lord H—(Harrowby), and the implication is that the Garricks attempted to find her some sort of patronage.[40]

But what is striking about the correspondence is Mrs. Cowley's desolation about her perceived abandonment by Garrick. Evidently the combination of his retreat into private life and his illness had played havoc with her sense of his protection. She seems unable to imagine continuing work without him. This sense of loss must have been peculiarly complicated by the fact that Hannah More, whose attitude towards playwriting was quite ambivalent, was the sole female recipient of Garrick's limited energies after his retirement. To add insult to injury, More's friendship with the Garricks gave her an easy mobility in distinguished literary circles which included Samuel Johnson and Richard Brinsley Sheridan. The fact that the intercourse between Garrick and More was less a professional exchange than a personal one would probably have been cold comfort to Hannah Cowley. She had been displaced as the favored daughter, when in fact her skills were far superior.

The second document that throws light on the situation is Cowley's preface to *Albina*, which oscillates curiously between her charges of plagiarism, and her accounts of repeated failure to find a foothold with the new winter managers, Harris and Sheridan.

> Should it, after all, appear to the Public, that there is nothing more in these repeated resemblances, than what may be accounted for supposing a similarity in our minds; and that, by some WONDERFUL coincidence, Miss More and I have but one common stock of ideas between us, I have only to lament that the whole misfortune of this similarity has fallen upon me. Now, as in this case, we must continue writing in the same track, it seems reasonable that we should have our productions brought forward in turn; instead of which Miss More has had TWO tragedies brought out, both of which were written since mine, whilst I struggled for the representation of ONE in vain. But, as there seems to be little hope of my obtaining this, or any other favour from the Winter Managers, I presume at least, that, as I do not pretend to prove – what is impossible for me to know – that Miss More ever read, or copied me, it will be admitted that I have not copied her.[41]

The charges and counter-charges of plagiarism, above and beyond the impugnment of personal integrity, were inextricable from the issue of profit: "by the conduct of the Winter Managers, I have been deprived of a reasonable prospect of several hundred pounds, and have spent years of fruitless anxiety and trouble." She closes grimly: "My productions have been uniformly received by the Public with applause; yet I find the doors of the Winter Theatre shut against me. – To this severe fate I most reluctantly submit."[42]

Ultimately, we must understand the preface to *Albina*, and the paper war as a whole, as having had less to do with plagiarism than with a deep-seated anxiety about authorship itself; that Cowley's and More's dependence upon Garrick's editorial and production assistance had raised unconscious questions after his departure about who the real author of their successes was. Had they written their plays, or had Garrick? This anxiety about authorship took the form of a very public debate which sought to persuade London that *in both cases*, More's and Cowley's, one playwright had generated original work, and the other playwright had borrowed or stolen her ideas. Unable to name

Garrick, they named one another. It was a form of burial: they were both participating in an effort to distance themselves from the presence of the male mentor. Both women, but Cowley in particular, felt robbed, and both women sought to reclaim their texts. The peculiarity and complexity of their story is that they sought redress through one another, rather than from the canonized patron whose memory they were socially and politically constrained to honor.

Cowley's conspicuous success for many years after Garrick's death suggests that, for her, the separating and healing process was successful. In More's case the departure of the mentor and the end of her commercial playwriting efforts were simultaneous, although her literary efforts continued to be successful in other areas, with other male mentors.

In retrospect, the paper war had the unfortunate side effect of further imperiling the precarious position of women playwrights in general by inviting all of London to witness divisiveness among them. This divisiveness had the special complication of gender: it added to the questionable wisdom of writing and public "speaking," the tastelessness of public acrimony in a culture which rewarded women for maintaining privacy. It further succeeded in shifting the focus of the debate from the similarity between the two plays to the questionable wisdom of allowing women playwrights in the theatre at all. As Charles Dibdin wrote for all posterity on the subject of this paper war:

> Nothing can be more ridiculous than literary quarrels even among men, but when ladies, fearful lest their poetic offspring should crawl through life unheeded, publicly expose themselves to the world, in order to ascertain their beauty and legitimacy, who does not wish they had occupied their time with a needle instead of a pen.[43]

But the underlying issue was invisible not only to the public but to the principals themselves: that Garrick's praiseworthy guidance and help to women playwrights during his career as manager had created in them a correspondingly strong need to distance themselves and their work from his authority and authorship in order to continue working after his death.

# 4

# SOPHIA LEE
## Documenting the Post-Garrick Era

Sophia Lee has particular importance for this study because she enters professional playwriting for the first time in 1780, shortly after Garrick's death. Her story, or the fragments of it that survive, provides a point of departure for discussing this "post-Garrick era" and understanding what his absence might have meant for women entering playwriting as a career.

Lee is the only playwright in this study to have come from a theatre family. Her father was John Lee, a manager and actor, who alternated in the latter portion of his life between managing at the Bath Orchard Street Theatre, and performing seasons in London, for Garrick and for Harris. He landed in debtor's prison twice, once in Edinburgh when Sophia was six, and again when she was in her early twenties; during her visits to him in prison she began writing the play for which she later became famous, *The Chapter of Accidents*, based in part on Diderot's *Père de Famille*. Her mother, Anna Sophia, was an actress for some years with the Bath company until her death in 1770. Sophia Lee's exposure to theatrical goings-on, whether through hearing her parents rehearse lines at home, listening to theatre gossip over the dinner table, or watching them perform, would have been unavoidable. In addition to absorbing some fundamentals of dramaturgy and stagecraft, she also was familiar with many of the players and managers, not only in Bath but also in London.

Sophia Lee has the odd distinction of having had a runaway success for her first production, and then quitting the field and keeping theatre at an arm's length ever after. She invested the proceeds of her benefit nights into a highly successful boarding-school venture (Belvedere House) with her sisters, and did not

*Plate 5*
George Colman the Elder
1732–1794
Occupations: Theatre Manager, Playwright

Colman's long and complicated relationship with Garrick almost certainly influenced his own developing style of management. Garrick mentored Colman through the revisions to *Polly Honeycombe* in 1760, and the production of Colman's first full-length play, *The Jealous Wife*. Subsequently there was a difficult period of dispute and reconciliation in 1765 and 1766 over the authorship of their collaboratively written *The Clandestine Marriage*. In the midst of this dispute, Colman wrote Garrick: "I understood it was to be a joint work, in the fullest sense of the word; and never imagined that either of us was to lay his finger on a particular scene, and cry, 'This is mine!' [I] cannot help being hurt at your betraying so earnest a desire to winnow your wheat from my chaff, at the very time that I was eager to bestow the highest polish on every part of the work, only in the hopes of perpetuating the memory of our joint labours, by raising a monument of the friendship between me and Mr. Garrick." Garrick apparently hoped that Colman would take his place as manager of Drury Lane when he stepped down in 1776, but Colman, with characteristic independence, decided instead to manage at the much less prestigious Haymarket. (Quoted from *The Private Correspondence of David Garrick*, ed. James Boaden, London, Henry Colburn and Richard Bentley, 1832, vol. 1, pp. 214–216.)

*Plate 6*
Sophia Lee
1750–1824
Occupations: Educator, Novelist, Playwright

Feminism, as it was introduced into late eighteenth-century thought, was often regarded with anxiety and suspicion by the very women who stood to gain the most from it. Then as now, the tendency was to focus on the sensational aspects of dissolving gender roles, rather than on underlying substantive issues like employment and education. In 1804, as part of her introduction to her novel *The Life of a Lover*, Sophia Lee wrote: "During the many years which these volumes have remained in my closet, such changes in nations, manners, and principles have been made, as defy all calculation. The revolutionary system has pervaded literature . . . The rights and character of woman have been placed in lights by which the delicacy of the sex has often been wholly sacrificed to the assertion of a hardy equality with man, that, even if it assured an increase of esteem, would cause an equal deduction of tenderness; a bad exchange for the sex upon the great scale. It was, I own, my girlish intention, to draw my heroine a female, possessing, without a masculine mind or manners, some decided opinions, which at the time when this work was written [sometime during the 1770s], would have been thought new and bold." Lee's description here of a female, without a masculine mind or manners, but possessing some decided opinions, nicely characterizes the limits to which she was prepared to go in battling to produce her plays (Quoted from *The Life of a Lover: In a Series of Letters* by Sophia Lee, printed for G. & J. Robinson, Paternoster Row, 1804, n.p.)

attempt another professional production for sixteen years.[1] This first play, *The Chapter of Accidents*, was produced by George Colman in August of 1780 at the Haymarket. It was a title that neatly described her own efforts to get her play produced. She published the play in September of 1780 with a detailed and angry preface which may offer some insights into this period for women as a whole. What follows is her preface with only a few small deletions:

> The aversion a woman ought to feel at the necessity of engaging even in a literary contest, has induced me to endure a variety of imputations; yet, to publish a piece, and leave all unanswered, might at once give a sanction to the past, and encourage future slanders: – let this plead my excuse for introducing myself to those who have so generously received a comedy I could wish more worthy [of] their patronage.
>
> Charged early in life with the care of a family, I accompanied my father eight years ago in the rules of a prison, where the perjury of an enemy and the injustice of a judge for a time confined him [summer of 1772]. To amuse some of my melancholy leisure, I there (from a fondness for Marmontel's beautiful tale of Lauretta) first conceived a design of introducing into the Drama a female heart, capable of frailty, yet shuddering at vice, and perhaps sufficiently punished in her own feelings. A lover, whose error was likewise in his heart, not head; and even for him I contrived a chastisement in the agony of losing her: nor did I imagine, in adopting a religious tenet, I could ever be accused of offending morality. Subsequent characters and incidents arose in the manner they now appear, except that the governor had then no place in it. It is now seven years since the piece was brought thus forward; soon after which a friend lent me a translation of Monsieur Diderot's *Père de Famille*. – This fine performance gave me infinite pleasure under all the disadvantages of a translation; and the chance-similitude which now and then occurred between that and mine rather flattered than grieved me, since, conscious of my own originality, and imagining even my worst enemy, if he charged me with plagiarism, would at least allow, while the subject was new to our stage, my only crime was in denying

it. – I returned the translated play, and mine lay dormant for several years. Sentiment was now exploded, and I therefore sought to diversify it with humour. The character of the austere Commander in Monsieur Diderot's play had particularly pleased me; and not being mistress of the French language, I sought in vain for a translation, on purpose to interweave him into mine. Not able to meet with any, I created the character of Governor Harcourt, (whose chief likeness to the French uncle is in name) and heightened the piece with every event relative to him . . .

In the interim my father had been engaged as a capital Actor by Mr. Harris [at Covent Garden, 1774–1777]. Life opened gradually upon me, and dissipated the illusions of imagination. I learnt that merit merely is a very insufficient recommendation to managers in general! and as I had neither a prostituted pen or person to offer Mr. Harris, I gave up, without a trial, all thoughts of the Drama, and sought an humble home in Bath, resolving to bury in my own heart its little talent, and be a poor anything rather than a poor author. Some valuable friends, I had long possessed there, insisted I should be wanting to myself in consigning this piece voluntarily to oblivion, and offered me a recommendation to Mr. Harris, with a promise of concealing my name, unless it was accepted. I could desire nothing more: and under these circumstances it was put into that gentleman's hands above a twelvemonth ago. The praises he gave it induced my friend to own my name, and from that moment (let his conscience tell him why) it sunk in Mr. Harris's favour. He said he had frequently refused a play of Mr. Macklin's taken from *Le Père de Famille*, and could not accept another on the same subject; insisted that the serious part of mine was all Diderot's; advised me to cut it entirely out, and convert the humorous part into an after-piece, which he would bring out in the course of the season. Reasons very remote from the Stage could alone induce me to listen a moment to his proposal, and those brought me a hundred miles to converse with him on the subject; when he produced me the copy sent him, so worn out and dirty, that I had reason to conclude he had lent it to every one he knew, at least – I was enough mistress of myself to listen with complaisance to the most supercilious and unmeaning criticisms, and agreed to mutilate it according to his ideas. The Actors were now named; I had every reason to imagine it a settled thing; and returning to Bath, sent the reduced copy at the appointed time, viz. early in September. A month elapsed without my even knowing he had received it; when, with the continued ill manners of addressing me by a third person, (for he never wrote a single line in answer to several letters) I was shewn a paragraph from Mr. Harris by the friend already mentioned, importing, that I "had sent him four acts instead of two, and must still take away half; adding, that he advised me by all means to retain my own, disregarding Diderot's." I did retain my own; for as the manuscript was luckily returned for another alteration, I thought it time to consider what was due to myself, and that the character of mildness and complacency would be rather dearly bought if I gave up all merit for it; I therefore wrote him a civil letter, and finally withdrew it.

I shall not expatiate upon this treatment. I was perhaps in some degree blameable, for believing that man would set any value on my time or my money, who knew not the value of his own; nay, I may be in reality obliged to him in one sense, since his acceptance of my Comedy would inevitably have consigned to oblivion those parts of it honored with the most lavish applause.

What pleasure do I feel in retracting the general aspersion cast upon managers when I speak of Mr. Colman! – Obliged to get the piece represented if possible, lest the subject should be borrowed (an evil too common of late) I enclosed with it an anonymous letter to that Gentleman, briefly relating these particulars, and it was left at his house early in the year by an unknown person. At the expiration of a fortnight the manuscript or his answer was demanded, and the latter by this means rendered both impartial and decisive. Mr. Colman thought the general name of Author entitled to the compliment of his own hand-writing; and, by flattering opinion, and immediate acceptance of my piece, encouraged me to avow myself. By his advice I cut the songs, and lengthened it into five acts. Nor did his kindness end there. He gave me the benefit of his judgment and experience, both in heightening and abbreviating the business, with every attention in casting and getting it up;

generously uniting to the name of Manager that of Friend, Mr. Colman has brought into notice a woman who will ever with pride and pleasure acknowledge the obligation.[2]

As a whole, Lee sounds embattled in very much the same way that Cowley did in her preface to *Albina* the year before.[3] Even repeated hardship growing up in a theatre family had not prepared her for trying to get her play produced. Colman's kindness to her and their successful collaboration were not enough to make it worth her while to venture back in. What can we infer from this preface about the reasons for Lee's early withdrawal?

# 1

Lee's preface suggests that the *first experience* of producing a play was a critical one and had a lasting effect. Hannah Cowley, for example, wrote in her preface to Garrick for *The Runaway*: "Had you rejected me, when I presented my little Runaway, depressed by the refusal, and all confidence in myself destroyed, I should never have presumed to dip my pen again."[4] Cowley's text underlines the importance of having felt warmly welcomed, and the way it created for her a certain momentum. Lee's first experience was a difficult one, for a host of reasons, and her response afterwards was to stay away from theatre, prematurely ending what might have been a productive career.

# 2

*. . . the chance-similitude which now and then occurred between that and mine rather flattered than grieved me, since, conscious of my own originality, and imagining even my worst enemy, if he charged me with plagiarism, would at least allow, while the subject was new to our stage, my only crime was in denying it.*

One of the first things we hear about Mrs. Hazard in Clive's satire *Bays in Petticoats* is that her play is not original: she stole all her ideas from a man. The maid reports: "Why, do you know 'tis none of her own? a Gentleman only lent it her to read; he has been ill a great while at Bath; so she has taken the Advantage of that, made some little Alterations, had it set to Music, and has introduc'd it to the Stage as a Performance of her own."[5]

Accusations of plagiarism seem to have carried extra weight for women playwrights. A survey of prefaces to plays by a dozen contemporary male playwrights[6] shows that when male playwrights responded to charges of plagiarism, they tended to frame their rebuttals in ways that were witty or satirical, rather than serious and defensive. Richard Cumberland, for example, in his dedication to *The Choleric Man* (1775) writes with dripping irony to "High and Mighty Sir":

> Thus you stand, like the admonishing slave in the triumph, to remind the conqueror [any successful playwright] that *he is a man* . . . It is to you therefore, *ingenious Sir*, I am indebted for the discovery that I have lost sight of an original which I pretended to have copied, and copied one which I really never saw.[7]

A more moderate but equally controlled tone characterizes James Boaden's retort to detractors in his preface to *Cambro-Britons*:

> By the introduction of a supernatural agent, I may be by some deemed the plagiarist of *The Castle Spectre* . . . it is an affair of *chronology*; if there be any imitation (which I neither suppose nor charge), they who remember my play of *Fontainville Forest* will imagine Mr. Lewis conceived his phantom from mine.[8]

The two prefaces denying plagiarism by Lee and by Cowley have no such rhetorical distance or control. The rebuttals by the women have the solemn precision of giving evidence before an imaginary jury. They lack wit because the stakes are high, and the occasion is too serious. An accusation of plagiarism impugned a woman's integrity, as it did anybody's, but it also impugned the woman's ability to write at all, and this, more than anything, made repartee under pressure impossible.[9] Furthermore, disputing charges of plagiarism necessarily forced a woman into a public defense of her work, either in prefaces or in journals and newspapers. There was a high price to be paid for this kind of public defense: the major chroniclers of theatre activity during this period chide Lee for "irascibility," "petulance," and a failure to conduct herself appropriately.[10]

In any case, the rules regarding what constituted plagiarism were murky in the latter eighteenth century, and the anecdotal evidence indicates that where there was ambiguity, events did not play out in favor of women. Roughly speaking, it was felt that if an author made appropriate acknowledgements, he or she could not be charged with having plagiarized (the term used instead for legitimate use was "borrowed"). For example, John Burgoyne wrote a play (*The Heiress*, Drury Lane 1785–1786), which he appropriately acknowledged as having been based partly on *Le Père de Famille*. Far from calling it plagiarism, Genest commented that although he wishes the script had been more original, it was "the best new comedy since *The School for Scandal*."[11] *The Heiress* had also borrowed substantially from a work by the novelist and playwright Charlotte Lennox; but here Burgoyne's printed version made only a vague allusion to having borrowed from "novelists" without saying which ones. Genest doesn't take him to task for this omission, although he does set the record straight by naming Lennox and the characters in question. However, in a rather starchy letter to Burgoyne's daughter Caroline, after the identity of Burgoyne's unnamed "novelist" had emerged in the newspapers, a friend of the family's, a Miss Warburton, wrote:

> I happen to *know* that your father took the idea of the *The Heiress* from Mrs. Lennox's novel of *Henrietta*, which he reckoned one of the cleverest works of its class that had appeared; and I think what he says in his preface about acknowledging obligations to novelists was aimed at Sheridan, who could never bear to be told (what was, however, perfectly true) that his Sir Oliver Surface and his two nephews were borrowed from his mother's beautiful novel of *Sidney Biddulph*.[12]

There are two issues: the first is that Burgoyne does not get slapped with charges of plagiarism, but only a much lesser charge: lack of originality. The second, based on Miss Warburton's observations, is that male playwrights appear to have had a singularly difficult time acknowledging their sources when that source happened to be female, and there is some sanction for that omission being provided here after the fact, in this case by the critic.

By contrast, when a play by Hannah Cowley made a similarly vague gesture of acknowledgement, Genest did not hesitate to try to prove plagiarism. Instead of chastising her in general terms as he had done Burgoyne for not being more forthcoming about her sources, Genest did a line-by-line comparison of Cowley's *The School for Greybeards* (Drury Lane, 1786–1787) with Aphra Behn's *The Lucky Chance*, almost as if he were mounting a legal brief. Mrs. Cowley had named an "obsolete play" as her source in the preface, but apparently did not dare link her name with Aphra Behn's in public. "Mrs. Cowley was ashamed to advance a direct lie, but she was not ashamed to insinuate a falsehood."[13] In fact Genest's comparison inadvertently reveals how distinct Mrs. Cowley's play is from the original. This double standard for women playwrights becomes even more apparent when Genest sings John Philip Kemble's praises for having brought out Mrs. Behn's *The Rover* under his [Kemble's] name and with a new title (*Love in Many Masks*, 1789–1790). Kemble's version, if it can be called that, is in large sections a verbatim reproduction of the original, with the disclaimer it was "taken from Mrs. Behn with considerable alterations." Far from citing Kemble for plagiarism, Genest comments that

> this alteration of Mrs. Behn's *Rover* is a most judicious one, and might serve as a model for any person, who undertakes to alter an old play – Kemble has omitted what was exceptionable, added some few lines when absolutely necessary, and made many slight changes in the dialogue, but without changing anything from caprice.[14]

Genest's inconsistency in these instances suggests that charges of plagiarism could be loosely construed and utilized at the critic's discretion to improve or damage a playwright's reputation.

Fully twenty-four years later, in a preface to one of her novels (*The Life of a Lover*), Sophia Lee was still processing the pain of having to defend herself publicly against charges of plagiarism:

> When the Comedy of Chapter of Accidents was first represented, I was inexperienced enough to imagine that I might submit the little product of my fancy to the public, without appearing personally at its bar; but I soon discovered that the very success to which I owed so many friends, necessarily created me an equal number of enemies. Rendered timid from this conviction, as well as from my sex, I am now anxious to interest the candid and deprecate the severe. . . . [15]

Lee's choice of the word "bar" is suggestive. It is as if she had been tried in a court of law for criminal activity.

Women playwrights like Sophia Lee were in an unenviable position. What fragments of their professional history survived from the Restoration and the early eighteenth century had explicitly branded early pioneers like Aphra Behn and even Susanna Centlivre as sexually promiscuous and morally unfit. Women entering playwriting in the late eighteenth century were in the peculiar position of having to prove their respectability and moral fitness *along with* their competence as playwrights, which partly explains why the dramatic content of women's plays during this period was scrutinized so obsessively for signs of plagiarism or moral decay.

**3**

For all her exposure to the inside workings of theatre, Lee seems unable properly to interpret and place Harris's "critique" of her play, particularly his charges that she should cut "all the serious part" which he claimed was Diderot's anyway, and size the play down from a full-length comedy to two acts. Her play and Diderot's bear only the most superficial structural resemblances; Harris either has not read the French play, or he is being deliberately obtuse. The thrust of Lee's play is whether or not a woman who has had premarital sex with her lover is still capable of the virtue needed to be his wife. Diderot's play, from start to finish, is about what constitutes appropriate paternal control in the family.[16] In any case, Harris's quibbles about artistic merit actually are a cover for one of his favorite strategies, which was to downgrade a full-length play into a two-act afterpiece.

Harris's motives were purely financial: the author of an afterpiece received only a fraction of what the author of a mainpiece could expect from three benefits. In this way, the theatre got the use of a new script at a bargain price. But Lee's preface gives no indication that she understood what Harris was up to. Business motives masqueraded as artistic critique, and nothing in the more paternal style of Garrick had prepared women for this kind of manipulation.

**4**

I find it interesting that Hannah Cowley's preface to *Albina* (1779) and Lee's preface to *The Chapter of Accidents* (1780) have remarkable structural similarities to one another. They both begin with an apology for speaking publicly, and then they outline the actual sources of their respective plays and the difficulties they encountered with managers. Cowley's is longer and more detailed, but the sequence of her anonymous submission to Harris, her victimization at the hands of Sheridan and Harris, and her rescue by Colman are the same. One clear difference between the two prefaces is that Lee never mentions Sheridan at all, and one senses that she may have decided ahead of time, based in part on Cowley's preface, that an application to him was simply was not worth the effort. The similarities between the two prefaces lead me to wonder if would-be playwrights like Lee weren't reading prefaces like Mrs. Cowley's as they were published and using them as a kind of map, a way to plot a course for themselves through a mine-field. Certainly at this point we have no evidence of any kind to suggest that women playwrights had identified themselves as a group, or were in contact with one another or working cooperatively.[17] These prefaces, however, offered a forum in which grievances could be aired and circulated, like a nascent form of professional newsletter. The women were charting this post-Garrick landscape, if not in concert, at least with some awareness of what had happened to other women.

**5**

*Some valuable friends, I had long possessed there . . . offered me a recommendation to Mr. Harris, with a promise of concealing my name, unless it was accepted.*

Sophia Lee subsequently submitted her manuscript to Colman anonymously, and wrote him after he had accepted it to reveal herself: "The letter which introduced the opera was so true an account of my situation that it wanted only my sex and name . . . "[18] Hannah Cowley, in her preface to *Albina*, remarked: "as I had some reason to dread Mr. Harris's opinions, it was presented to him, in the Summer of 1777, by a Lady of Rank, with the name and sex of the Author concealed."[19] Elizabeth Inchbald's identity as the author of *The Mogul Tale* was kept strictly secret, even from the actors, up until the middle of opening night. In 1779, when Frances Burney told her good friend Samuel Johnson that she was about to write a play, he responded with the warmth and generosity that were characteristic of his dealings with Burney, and offered her this advice about the process of writing itself:

> He then gave me advice which just accorded with my wishes, viz., not to make known that I had any such intention [of writing a play]; to keep my own counsel; not to whisper even the name of it; to raise no expectations, which were always prejudicial, and, finally, to have it performed while the town knew nothing of whose it was.[20]

Mrs. Piozzi told a friend once that when Joanna Baillie finally came forward to claim authorship for her first collection of plays, the book sales plummeted.[21] The decision to publish and produce anonymously may have had less to do with maidenly modesty than with remuneration. Women's writing – even if it was acceptable – was considered to be worth less, both artistically and economically, than men's. This was a prejudice which would have had a powerful effect on how a manager read a new play. Certainly, the way Harris's opinion of Lee's *The Chapter of Accidents* changes in midstream, and the way he then presses her to turn her opera into an inexpensive (for him) afterpiece after learning who she is, is highly suspect in this regard.

### 6

*I learnt that merit merely is a very insufficient recommendation to managers in general! and as I had neither a prostituted pen or person to offer Mr. Harris, I gave up, without a trial, all thought of the Drama.*

We cannot ignore Lee's veiled accusations about Harris's personal conduct, especially given the fact that a report has come down to us of his having attempted to rape Elizabeth Inchbald during this same period when she too had approached him with a play.[22] It is actually fairly rare for reports of sexual harassment to surface during this period; one historian explains that if a woman reported abuse to her family, her father or brothers were duty-bound to defend her honor by duelling with the offender, and the prospect of death or injury to a member of the family was usually a powerful silencer. One historian comments: "The custom of duelling, supposed to protect women from insult, really exposed them to it."[23]

When Lee speaks of having "neither a prostituted pen or person" to offer Harris, it is difficult to avoid drawing conclusions of sexual harassment. In fact, however, her reference to prostitution refers to a period *prior* to the one in which she had submitted her manuscript to him ("I withdrew without a trial") and so whatever Harris's peccadilloes, they were not inflicted on Lee personally so far as we can tell. However, her report adds to a general tone of alarm and disapprobation ("the general aspersion cast upon managers"), of women in need of protection *from* managers, rather than of being protected by them.

Prostitution is a strong, ugly word, and Lee does not use it lightly. Her narrative implies that part of the bargaining process of getting a play "up" may include the female body of the playwright as barter. It was a state of affairs that would have been unthinkable under Garrick, who, whatever his private impulses, maintained an unimpeachable decorum around such matters.

By contrast, Harris, Colman, and Colman the Younger all lived with women for many years without benefit of marriage, and had numerous children by them.[24] These liaisons were quite public and do not seem to have carried any particular liability for the men. Lee's concerns about Harris's moral probity may have been related to his irregular domestic arrangements, but it is unlikely to have been the focus of her concern, since Colman's arrangements had for years been equally irregular, and she obviously regarded him very highly. It is much more likely, in the context of a general disregard for middle-class propriety by both Harris and Colman, that Lee has become privy to information about Harris's conduct outside of his official liaisons that was disturbing enough to prevent her from approaching him in person. A woman's ability to survive this rough-and-tumble process of negotiation may also have included knowing how to neutralize overt sexual overtures.

## 7

Something begins to take shape in Lee's preface which we have noted briefly in the first chapter: that the *writing* of a play, and the *producing* of a play have to be handled as two separate entities where women dramatists are concerned. Writing plays, in and of itself, allowed a woman to preserve the kind of socially constructed feminine persona promoted by the conduct books, as long as it did not interfere with her primary responsibilities to husband and family. A woman could write plays quite privately, and even publish them, without compromising her claims to femininity. The problems lay in the process of getting them mounted, because producing plays forced women into the public arena, and into adversarial postures with managers, with critics, with actors, and even with audiences. Cowley commented once that *writing* her plays was nothing compared to the "anxious warfare" of seeing them into production.[25] This adversarial positioning was not simply the result of random personality conflicts; it was intrinsic to theatre as a collaborative art form. The playwright and the manager were potential adversaries from the moment of a play's submission, through the revision process (witness Harris's determination to demote Lee's script to an afterpiece), and into production. If a playwright saw her script moving out of focus for any reason, as in fact Lee did early on when Harris required her to get rid of the "serious" parts, it was her job to fight for her original vision. If a playwright and a manager were in complete agreement about what needed to take place, no such conflicts might arise. But those instances were comparatively rare. As a rule, production meant moving from a moment of artistic privacy and pleasure into an arena of business deals, name-calling, and artistic wrangling. The ideals of eighteenth-century womanliness were poor equipment for fighting these battles. If a man engaged with another man in a dispute over something, publicly or privately, it was not loaded in the same way that it was for a woman. Hannah Cowley describes women who engaged in battles as exhibiting "an unsexual hardiness." Women playwrights in conflict with their manager's judgement had to make a precipitous choice about whether to acquiesce, confront, or pull out. It left very little room for the normal, sometimes heated negotiations that attend any production process. In the absence of finding a socially acceptable way to negotiate with a manager, one on one, Lee and Cowley resorted to the angry preface as a rhetorical substitute.

**8**

*. . . not being mistress of the French language, I sought in vain for a translation.*

There is an apology implicit here that echoes throughout the surviving papers and prefaces of virtually all eighteenth-century women playwrights, and that is the sense of being inadequately educated. This excerpt from Eliza Haywood's preface to her tragedy *Frederick*, published in 1729, resonates with the kinds of anxieties women writing plays experienced throughout the century:

> As to the Merit of the Piece, I have little to say, but that Nature, the only Instructress of my unlearned Pen, has, I hope, furnish'd me with Expressions not altogether incongruous to the different Passions by which my Characters are agitated; and tho' I know myself beneath the Censure of the Gyant-Criticks of this Age, yet have I taken all imaginable Care not to offend the rules they have prescrib'd for Theatrical Entertainments: The Scenes being unbroken, the Time of Action not exceeding twelve Hours, and the whole Business contrived and executed within the Walls of the Castle . . . Since then my chief faults consist in the Diction, I depend the candid Reader will forgive the Want of those Embellishments of Poetry, which the little Improvements my Sex receives from Education, Allow'd me not the Power to adorn it with.[26]

Catherine Clive's character, Mrs. Hazard, struggled with the same problems where education was concerned. One of the characters in *Bays in Petticoats*, a windbag named Sir Albany, makes this observation as Mrs. Hazard struggles to see her new play into production at Drury Lane:

> If Men, who are properly graduated in Learning, who have swallow'd the Tincture of a polite Education, who, as I may say, are hand and glove with the Classics, if such Genius's as I'm describing, fail of Success in Dramatic Occurrences, or Performances, ('tis the same Sense in the Latin) what must a poor Lady expect, who is ignorant as the Dirt?[27]

Certainly education for women was improving as the century unfolded (Sophia Lee's school being one important example), but there were often large gaps, in the classics and history particularly. For example, the Misses Lees (Sophia, Harriet and Anna) advertise the subjects taught at their school for girls as "English, French, Writing, Arithmetic, and fine Work"; there is no mention of Greek, Latin, or classical history.[28] In a country which since 1737 had prohibited by law any reference to contemporary politics in drama, these educational gaps constituted a serious handicap, since materials for plays had to come from other sources in classical literature or history. Sheridan's *Pizarro* is a perfect example of how contemporary political commentary in a play had to be carefully couched in a historical context.

Lack of education may partly explain why women dramatists tended to gravitate towards comedy rather than tragedy, since comedy could utilize contemporary domestic situations with little risk of exposing their ignorance of classical references. But even women writing comedies were not protected from the kind of critical carping that sought to remind the reader that women had to be handled in a separate category, as uneducated persons. Hannah Cowley's popular afterpiece, *Who's the Dupe?*, received this treatment from Genest:

Gradus says – "Zanthus! I remember but one being of that name, and he was a horse" – it is very excusable in Mrs. Cowley, as a woman, that she should not know that Homer mentions the River God Xanthus, as well as Achilles' horse, but it is an unfortunate mistake, as it is one that Gradus could not possibly have made – besides Xanthus is absurdly spelt with a Z. – Why did not Mrs. Cowley consult the person who furnished her with the Greek epigram? – an attempt to correct this mistake seems to have been made in the later editions of this Farce.[29]

The subject of education comes up again in Genest's discussion of Cowley's tragedy, *The Fate of Sparta*, which was produced ten years later in 1788. This time, Genest is not so broad-minded and tolerant of Mrs. Cowley's educational deficiencies:

It is a very poor play, with now and then a good speech – so egregiously absurd, that no excuse can be made for Mrs. Cowley on the score of her being a woman – she does not seem to have borrowed anything from Southerne, whose *Spartan Dame* is written on the same story . . . Southerne and Mrs. Cowley have both deviated from the story considerably, and Mrs. Cowley is still more ignorant of Spartan manners than Southerne – . . . she speaks of Leonidas and Cleombrutus as having reigned together, tho' there never had been an instance in Sparta of two kings of the same family reigning at the same time, till after the date of this play.[30]

Membership had its penalties. The difference between Genest's first and second set of comments is that by 1788 Mrs. Cowley had achieved the (uneasy) status of a professional in the field, and that if she were going to continue to write plays, her work was going to have to be judged by the same standards that apply to the men. It was, of course, a strategy for containment; women did not have adequate access to education, and necessarily could not be held accountable for the historic failure of their culture to see them as educable (although this apparently did not affect Cowley's success at the box office). But these complications did not trouble Genest, who as self-appointed watchdog on matters of plagiarism and accuracy, made it his business to remind his readers of the egregious limitations of women playwrights. By 1832 most of the productions had rotated out of the repertory, so readers had no opportunity of judging their merits for themselves.

## 9

*He* [Colman] *gave me the benefit of his judgment and experience, both in heightening and abbreviating the business, with every attention in casting and getting it up; generously uniting to the name of Manager that of Friend.*

The word "friend" and "friendship" in reference to managers recurs over and over in the surviving prefaces and letters. Hannah Cowley's plaintive cry in her letter to Garrick in 1777 was "I have lost your friendship!"[31] In 1779, Mrs. Griffith wrote in her preface to *The Times* the following statement about Thomas Sheridan, Richard Brinsley's father and sometime acting manager at Drury Lane: "I gladly take this opportunity of returning my thanks to my much-esteemed friend, Mr. Sheridan, senior, for his kind attention to the getting up my Play, my ill health not permitting me to attend one Rehearsal."[32] She used the same term in 1769 in her preface for *The School for Rakes*, which she inscribed to David Garrick, "declaring to the world, that you are my friend."[33] Colman once remarked to Mrs. Gardner in 1777, after she made a direct solicitation to the audience for their support for her play, that "she had taken a very improper mode to gain his friendship."[34] However, after Lee's 1780 preface, the word almost disappears from the literature. Elizabeth Inchbald made no public displays of gratitude to Colman or anyone else, and Cowley's prefaces became much more circumspect. We note that in 1781, Mrs. Brooke did *not* use the term "friend" in her thanks to Harris in the preface to *Siege of Sinope*. Even Joanna Baillie, though she was careful to thank Kemble in the introductions to her later editions of *De Monfort*, never used the word "friend." Something of the earlier concept of the manager as patron, mentor, advocate and friend, had dropped out of parlance and out of the general expectation. Lee's reference to Colman as "friend" is an attempt to reinvoke that earlier model of mentor and protector, but it was already gone. The new era was a little less friendly, but also a little less monolithic.

## 10

Lee's preface is very persuasive, both about Harris's boorish conduct, and about Colman's skill and generosity. And her remarks are echoed in substance by Cowley's preface to *Albina* the year before: Harris is obstructive; Colman is respectful and enabling. But there is something in the easy dichotomy of these two managers, the one as evil obstructor and the other as saintly benefactor, that should alert us. It's too simple, rather like the dramatic structure of a melodrama. Furthermore, Lee's characterizations of these two men don't hold up, even among the women themselves. Harris never earned a reputation for sensitive handling of new plays in the way that Colman and Garrick did, but nonetheless he produced the work of a considerable number of women playwrights over the years.[35] Frances Brooke, after years of frustrated effort, first got produced (*The Siege of Sinope*) at Covent Garden, and wrote:

> To Mr. Harris my obligations are great: his good sense and taste called my attention to more than one impropriety in the conduct of the piece, when first offered; his liberal turn

of mind gave it every advantage of decoration; whilst his candour and politeness removed the dragons which have been supposed to guard the avenues to the theatre, and which have too long deterred many of our greatest writers from taking this road to the Temple of Fame.[36]

"Dragons" is almost certainly a reference to Garrick and Colman;[37] and here again we see how complicated any effort to categorize the managers rapidly becomes. Harris, who figured as a dragon for Lee, was Mrs. Brooke's dragon-slayer. She had a history of business relations with Harris anyway, which may have helped make him a less imposing figure than he was for Lee or for Cowley.[38] Whatever the reasons, this was Brooke's first successful working relationship with a manager, and Harris continued to produce her work until her death in 1789.

There is other evidence which now brings Colman's sainthood into question. In the early 1950s, in the walls of an old house in Devon, a manuscript was discovered which included a play by Sarah Gardner called *The Advertisement* ("a comedy in Three Acts, as perform'd at the Theatre Royal, Haymarket, 1777") together with a lengthy preface explaining why the play only lasted for one night. Mrs. Gardner's preface is a diatribe against Colman the Elder, and echoes Lee's and Cowley's worst anxieties about submitted manuscripts being plundered by managers for ideas. In addition, she reports that Colman took offence at the way she had pressed him for production, and that he communicated his displeasure to the cast, giving them tacit permission to perform badly, which of course they did with relish. The audience came to Mrs. Gardner's rescue by hissing the actors and demanding that they "go back for their book," and cheering her when she made her entrance and again at the end when she addressed the audience. Backstage, "the Manager said little: but if frowns could have struck her dead she would have expir'd on the spot. However he gave her to understand that . . . on no consideration the play should ever be perform'd again."[39] The war did not end there. In 1782, when Colman's son, George Colman the Younger, produced his nasty little farce satirizing women playwrights (*The Female Dramatist*) and it failed miserably, it subsequently was rumored to have been written – not by young George – but by *Mrs. Gardner*.[40] The rumor was elegantly engineered to simultaneously protect the rising playwriting career of the favored son, and to further indemnify the languishing play-writing career of Mrs. Gardner.

My objective here is not to make a case against Colman, or conversely, a case in support of Harris, but simply to complicate Lee's claims and to argue that underlying these apparent conflicts of personality lay the much graver issue faced by all playwrights, which was that theatrical activity had been artificially restrained, and was controlled by a tiny cadre of very powerful men. Since there was nothing to be done about the Crown's determination to keep close control over the theatres, it is not surprising that some of the legitimate frustration felt by playwrights over those limitations would get transformed into something more manageable, like personal conflict. But in point of fact, the two-pronged control of severely limited numbers of theatre patents on the one hand, and of the censor on the other, had created a situation for playwrights – male or female – that posed extraordinary difficulties. Lee's characterizations of Harris and Colman are inconsistent with the reports of other women playwrights because the personalities of the men were not the real problem. The problem was the system that had put them in place to begin with. Whether a manager chose to be encouraging or discouraging to a playwright was immaterial at one level, since both operations constituted a prodigious display of power.

In economic terms, these men constituted an eighteenth-century version of an oligopoly, in which a few large suppliers predominate but cover their tracks by saturating the market with messages about product differentiation.[41] But because they were not simply businessmen, although theatre certainly was a business, but also people whose decisions determined what the public would see in representation, we must also acknowledge that this was an artistic oligopoly. To the extent that it was uniformly dominated by the unconscious tastes and interests of a handful of white middle-class men, it was an oligopoly that had important implications for the way gender was constructed, challenged, or reinforced onstage. When David Garrick, for example, turned down Frances Brooke's *Virginia* all those years before, the theatre lost a tragic female lead that could have delivered a devastating critique of a patriarchal double standard. Even if the rumors were not true, that Garrick had turned the play down because the male lead was flat by comparison and he didn't want to play it, the loss is still a significant one. James Boaden, in his biography of Kemble, observed that even in plays by men, Garrick's sometimes unaccountable decision not to produce a given script (which later became a hit elsewhere) could be traced directly to this issue of the female role getting primacy:

> The true reason in all of these [*Douglas* by Home, *Cleone* by Dodsley, and *The Orphan of China* by Murphy] of [for] his coldness was, that the <u>female</u> interest predominated – that Mrs. Cibber would have entirely overwhelmed him. This reason he was not bold enough to assign; so that the first was too "<u>simple</u> and <u>undramatic</u>," the second was "<u>cruel</u>, <u>bloody</u>, and <u>unnatural</u>," and the third, after Murphy had complied with all his strictures, was "<u>totally</u> <u>unfit</u>" for the stage. His answers might have been couched in three [*sic*] words – "Lady Randolph," "Cleone," "Mandane."[42]

Scholars have also argued that Garrick had a profound effect on Mrs. Griffith's plays, and that in the end the energy and declarative power of her female characters were diluted in order to meet his requirements.[43] Mrs. Piozzi commented once that she knew Joanna Baillie's anonymous collection of plays (1798) had been written by a woman because their heroines were middle-aged women, and that "*a man has no notion of mentioning a female after she is five and twenty*" [my italics].[44] Sophia Lee's preface gives us one more in a long series of such small incidents, when she reports that Harris wanted her to rewrite her play, getting rid of all "the serious parts" that were "Diderot's." The part of Lee's play that would have been lost to representation if negotiations with Harris had proceeded, was precisely that part in which Lee was consciously challenging a culturally accepted norm regarding women who have sex before marriage. In the context of its day, Lee's play was a bold stroke, and in spite of critics charging her with immorality, her audience, as she reports in the preface, responded powerfully and positively to that part of the plot. Harris would have gotten rid of it, probably not from any conscious notions of obstructing new ideas about women and virtue, but because he had his eye on turning a profit, and this section of the play seemed to him expendable. It was that simple. In some sense, the most serious damage to women's work happened quietly, unconsciously, before the fact, in the way the culture out of which these managers had emerged manifested itself in their routine daily decisions.

Sophia Lee's preface gives ample demonstration of the anxiety, alienation, and lack of control that women playwrights experienced during this period after Garrick. Garrick's sympathetic presence had created an opening for a select group of women, and had helped legitimize the presence of women as playwrights inside the theatre, but it had not shifted the underlying power structure. The unchallenged power of managers, together with the disabling pressures of social decorum, continued to make it difficult for women playwrights to make their way forward. And so once he was gone, women's anxieties about finding access through an empathetic mentor asserted themselves in force.

But at this juncture another pattern emerges that is in its own way instructive and contradictory. If we look at a graph of productions by women playwrights at Bath, where Sophia Lee spent most of her life, something peculiar emerges. There is a small but noticeable surge in the number of productions by women beginning in about 1779, that is, *after* Garrick's retirement and death (see Figure 1). Given Garrick's much-publicized generosity toward women, and the evident difficulties encountered by playwrights like Lee after his retirement, this surge runs exactly counter to expectations and needs some explanation.

It is useful to reconstruct as closely as possible what kinds of plays a young woman like Sophia Lee might have seen or heard about while growing up in Bath as a general audience member. Bath's Orchard Street Theatre is a useful one to follow for this study because it began operations in 1750, shortly after Garrick took over Drury Lane in London, and closed operations in 1805, just after the turn of the century. As such, its production history gives the historian an opportunity to examine what was being produced by the provincial theatres during and after Garrick's tenure at Drury Lane. Bath is a particularly interesting provincial theatre to look at because it was a second home for a number of socially prominent Londoners, and the choice of plays for any given season constituted a distillation of the new plays and the revivals that were current in London. Bath was not a try-out town for new plays; it was the place new plays were produced once they had succeeded in London. There were occasional productions written by local people (actors or theatre

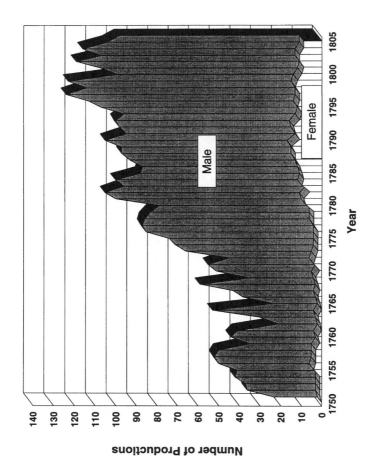

*Figure 1* Productions by men and women, combining numbers for active and deceased playwrights, at Bath's Orchard Street Theatre over the period 1750–1805

staff sometimes wrote something original for their benefit nights), but the overwhelming majority of plays at Bath were already in the public domain, and many of them were recent hits: "it is clear that the managers [of Bath] kept in touch with London, and new plays were often mounted very quickly."[45]

Beginning in 1771–1772, the year in which Lee wrote a first draft of *The Chapter of Accidents*, the calendar shows an occasional production by Susanna Centlivre: *The Wonder, The Busy Body,* and *The Ghost* (somewhat uncertain attribution), and one by Elizabeth Griffith in the season before, *School for Rakes*. By 1779–1780, the season in which Lee decided to find a producer for *Chapter of Accidents*, the picture was noticeably altered. In addition to the usual plays by Centlivre, Cowley's *The Belle's Stratagem* and *Who's the Dupe?* were playing regularly alongside Hannah More's *Percy* and *The Fatal Falsehood*, and Griffith's *The Times*. When Lee produced her *Almeyda* in 1796 in London, the 1795–1796 season at Bath included Centlivre's *The Wonder* and *The Busy Body*; More's *Percy*; Brooke's *Rosina* and *Marian*; Inchbald's *Every One Has His Fault, The Child of Nature,* and *The Midnight Hour*; Cowley's *The Belle's Stratagem, Bold Stroke for a Husband, Which is the Man?* and *More Ways than One*; and Lee's own *The Chapter of Accidents,* which by then had become a recognized part of the eighteenth-century repertory. In fact, of the plays listed above, four find their way into Hogan's lists of most popular entertainments for this last quarter of the eighteenth century: for mainpieces, *The Belle's Stratagem* (eleventh in his list of the top twelve); among afterpieces, *Rosina* and *Who's the Dupe?* (second and twelfth in the list of top twelve), and Sophia Lee's *The Chapter of Accidents* (first in an additional list of six new mainpieces).[46]

If for a moment we imaginatively project ourselves into the audience at the Bath Orchard Street theatre, one of the things the graphs show is that the probability of encountering a production by a woman increased noticeably starting in about 1779.[47] In other words, the chances of a woman going to the theatre and seeing a play by another woman, or reading about a production by a woman in the newspapers, began to improve. It is interesting in this context to notice that Sophia Lee's play, which she had begun writing in 1772, some seven years prior to this change, lay dormant until 1780, the point at which plays by Hannah Cowley, Hannah More and Elizabeth Griffith were being routinely produced as part of the repertory. It suggests the possibility that their collective presence constituted access of a different kind, that they made it possible for a woman with secret ambitions to write for the stage to begin thinking more concretely about actual production. In 1769, a woman, a poet, put the case quite neatly in her own preface: "I see many female writers favourably received, admitted into the rank of authors, and amply rewarded by the public; I have been encouraged by their success, to offer myself as a candidate for the same advantages."[48] This new sense of access and even of entitlement had also been felt by women interested in writing for the theatre. As early as 1768, Charlotte Lennox wrote to David Garrick, enclosing her play entitled *The Sister*:

> The success which has lately attended writers for the stage, and some of them too, of my own sex, has encouraged me to write a comedy, which I beg you will read with your usual candor, and that indulgence you have always shown for my writings.[49]

The graphs (see Figures 1–3) also show a marked increase in activity overall, for male and female playwrights, beginning in about 1779. There are two ways to interpret this increase and the subsequent smaller increase in productions by active women playwrights. One is to argue that the increase in activity by women was made possible by the increase overall. The second is to note that the only place there is a decline in activity is in the number of revivals of plays by *deceased* males: their numbers in fact decline in direct proportion to the degree to which women's numbers rise. So if anyone was moving over to make room for this new group of active women playwrights, it was not the active male playwrights, whose numbers continued to climb undisturbed, but the deceased ones. This accommodation to women, then, was a function of an expanding market overall, and in no way inconvenienced or replaced active men entering the same profession.

But the earlier question still remains. How is it possible that the increase in productions by women takes place *after* Garrick is gone? One answer might be to think of women like Cowley, More and Griffith as his legacy to the profession, since they continued to work after his retirement. But More actually quit the field promptly after he was dead, and Griffith only produced one more play in 1779 (*The Times*). In fact, of all the women he

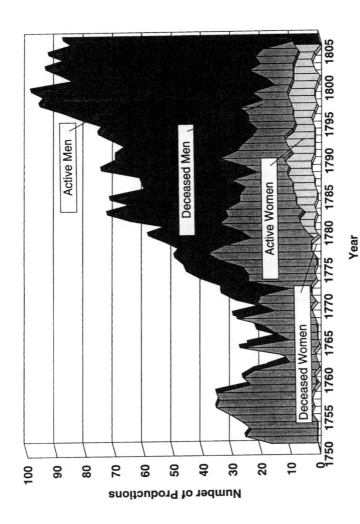

*Figure 2* Productions by men and women at Bath's Orchard Street Theatre over the period 1750–1805, showing whether the playwright was deceased or active in the second half of the eighteenth century

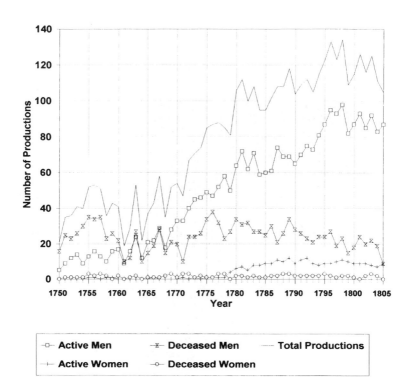

*Figure 3* Actual rise of productions by female playwrights beginning in
1779 at Bath's Orchard Street Theatre

worked with, Cowley is the only one who emerged later as
someone with a career and a professional identity that outlived
the man himself. But it is also important to remember that plays
written by these women were in many instances produced year
after year, both in and out of London, and the influence of those
plays continued well after the woman herself had long since quit
writing for the stage. The result was that even a handful of
successful women playwrights with one or more viable plays to
their names could make a substantial difference in the repertory.
There was a cumulative pile-up by the mid-1790s that enor-
mously increased the probability of any female spectator seeing a
play by a female dramatist.

There were also concurrent shifts in the receptivity of the audiences for plays by women, shifts which the managers themselves were not always able to keep up with. As early as 1776, Hannah Cowley wrote of her first play:

> I perceive how much of this applause [for *The Runaway*] I owe to my *Sex*. – *The Runaway* has a thousand faults, which, if written by a Man, would have incurred the severest lash of Criticism – but the Gallantry of the English Nation is equal to its Wisdom – they beheld a *Woman* tracing with feeble steps the borders of the Parnassian Mount – pitying her difficulties (for 'tis a thorny path) they gave their hands for her support, and placed her *high* above her level.[50]

Cowley's preface is apologetic and throws her play on the mercy of her (by implication, male) spectators, but it also thanks them for their tolerance and support. We have seen already in Chapter 3 how Sheridan's nasty epilogue to *The Fatal Falsehood* in 1779 satirizing women playwrights met with fairly stiff opposition, both in the audiences and in the newspapers. George Colman the Younger met a similar fate: his two-act farce *The Female Dramatist* (1782), which also satirized women playwrights, was "uncommonly hissed in the course of its performance" and never revived again.[51] And in January 1793, the following prologue attended the opening of Mrs. Inchbald's *Every One Has His Fault* (it is interesting to note how the issue of education plays an important role in this address):

> But since the Sex at length has been inclin'd
> To cultivate that useful part – the mind;
> Since they have learnt to read, to write, to spel [*sic*]; –
> Since some of them have wit, – and use it well; –
> Let us not force them back with brow severe,
> Within the pale of ignorance and fear,
> Confin'd entirely to domestic arts,
> Producing only children, pies, and tarts.
> The fav'rite fable of the tuneful Nine,
> Implies that female genius *is divine.*
> Then, drive not, Critics, with tyrannic rage,
> A supplicating Fair-one from the Stage;
> The Comic Muse perhaps is growing old,
> Her lovers, you well know, are few and cold.

'Tis time then freely to enlarge the plan,
And let all those write Comedies – that can.[52]

These instances collectively mark a significant change from the hilarity and applause which greeted Mrs. Clive's broad satire on women playwrights in 1750,[53] or, reaching back even further, the ruthless censure that was levelled at Aphra Behn both personally and professionally.

In 1768, Garrick turned down Mrs. Lennox's comedy *The Sister*, and she subsequently offered it to Covent Garden, which was then being run by Thomas Harris and George Colman the Elder. The play opened on 18 February 1769. It was a respectable script and decently produced, but it met with an avalanche of hissing on opening night. The opposition was so intense that by the beginning of the fifth act forward, it was impossible to hear the actors, and they simply stopped trying to perform. Powell came forward and attempted to reason with the audience, but in the end the show was condemned. Mrs. Lennox never received so much as a single night's benefit. It was later discovered, in a meeting of Goldsmith, Dr. Johnson and Colman, that this hissing audience had been maliciously organized. Goldsmith reported that he had been approached before the show and advised to hiss it, ostensibly because of Mrs. Lennox's recent writings on Shakespeare. But Mrs. Lennox later acknowledged to Johnson that she suspected the entire operation had been organized by the playwright Richard Cumberland. If she was right, the underlying motive probably had nothing to do with her writings on Shakespeare but was almost certainly an effort to eliminate her as a potential threat to his primacy in the profession. Cumberland was famous for this kind of spiteful behavior; his treatment of Frances Burney ten years later was viciously competitive. But the issue is not his personality, but the fact that this small insurgence of women into the field was not greeted with unmixed enthusiasm. The market, because it was artificially limited by the patent system, could not expand indefinitely to accommodate the women who wanted to write without some eventual loss to the male incumbents. Under the circumstances, Cumberland's cabal was a crude but predictable strategy to preserve his own interests.[54]

Part of Garrick's legacy, then, was a change in public attitude. It would be imprudent to characterize this change as universal;

the evidence indicates that it was not, but by the late 1770s, it was no longer fashionable to ridicule casually and publicly the idea of a woman playwright. Garrick's prologue to Hannah More's *Percy*, written the year after his retirement, had the quality of an injunction to the audiences that would follow:

Summon your critic powers, your manhood summon,
A brave man will protect, not <u>hurt</u> a woman;
Let us wish modestly to share with men,
If not the <u>force</u>, the feather of the pen.[55]

The prologue for Mrs. Inchbald's play indicates that audiences in 1793 still needed some convincing, but that the idea of a woman playwright was one whose time had come: " 'tis time then freely to enlarge the plan." It is not clear whether this shift in public attitude, toward an ethos of gallantry, was the cause or the result of increasing numbers of productions by women, but it does appear to be related in some way to Garrick's patronage, and to have survived his departure.

However, Garrick's fostering of women had some internal inconsistencies, which may provide an explanation for the surge in productions by women after his death. In a letter to Elizabeth Griffith in 1775, David Garrick explained why he was about to reject her most recent play:

Mrs. Lenox [*sic*] who was so unfortunate at Covent Garden Theatre, put into my hand last Year an alterd play, which upon my honour I have not yet had the leisure to consider as I ought – another Lady of great merit [probably Mrs. Cowley] has likewise intrusted me with a performance of 5 Acts, which I must immediately look over, with all the care and delicacy due to her Sex & her talents – these matters with my other necessary business will, I protest to you most Solemnly, engage more time than I can possibly spare . . .[56]

Betty Rizzo has interpreted Garrick's letter to mean that he was operating on a quota system, and that even as he was bringing women forward, he was carefully limiting and controlling their numbers and their level of activity. His letter clearly implies that he thought of female playwrights as a category distinct and separate from male playwrights. Was he, in fact, carefully regulating the number of women that he brought out in any given year, thereby imposing an artificial ceiling even as he was creating access? The interpretation is a provocative one, not only in the way he may have been controlling numbers, but in the kinds of women he chose to work with. It is intriguing to speculate, for instance, just how long his generosity would have continued if this trickle of debutante playwrights had turned into a landslide of career professionals. When Mrs. Griffith had the bad taste to come back to him with more plays after her first successful debut, his generosity cooled a little and things became slightly awkward.

The most important generalization that can be made about the post-Garrick era is that there is a subtle shift in emphasis from individual patronage like Garrick's to a more open-market policy. This was in part the result of broader social acceptance of women as playwrights, and a broader representation of their work in the repertory. Garrick's legacy was a complicated one. In one sense, he had departed leaving these women to the uncertain ministrations of the other managers, but on the other hand, the idea of the woman as playwright seems to have been more securely anchored in the public imagination. Everyone, but especially young women, could attend the theatre and see for themselves concrete evidence of other women's success and recognition. That had the potential for creating a momentum that made women playwrights slightly less dependent upon the chemistry or good will of any one particular manager, and more focused on taking their rightful place in the profession. In Mrs. Inchbald's case, for example, playwriting was never a personal contract based on friendship; it stayed strictly within the realm of business.

In the post-Garrick era, it was harder for women to have their plays considered seriously and sensitively in the first place, but if they survived the initial mayhem of getting a script accepted and produced, they stood a better chance of turning a debut into a career under this new system than they had under Garrick. Things were not simple for women playwrights still; the factors which conspired against women becoming playwrights – some related to social constraints and others to economic competition – were strongly rooted, as Frances Burney's and Joanna Baillie's stories will show. But there is a useful lesson here, which is that one person can make a difference, even one that he himself might not have predicted or fully approved.

After 1779, the climate for women like Sophia Lee was a fragile ecology in which change could tip the balance and allow the new species to thrive or eliminate it all together. In the end, the factors which had given Lee the confidence to take the plunge into playwriting were not enough to keep her there. Partly, I think, her father's desperate struggles with bankruptcy must have dampened her willingness to continue taking risks in the theatre. Moreover, the accusations afterwards of plagiarism and immorality were deeply wounding, and probably intended to be. In a sense, they were a measure of the degree to which women had brought pressure to bear on the market. Harris's unpleasant manipulations of Lee's *Chapter of Accidents* could be processed and brought into perspective over time, but the corrosive charges of plagiarism and immorality lingered and were probably decisive in her refusal to turn playwriting into a career.

Since broad ridicule of women playwrights, or outright opposition such as Cumberland's cabal, were no longer generally tolerated, more sophisticated ways had to be found in order to neutralize and manage their activity. Charges of plagiarism or immorality were one such strategy; calling women's educational qualifications into question was another. Garrick's legacy to women playwrights like Sophia Lee included not only their greater public acceptance, but also a developing arsenal of new strategies for keeping their activities under control.

# 5

# ADVANTAGE, MRS. INCHBALD

Elizabeth Inchbald arrived in London in 1780, after working for eight years as an actress in the provincial theatres. Garrick was gone. Richard Brinsley Sheridan had been managing Drury Lane since 1776, and Thomas Harris was in sole command of Covent Garden, since Colman's decision to manage the Haymarket summer seasons.[1] Mrs. Inchbald had a contract to perform some minor roles at Covent Garden as a member of Harris's company. Harris, however, was getting more than he had bargained for. Tucked into her luggage were two manuscripts: one a novel, and the other a play.

Mrs. Inchbald subsequently became one of the most prolific and successful playwrights of her time. Between 1780 and 1805, she wrote twenty plays, ten of which were adaptations, and ten of which were original. Of the twenty, seventeen were conspicuously successful onstage.[2] She published two successful novels, and eventually became a prominent critic and anthologist of drama. Her career is unique in this study because it exposes gender hierarchies *within* theatre that might have otherwise gone unremarked. Hostilities that stayed covert when she was a playwright became manifest when she became a critic and anthologist, no doubt because these later career developments effectively put her in charge of shaping the contemporary canon.

But how Mrs. Inchbald became one of England's most prolific and successful playwrights without the benefits of eighteenth-century mentoring is the primary concern of this chapter. She is a product of the period that I have called the "post-Garrick era," meaning that the paternal style of mentoring which had been Garrick's trademark, had been replaced by no system at all. Women were back on the open market, applying to managers at random in much the same way that they had been prior to Garrick's arrival on the scene. There were two important differences, however. One was that Garrick's support of specific women had given a certain legitimacy to the idea of women playwrights in the public mind, a legitimacy which definitely was not in place prior to his tenure at Drury Lane. The second difference was that women playwrights were part of a larger surge of women writing in all genres. Elizabeth Inchbald wrote novels, as did Frances Brooke, Frances Burney, Sophia Lee, Charlotte Lennox, and Elizabeth Griffith. Joanna Baillie wrote verse and essays; Hannah More wrote essays on education and religion. Inchbald and Brooke also wrote critical commentary about the theatre. Legitimacy, then, could be borrowed from this larger surge until such time as the number of women playwrights reached critical mass and they could create momentum for one another, which is indeed what happened. Mrs. Inchbald's two manuscripts, her novel and her play, attest to the connectedness of all areas of writing for women in this transitional period. Every playwright in this study, with the sole exception of Hannah Cowley, wrote in more than one genre, and consequently participated in that larger membership.

Now to the specifics of Elizabeth Inchbald's career. Having a sense of legitimacy was one thing; getting produced was quite another. How did she persuade managers to produce her work? How did she learn stagecraft and dramatic technique sufficiently to bypass the need for expert editorial help? In the rough-and-tumble climate of this "post-Garrick era," where did her morale and a sense of herself as a developing artist and professional playwright come from, if not a mentor?

One of the most distinctive features of Inchbald's career is that she was also an actress. During the winter seasons, she was a member of Harris's company; during the summers, she was a member of Colman's. This pattern is atypical for the period; actresses and playwrights almost never wandered into each other's professions. When they did (Catherine Clive is a conspicuous example), they never maintained professional status in both areas at the same time. Actresses who occasionally wrote for their own benefit nights were careful to maintain amateur status as a dramatist; to my knowledge, only one actress, Sarah Gardner, undertook the risk and exposure of identifying herself as an actress *and* a playwright during the late eighteenth century,[3]

*Plate 7*
Thomas Harris
17??–1820
Occupation: Theatre Manager

Sometime after Elizabeth Inchbald's arrival in London in 1780, her employer Thomas Harris attempted to rape her. The details of this attempt are recounted by John Taylor, who was a chronicler of the period and a longtime personal friend of Mrs. Inchbald's: "It is well known that the late Mr. Harris, then the chief proprietor of that theatre [Covent Garden], was a very gallant man, and did not find the virtue of several of his fair performers impregnable. At his desire, Mrs. Inchbald attended him one morning at his house at Knightsbridge, to consult on one of her plays which was soon to be represented. When the consultation was ended, Mr. Harris, who was a handsome man, and had found so little difficulty among the theatrical sisterhood under his government, thought that he might be equally successful in an attack on Mrs. Inchbald; but, instead of regular approaches, he attempted to take the fort by storm, and Mrs. Inchbald found no recourse but in seizing him by the hair, which she pulled with such violence that she forced him to desist. She then rushed out of the house, and proceeded in haste, and under great agitation, to the green-room of the theatre, where the company were then rehearsing. She entered the room with so wild an air, and with such evident emotion, that all present were alarmed. She hastily related what had happened as far as her impediment [a recurrent stutter] would permit her, and concluded with the following exclamation: 'Oh! if he had wo-wo-worn a wig, I had been ru-ruined.'" (Quoted from *Records of My Life* by John Taylor, New York, J. & J. Harper, 1833, p. 224.)

*Plate 8*
Elizabeth Inchbald
1753–1821
Occupations: Playwright, Novelist, Critic, Anthologist, Translator

Elizabeth Inchbald was famous for thrift and for being a canny negotiator with theatre managers and publishers. But women who demonstrated this kind of business acumen were ridiculed because they had blurred certain gender boundaries. Business sense had been designated male. In 1805, the year Inchbald produced her last play in London, her friend John Taylor wrote her to report disturbing gossip by former theatrical connections and friends. She was now being mocked as an eccentric, censured for the very habits that had not only kept her solvent but also allowed her to support two destitute sisters (one a prostitute) and quietly assist countless others. Mrs. Inchbald's reply to Taylor was characteristically measured and shrewd: "That the world should say I have lost my senses, I can readily forgive, when I recollect that a few years ago it said the same of Mrs. Siddons. I am now fifty-two years old, and yet if I were to dress, paint, and visit, no one would call my understanding into question; or if I were to beg from all my acquaintance a guinea or two, as subscription for a foolish book, no one would accuse me of avarice. But because I choose that retirement suitable to my years, and think it my duty to support two sisters instead of one servant, I am accused of madness. I might plunge in debt, be confined in prison, a pensioner on 'The Literary Fund,' or be gay as a girl of eighteen, and yet be considered as perfectly in my senses; but because I choose to live in independence, affluence to me, with a mind serene and prospects unclouded, I am supposed to be mad." (Quoted from *Records of My Life*, by John Taylor, New York, J. & J. Harper, 1833, pp. 227–228.)

although unfortunately for her, her efforts to write plays were forestalled by the elder George Colman.

Mrs. Inchbald was the exception. She straddled two careers for well over a decade, watching plays from the wings, both as the actress waiting to make an entrance, and also as the playwright, sizing up the moment-to-moment impact of her own work and other people's. The term she used in her diaries for this backstage perspective on the theatre world was "I behind." It was her way of noting an evening spent watching a play from behind the wings.[4] But her term has larger meaning for this study, because it suggests for women an alternative route to becoming a playwright, one which bypassed the mentor entirely. By utilizing her inside position as an actress, Inchbald was able to create professional access *for herself.* This transition, from actress to playwright, constituted lateral mobility within the institution of theatre itself, as an alternative to the vertical path implied by a direct application, as female playwright, to the manager.

One result of this lateral mobility was that when it came time to offer managers her manuscripts, she was already on the inside. Should one script be turned down, she could try a second manager, or a second or third script, until finally someone said yes. But she was not in the awkward position of having to start from scratch each time, hoping a manager would remember her name and grant her an interview, and anxious about rebuffs by seasoned butlers. Inchbald's early diaries record countless instances in which she ran into a manager backstage, in between rehearsals or during a performance, and offered him a script or reminded him about one she had submitted. For example, on 26 December 1780, when she had only been in London for a few months, her diary records the following encounter: "Saw Mr. Wilson [a fellow actor] and Mr. Harris spoke very polite and mentioned my farce."[5] The telegraphic style of her writing makes it difficult to know who was speaking politely to whom, but the cumulative effect of these chance encounters over a period of four years was that she finally got one of the managers to agree to give her farce a trial. When I speak of access, and of lateral mobility, this is what I mean.

A more detailed look at Inchbald's working relationship with both Colman and Harris helps to explain more precisely how this inside position provided the access, training and encouragement that we associate with mentoring. Certainly in the early days of her career as playwright, the natural candidate for mentor would have been George Colman. Colman, as we know from both Hannah Cowley's and Sophia Lee's testimony, was an able and experienced playwright and a tactful editor, in addition to being a manager. Colman's plays had been edited and critiqued by Garrick in the early days, and so his style of working with women was probably as close to Garrick's as anyone's. The working relationship that developed between him and Mrs. Inchbald harked back to Garrick's style of patronage, but evolved into something quite distinct, and has important implications for understanding this period as a whole. In summary, Colman's tentative efforts to position Mrs. Inchbald as a literary daughter failed. She rapidly positioned herself, after a rocky start, as a literary colleague.

Colman was instrumental in helping Mrs. Inchbald get her first play produced, a short afterpiece called *The Mogul Tale* about an adventure in a hot-air balloon. From the beginning, he was at some pains to make sure Mrs. Inchbald's identity stayed concealed. It is not clear if he thought the play would fail, or if he felt it had a better chance if the dramatist's gender was not revealed. In March of 1784, he wrote her the following note:

> Mr. Colman presents his compliments to Mrs. Inchbald, and assures her that he never mentioned her name to any person whatever on the subject of the Mogul Tale, and was yesterday extremely surprised at his son and Mr. Jewell both suggesting her as the author, which suggestion however he did not in the least confirm, nor was it in the green-room. He really thinks it better for the author not to be avowed at present, though he thinks the piece cannot be injured; and to attempt to injure the reputed author would be infamous.[6]

In any case one senses in the correspondence that Colman undertook to produce this play for Mrs. Inchbald as a kind of personal favor, to give her a chance. If she stayed anonymous and the play was unsuccessful, the whole business could die a quiet death with as little embarrassment to her (and Colman) as possible. She was even cast in the play, ostensibly to preserve her anonymity as playwright, but also, I suspect, to remind her that her real job in the company was acting. It was hardly the robust send-off that characterized the Garrick era.

Colman may have been registering his ambivalence about the development of their working relationship. Even on this first production, Mrs. Inchbald was proving somewhat intractable. Certainly their early work on the play developed along fairly traditional lines, with Colman offering editorial advice and encouragement in his notes to her and Mrs. Inchbald making changes and waiting eagerly for her chance to be produced. But as the season commenced, the week of 28 May 1784, Mrs. Inchbald was making the transition from the winter season at Covent Garden to her third summer season at the Haymarket, so the events surrounding her first production unfolded more or less under her nose. This was to have an empowering effect on her relationship with Colman.

What follows is the sequence of events leading up to production, reconstructed from diaries and letters:

*4 March 1784*: Mrs. Inchbald sent Colman *The Mogul Tale* under her own name. According to Boaden, it had been submitted earlier and refused under the pseudonym "Mrs. Woodley;" her successful resubmission suggests that her personal acquaintance with Colman as one of his actresses had definitely worked to her advantage.[7]

*7 March*: Colman agreed to buy the play for 100 guineas (afterpieces like this farce usually were bought outright, rather than being paid for through the three-night benefit system). Colman's payment is extremely generous, particularly given the fact that Inchbald had no reputation as yet.

*17 March*: Colman sent the play back to her with a note "that pleases her."[8]

*19 March*: She sent the manuscript back to him with alterations, and he took it to the country with him.

Colman's notes to Inchbald from this period include references to his "scrawls on the blank leaf," and "dark hints," as if deliberately to make light of his potentially intimidating authority as manager. He writes: "The idea is droll . . . with a little help, I think it can't fail." And "He [the Mogul] is not yet quite the thing; but Mr. C. will try to bring him back the better for his excursion."[9]

After an initial honeymoon with letters back and forth containing suggestions and encouragement from Colman (hers to him do not survive), the fair copy of the play was duly submitted to the Licensing Office on 29 May 1784, just a day after the opening of the Haymarket's summer season. Legally manuscripts were supposed to be filed fourteen days prior to opening night, so it would have been Mrs. Inchbald's justifiable expectation that her farce be presented at the end of the second week in June. No such thing happened. The play was finally produced five weeks after licensing, well into the summer season, a lengthy wait by the standards of the day. Under normal circumstances, a woman playwright on the outside, waiting patiently for her career debut, might have been driven into an anxious depression over such a delay; certainly this was the case when Hannah Cowley's farce *Who's the Dupe* was deliberately delayed by Sheridan in 1779 until it became a financial liability to her.[10]

But Mrs. Inchbald was a member of Colman's acting company (not to mention a member of the cast of *The Mogul Tale*), and she was in a prime position to watch certain internal politics play themselves out. To wit, of the thirty-three nights of performance that elapsed between the licensing of her script and its actual production, twenty-five of those nights were taken up by performances of scripts that had been written either by Colman himself or by his son, George Colman the Younger (now twenty-two years old to Mrs. Inchbald's thirty-one). One of the plays, *Two to One*, was a new production for Colman the Younger, requiring a new cast, full rehearsals, and scenery. In five instances, both mainpiece *and* afterpiece were by the Colmans. There was a total of eight different Colman productions, each repeated several times, which virtually monopolized the resources and personnel of the theatre.[11]

Mrs. Inchbald was herself cast in a number of these productions, one of which was Colman's *The Separate Maintenance*. This play featured a Mrs. Fustian, a woman with delusions of being amorously pursued by an unnamed theatre manager who promises her a production of her tragedy. She makes a fool of herself by trying to read her tragedy aloud to her friends, who are saved from the ordeal by the repeated interruptions of visiting acquaintances and relatives. Mrs. Inchbald played the ingenue,

Miss English, whose efforts to temper her friend's enthusiasm are wasted:

MISS ENGLISH. There are some good Judges here that may give you some good hints and advice, Madam.

MRS. FUSTIAN. Oh! as to hints and advice, I stand in no need of them – my Tragedy is finish'd, and I never omit or alter a line, Madam. The subject is most happily chosen, the situations striking, the incidents interesting, the sentiments noble, and the versification flowing and spirited – I'll sit down at this Table – [she clears her throat before beginning] hem! hem![12]

The messages for Mrs. Inchbald were complex. On the one hand, the play acknowledged that female playwrights existed. But on the other hand, the female playwright in this piece was a fatuous fool. However, male playwrights had been represented as fatuous fools, so this was perhaps the ritual roasting that went with membership. Might one be a female playwright and *not* be a fatuous fool?

Elizabeth Inchbald's position as playwright, and especially as novice playwright, was a complicated one. There was Colman's editorial support and his generous payment on the one hand; on the other hand, there were the delays, the superior status of the favored son, the anonymity surrounding her first production, and the misogynistic implications of Colman's own play. These various factors might have added up to a negative first experience, except that Mrs. Inchbald's position as an actress, on the inside of this company, must have lent her a certain philosophical calm. She could monitor Colman's attitude, watch the season develop, and bide her time.

Ironically, the five-week delay may have been to her benefit anyway. It made possible a number of alterations on the script which grew out of her first-hand experience with the company during the rehearsal process. A diary entry dated 23 June marks the first time she heard her play read in the green room, and Boaden reports that she felt encouraged. But on 28 June, "she thought she did not like the alterations."[13] Technically it was not legal to make alterations on a script once it had been submitted to the Licensing Office, but in practice, virtually everyone did, and the Licenser turned a blind eye as long as none of the changes was drastic.[14] In the end, the alterations were a

118

success; when *The Mogul Tale* did finally open, on 6 July 1784, it was a hit. In fact, Inchbald played one of her own characters, and was so nervous that she began to stutter, whereupon she broke character and laughed out loud.[15] The audience quickly discovered that the stuttering actress was also the "anonymous" playwright, which greatly increased the play's cachet.

Mrs. Inchbald's relationship to Colman is best summarized by two letters written in 1786. The letters were occasioned by his impending production of her latest farce, which eventually became known as *The Widow's Vow*. His initial suggestion for a title (Colman liked to name plays) was as follows: "But seriously, what do you think of christening it *The Neuter* – a title that suits the subject and yet conceals the plot?"[16] Evidently she thought very little of the idea, and although the suggestion was phrased mildly enough, it threw her into a tailspin. By this time Mrs. Inchbald was an experienced playwright and well-known figure, so the incident reminds us that any suggestion from a manager, given the power of the managerial position, had the impact of a command. Her letter back to Colman, which does not survive, must have been vehement. It elicited this response, in which he backs off and says with some asperity:

> Dr Madam, Tho I cannot acct [account] for yr <u>Pannicks</u> and think I am no unlucky Godfather, e'en christen yr Child after yr own liking, & be assured that I will still remain a Sponsor for its success, in spite of the terrors of your <u>Friends</u> [who have evidently advised her not to protest for fear of losing the production ].[17]

The tone of this letter contrasts strikingly with the much more urbane and self-possessed authority of similar letters by Garrick to playwrights. Colman is conciliatory, disposed to accomodate. His suggestions to her are framed as collaborative offerings rather than as directives. He is temperamentally and artistically more low key than Garrick. Colman's reference to himself as "godfather" is instructive; it suggests that he understood himself to have been chosen *by her* rather than the other way around. This configuration would not have been feasible under Garrick. He was invariably the father.

What started as a traditional mentoring relationship in 1784 had, by 1786, evolved into something else. It was Colman's position that was marginal to Mrs. Inchbald's activities as playwright. It was he who waited upon *her* approval for his suggestions. In other words, she understood herself to have a relationship with this manager, but it was not one in which, as playwright, she was created by him. The reason was simple: she had trained herself to be a playwright, by watching rehearsals and productions and audiences night after night, seeing what worked and what did not. She had given herself access to production by speaking directly to Colman backstage whenever the opportunity presented itself. She had provided moral support for herself, simply because she could see first-hand the reasons for delayed production.

I try to imagine Elizabeth Inchbald in the previous generation, working with David Garrick. I cannot. I think he would have regarded her as another Frances Brooke. She was someone with gift, tenacity, and independent opinions, and it was her good fortune in life to enter the London theatre scene at a time when a certain groundwork had been laid, but Garrick had already departed. That moment in which the woman playwright understood herself to be the privileged recipient of the mentor's largesse is missing from Mrs. Inchbald's narrative. Colman never got the opportunity to impose upon her an appropriate sense of gratitude. By the time *The Mogul Tale* turned into an overnight hit, the opportunity was lost for good. Ever after, she was able to negotiate with the kind of leverage that comes only from proven box-office success. For Elizabeth Inchbald, it was the thin end of the wedge.

As Mrs. Inchbald's career developed, she avoided cultivating an exclusive relationship with any manager, as Mrs. Cowley had initially done with Garrick. There had been no initial bonding with Colman as mentor, so she felt no particular sense of either gratitude or loyalty. Consequently, after the success of *The Mogul Tale*, Mrs. Inchbald immediately approached Thomas Harris with her next script. This move capitalized on an old rivalry. Colman and Harris had been adversaries since their attempts to co-manage Covent Garden in 1767 had collapsed some years before. Even after the rift was officially healed in 1771, a competitive dynamic persisted when Colman took over the Haymarket. Mrs. Inchbald lost no time taking advantage of the incipient rivalry, and played these two managers off one another for the duration of her career, by offering her plays first to one and then to the other. What one manager refused, the other was likely to accept.[18] Bit by bit she was able to cultivate a competition between the two, as Colman's slightly aggrieved letter in 1788 makes clear: "I wish you joy of the Child of Nature [her new play] at Covent Garden, but hope for as fine a Child at the Haymarket. Pray let me know if I may expect it."[19] Boaden notes the pattern as follows:

> The French piece which Mr. Harris had brought for her translation was rendered into English at the close of January, 1788, and returned for alterations; these being read, the Covent Garden manager made up his opinion, and refused to accept it. Nothing disconcerted by rejection, in February she sent it to Mr. Colman.[20]

In addition to avoiding an exclusive relationship with a manager, it was also her practice to seek outside criticism of her manuscripts. Her first full-length play, entitled *I'll Tell You What*, got its most acute and stringent criticism not from Colman, who eventually produced it in 1785, but from her good friend Francis Twiss, who wrote:

> As proof of my wish to give you my real opinion of its merits, I take the liberty of saying that I think the fifth act infinitely inferior to the others; the catastrophe is not without a considerable share of improbability, nor is it managed with that adroitness which I should have expected from your pen. The scene in the first act, between Lady Harriet and Bloom, rather drags.[21]

Twiss's letters also sought to temper Colman's tendency towards generalized enthusiasm, and to give Mrs. Inchbald a more realistic sense of her skills: "Let him [Colman] express himself in what terms of commendation he will (for that other high-flown stuff you must yourself know to be too ridiculous) my opinion will not be changed on that account."[22] This correspondence freed her at a formative stage to hear her harshest criticism not from the man who held the financial strings to her career, but privately, from someone she trusted and whose letters she evidently treasured. This strategy, conscious or not, had the effect of preventing a dependency from developing on a single figure like Colman. By consulting Twiss, she at once delimited the power of the manager and broadened her power base, by providing herself with critique from some source other than the would-be mentor.[23]

Thomas Harris posed an altogether different set of problems for a woman playwright. Harris, who was a former soap manufacturer and a seasoned businessman, had none of the genial avuncularity of Colman. Nor did he have Colman's skills in playwriting. And far from wanting to take chances on new plays, he tended to be quite conservative, and would usually only take on a new play if the playwright had a demonstrated record of success at one of the other houses. The development of Mrs. Inchbald's relationship with this manager was one in which her position as an insider was even more crucial to her survival and development as a playwright than it had been under Colman.

The story that sets the tone for her relationship with Harris is John Taylor's account of the attempted rape (see p.112).[24] Taylor's particular version of this story does not appear elsewhere so it may be apocryphal, but there are enough other indications in the diaries and letters to suggest that Harris's interest in her extended well beyond the professional.[25] Additionally Boaden reports that as early as the fall of 1782, Mrs. Inchbald offered a farce to Harris which was accepted, but never produced, and for which she received from him £20 as an advance.[26] Curiously, this payment appears nowhere in the Covent Garden ledgers for that year. If Harris made this payment to her from his own funds, which would have been highly irregular, it too suggests that he sought to involve her in some way that was not strictly professional. In any case, he took no chances on producing any of her plays until her successes with *The Mogul Tale* (1784) and *I'll Tell You What* (1785) at the Haymarket made her a much better risk. We can be fairly certain that in 1782 he had no intention whatever of producing her, payment or no payment.

It is unlikely that he continued to make aggressive overtures; she undoubtedly would have quit his employ as she had Richard Daly's summer season in Dublin for the same reason. But an adversarial tone characterizes their subsequent financial dealings, almost as if she were being made to pay for an initial rebuff. The ensuing business relationship was often an exhausting and infuriating one for Mrs. Inchbald, but it had the curious advantage of forthrightness. Whatever the problems of working with this man, demoralizing dependency and gratitude were not among them. Harris constituted management, and one senses that the adversarial stance Mrs. Inchbald took with him was paradoxically more comfortable for her than dealing with an avuncular character like Colman. In any case, if thinking about Colman as a mentor is difficult, in Harris's case it is impossible: he offered neither the protection nor the encouragement traditional in the Garrick era, nor was he competent to function as an editor.

The nature of Mrs. Inchbald's financial dealings with Harris can be illustrated as follows. On 28 November 1788, after five productions with Harris, Mrs. Inchbald opened *The Child of Nature*. After opening night, Harris downgraded it to an afterpiece and required that she shorten it accordingly. The financial implications of this downgrading were enormous. Instead of the benefits that would have accrued to a mainpiece on its third, sixth and ninth nights, Mrs. Inchbald was instead given a flat sum of £55.36 on 9 December, according to the disbursements in the ledger.[27] The rationale offered by Boaden for this extraordinarily low price (less than half what she received for *The Midnight Hour*, *The Mogul Tale* and *Animal Magnetism*, all afterpieces) is that the farce was a translation, but this clearly had not been negotiated before the fact. It was three years before Mrs. Inchbald produced another play with Harris. Mrs. Inchbald's mainpieces generally brought her in the neighborhood of £500 to £600 through her three benefit nights, so the compounded loss on this show was devastating.

The *Child of Nature* incident was not an isolated one. Similar kinds of dealings marked her efforts to translate and adapt the plays of the German dramatist, August von Kotzebue. Harris would commission her to translate a piece on the understanding that he would negotiate a fee later.[28] Mrs. Inchbald eventually got tough before the fact; for her *Wise Man of the East*, which was produced at Covent Garden in the 1799–1800 season, she demanded and received £500 up front, before the show even opened.[29] In 1805, she successfully negotiated for £600 on delivery for her last play, *To Marry or Not to Marry*. The risk was to be absorbed by management, not by her. At this late stage in her career, she was taking no chances on good will.[30]

These repeated thrusts and parries demonstrate the degree to which mentoring was becoming a charade. The relationship of playwright to any theatre manager was a fundamentally adversarial one. In this instance, it was Mrs. Inchbald's job to protect her interests by maximizing her profits. It was Harris's job to protect the financial viability of the theatre by driving a hard bargain. But it was to neither of their benefits if Mrs. Inchbald starved or if Harris went out of business. The financial pressures on playwright and manager alike were guaranteed to erode the initial gloss of goodwill and gratitude. This was particularly the case in the latter part of the eighteenth century as the rules concerning a playwright's remuneration became more and more open to negotiation.[31] Where there was room for negotiation, there was necessarily a kind of pushing and pulling between conflicting interests which was antithetical to the spirit of the mentor relationship.

Managers in general during this period were making the uncomfortable adjustment to the notion of the woman playwright as autonomous professional. There was a certain health in the sharp conflicts between Inchbald and Harris: they signalled a growth away from traditional mentoring, with all its publicized gratitude and covert animosities. Harris, for all his obtuseness in other areas, had the virtue of being a sharp businessman; he knew a good thing when he saw it and was consequently better equipped to adjust to this new businesslike relationship than others like Colman, who had grown up in the more genteel traditions of the old school.

It is interesting to consider how Mrs. Inchbald's employment at Covent Garden as an actress, her "inside position," played into this relationship with Harris. If Mrs. Inchbald's access to becoming a produced playwright under Harris's management had depended solely upon the outcome of his romantic overtures towards her, her work would never have been seen at Covent Garden, and her career as a whole would have been vastly curtailed. As it turned out, because she was also an actress in his employ, their relationship did not end over her rebuff of him. Nor did it end as the result of their repeated squabbles with one another subsequently. This inside position may have made her encounters with him awkward for a while, but at least it ensured that those encounters would continue until things smoothed out, and she could get on with the business of persuading him to read and produce her plays.

There is another crucial way in which her position as an insider played into her career as a playwright for Harris. In

1786, after just one successful production for Harris (*Appearance is Against Them* in 1785), Mrs. Inchbald commenced vigorous negotiations with him for a new contractual arrangement. But this time she was not negotiating for money related to her playwriting, but for a seven-year *acting* contract. Her bargaining chip was another new play, *Such Things Are*, which she had completed as promised, but which had not been delivered. Harris threatened to discharge her altogether as an actress unless she sent him this new play.[32] Boaden's account unfortunately falls short of giving us the actual outcome, but the implication is that Harris backed down and made some kind of compromise. The incident is important because it signals a covert structural relationship between Mrs. Inchbald's acting and her playwriting. Looking further, we discover that after the successful run of *Appearance is Against Them* in 1785, the demands on her time as an actress began to diminish markedly. For example, in her first season with Harris, during a single month (October 1780), she performed eight different times.[33] During the 1786–1787 season, Mrs. Inchbald continued on full salary for Harris.[34] But for this steady income, she appeared in speaking roles once in November, three times in December, twice in January and twice in February, and then not again until 15 March, for a total of eight appearances in *four and a half months*. To give some indication of what that meant, an actress named Mrs. Morton in the same company with a comparable salary (£3.10 weekly) appeared onstage in speaking roles a total of thirty-nine times in the exact same four-and-a-half-month period.

A similar pattern emerges at the Haymarket in the summer of 1789, her final season there as an actress. During this entire summer, she performed only once, as Irene in her own piece, *The Mogul Tale*, which was by now a standard part of the Haymarket repertory. The rest of the summer was presumably spent writing and revising her new piece for the Haymarket, *The Married Man*, which opened in July. As Boaden drily notes, "Her engagement in the summer with Mr. Colman went on; but as an actress she did nothing for her salary: she performed but once in his season . . . "[35] Boaden was technically correct, but he missed the point, which was that in this case and in the case of Covent Garden, Mrs. Inchbald's salary as an actress had been transformed into a subsidy for her playwriting. Harris and Colman both were indirectly coming to terms with the fact that she was more valuable to them as a first-string playwright than as a second-string actress. This unofficial subsidy may have constituted the first instance in theatre history in which a company retained what was functionally a woman playwright in residence.

This scenario goes a long way towards explaining her bold negotiations with Harris for a seven-year acting contract, on the heels of a successful production as playwright. The two events were causally connected. She may have felt that it would take her seven years to become financially secure enough not to need her actress's salary any more. As it turned out, she overestimated; her carefully accumulated securities enabled her to turn that corner only three years after these negotiations. But in the meantime, her salary as actress, however meager, allowed her to continue writing plays without the anxiety of having her entire year's income (or more, if it were a mainpiece) rest on the success or failure of a single opening night. The more secure that salary as actress, the more secure her career as a playwright.

If my assumptions are correct, it was an astonishing coup, and one that quite obviously could not have been achieved except as the result of her position inside the company. She had effectively engineered a way to have access to the managers, and on-site training in playwriting through exposure to actors, rehearsals, and performances. Now she also had some measure of long-term financial security, all without the "protection" of a mentor. This change laid additional groundwork for the paternal aspects of the mentor relationship to be gradually replaced by cleaner contractual obligations.[36]

One of the mysteries connected to Mrs. Inchbald's career is how she managed such an extraordinary degree of psychological independence and professionalism throughout. Certainly personality played a part; I wonder also if her Roman Catholicism (especially in the anti-Catholic atmosphere of the Gordon riots) contributed to her strong sense of independence. And historically the moment was propitious for this new kind of woman playwright. Garrick's aid to earlier women playwrights like Mrs. Cowley had shifted some of the prevailing attitudes. However, the mentor model he provided was based upon a relationship in which the woman never emerged past contingency status.

Elizabeth Inchbald, together with Hannah Cowley, took that model and transformed it into professional status for women.

One of the things that is disappointing in these histories is that over and over we find that the women failed to provide mentoring or support for one another.[37] For example, there are only two recorded instances in which Mrs. Cowley and Mrs. Inchbald were in direct professional contact with one another, one in 1780, which proved uneventful, and a second more interesting meeting the year after. In 1781, after a fine debut performing in Mrs. Cowley's hit *The Belle's Stratagem* the year before, Mrs. Inchbald was cast again in a Cowley play, this one called *The World As It Goes*. On 9 February, Mrs. Inchbald noted in her diary that a rehearsal of the new comedy had started, and that Mrs. Cowley had attended rehearsal. There was a certain irony in the situation; Mrs. Inchbald, the aspiring woman playwright, was cast as a minor character in a play by Mrs. Cowley, now an established woman playwright. On 22 February, Mrs. Inchbald records that she has been called for an eleven-o'clock rehearsal, and notes tersely "angry with Mrs. Cowley," although she doesn't say why.[38] On Saturday, 24 February, Mrs. Inchbald appeared as Sidney Grubb. The play opened and closed in one night. "Mr. Harris spoke to me in the green room some time after the Farce," she writes. It must have been to remove her from the role, because the play reopened on 24 March, after a flurry of rewrites and a new title (*Second Thoughts Are Best*). A Miss Satchell played Sidney Grubb; there was no role for Mrs. Inchbald at all. The play did no better the second time than it had the first, and finally closed for good.

There is no concrete evidence that Mrs. Cowley was responsible for Mrs. Inchbald's being removed from the role of Sidney Grubb, but the circumstantial evidence suggests that Mrs. Inchbald's anger with Mrs. Cowley in rehearsal may have been the result of conflict over the interpretation of the role. It would have been entirely appropriate for a playwright of Mrs. Cowley's stature to have insisted on such a change through the agency of Harris.

There are several things to be gleaned from these incidents. The first is that if my surmise is true, then Mrs. Inchbald must have felt acutely and with some pain the power of the playwright. It was the first time she had been relieved of a role and replaced by another actress at Covent Garden. But at the same time she must also have recognized the fragility of Mrs. Cowley's position, and the caution that descends when even a gifted and seasoned playwright produces a play that fails not once, but twice. In these moments Elizabeth Inchbald must have seen the need for extreme caution in making her transition out of acting into the much riskier but more remunerative field of playwriting. I wonder if she felt envy. Certainly she made no move to speak to Mrs. Cowley about her own ambitions for playwriting. They operated as if from two separate shores.

For better or for worse, Mrs. Inchbald had experienced the living and powerful presence of another woman playwright. However abrasive the experience, she cannot fail to have absorbed the fact of a woman playwright occupying a legitimate space in the theatre. This had not been the case several years earlier for Mrs. Cowley, who had had to reach back as far as Centlivre and Behn for her professional ancestors, and whose literary presence was validated only by the opprobrium of David Garrick, and the anxious competitive presence of another female playwright. But Cowley's seniority in the green room constituted an incontrovertible piece of information: that women playwrights had a place in this theatre. Mrs. Cowley, a survivor of this earlier form of patronage, by her endurance and success had made it possible for Mrs. Inchbald to feel her own ambitions legitimate and feasible. Energy that might otherwise have gotten diverted into legitimating her presence as a playwright was available to her for the writing itself.

There is an amusing postscript to this chronicle. In 1808, George Colman the Younger wrote Mrs. Inchbald a furious letter on account of an introduction she had written about one of his father's plays, which was to be published in the anthology, *The British Theatre*. Her remarks on the play were mild enough, but Colman was incensed.

> Oh! madam! is this grateful? Is it graceful from an ingenious lady, who was originally encouraged, and brought forward, as an authoress, by that very man on whose tomb she idly plants this poisonous weed of remark, to choke the laurels which justly grace his memory?[39]

Mrs. Inchbald responded serenely as follows:

> Let it be understood that my obligation to your father amounted to no more than those usual attentions which

*Plate 9*
George Colman the Younger
1762–1836
Occupations: Theatre Manager, Playwright, Critic, Examiner of Plays

From the beginning, Colman's relationship with Elizabeth Inchbald was either uneasy or overtly hostile. In the end, he waited until Mrs. Inchbald was dead in order to retaliate fully for a lifetime of insubordination. In his *Reminiscences* of 1818, he wrote this description of her, which adroitly recast her professional status as playwright as a form of domestic activity: "*The Mogul Tale*, which turned upon the new invention of balloons . . . was Mrs. Inchbald's first production, public one I mean, of which that fair lady as happily delivered; and her subsequent literary progeny have done great honour to their now deceased mamma." (Quoted from Richard Brinsley Peake, *Memoirs of the Colman Family*, London, n. p., 1841, vol. 2, p. 364.)

every manager of a theatre is supposed to confer, when he
first selects a novice in dramatic writing as worthy of being
introduced on his stage to the public.

Her reply echoes of Cordelia's "according to my bond, no more,
no less."

Colman was invoking a form of mentoring to which Mrs.
Inchbald had never subscribed, that in fact her career had
helped bring to an end. He was also registering his deep alarm
and antagonism to the fact that her career had eroded an
invisible gendered hierarchy within theatre itself. By becoming
a critic of drama and an anthologist, she now was exercising
some control over the canon itself. From Colman's perspective, it
was an intolerable situation.

Efforts to put Mrs. Inchbald in her place did not stop with the
younger Colman. As recently as 1981, the otherwise informative
documentation of her career in *A Biographical Dictionary* suggests
that she fell into playwriting as a kind of happenstance, that it
compensated for disappointment over her failure to achieve top
ranking as an actress. "At the end of the Covent Garden season
of 1788–89, with her articles [contract] expiring and hopes of
eminence as a first-line actress dimming, Elizabeth turned
resolutely from the stage to her writing."[40]

Carolyn Heilbrun, in her book *Writing a Woman's Life*, warns
against certain kinds of master narratives in women's biography
because they subtly reconstruct vocation as avocation and refuse
to grant women in history the status of ambitious professional.[41]
To imply that playwriting for Mrs. Inchbald was a kind of
forlorn career fallback is insidious as well as illogical. Mrs.
Inchbald stood to earn more in one benefit night as a playwright than in an entire year of salaried work as an actress.
When she died, she left behind a fortune of £6,000. Also her
diaries prove that she had come to London to be a playwright as
well as an actress; she had already submitted a play to Colman
by the time she arrived in 1780.[42] Our evidence suggests that at
the very least, the relationship between her acting and her
playwriting was complexly interdependent, not the simple mel-
ancholy tale that the *Dictionary* tells. A more plausible reading of
the evidence is that by 1789 her career as a playwright was so
firmly established that she could afford to quit acting altogether
and devote herself to writing.

But the real point is that the bogus sympathy in this biographical sketch imposes on Mrs. Inchbald's career the same kind of perspective that Colman's 1808 letter does. A narrative of ambition, gift, and tenacity is transformed into one of pitiful hope and inevitable failure. These biographers, like the eighteenth-century mentors, insist that she lean her tired head on their shoulders. Similar efforts to revise the narrative of her career can be found in the *Dictionary of National Biography*, and in James Boaden's *Memoirs of Mrs. Inchbald*, in which there are repeated references to her considerable earning power, and to the implicit unattractiveness of a woman who drives a hard bargain. Boaden speculates that Colman found her "keen after emolument," a critique that would sound incongruous applied to a man with the same degree of success.[43] The peevish tone of the biographers is not so much the result of how much Mrs. Inchbald gets paid, as of the fact that she gets paid at all.

What these biographers share with the early mentors is a resistance to the notion of the woman as professional. This resistance takes different forms, some fairly direct and aggressive, and some passively couched in sympathy towards the subject. The objective, however, is the same: in the absence of a contemporary mentor who could appropriately position Mrs. Inchbald as a literary daughter, these biographers take it upon themselves to do the job retroactively. Vocation is recast as avocation or accident. In this sense, biography becomes the kind of avuncular mentoring that Mrs. Inchbald successfully avoided for most of her career.

# 6

# FRANCES BURNEY AND THE PROTECTION RACKET

When Richard Brinsley Sheridan assumed the management of Drury Lane in 1776, a ripple of anxiety went through the playwriting community. What kind of treatment could playwrights expect from this new administration? There were disheartening reports of endless delays on submitted manuscripts. The unofficial consensus was that Sheridan was indifferent to all new drama except his own. That was bad news for everyone interested in having work produced. But for women, there was an additional anxiety. The paternal protection of women playwrights which had been Garrick's trademark at Drury Lane was now no longer a given. Would the protection and fostering of women's work continue under this new manager?

The unlikely focus of this chapter is Frances Burney. In the history of English literature, Burney is remembered as a novelist. Nevertheless, during her lifetime she made a sustained and serious effort to become a playwright. Among her papers are nine dramatic manuscripts, only one of which was actually produced at Drury Lane in March of 1795. Burney's failure as playwright is the central concern of this chapter because it tells us a great deal about the women who wrote plays but who were never produced and whose names have not survived. She presents us with a remarkable case history in which father, theatre manager, mentor and brother all converge into an interactive network of gatekeepers, facilitators, and permission-givers. Burney eventually made her way through this network and reached a kind of transcendence, although her revelations about artistic autonomy came too late, at least for a career in the theatre.

There are two aspects to Burney's story that are of particular importance to this study. The first, not surprisingly, is Sheridan himself. Like most men of his age, Sheridan's attitudes about women were a conflicted combination of chivalry, control, condescension, and passionate loyalty. He alone among the managers in this book was the son of a female dramatist: his mother, the gifted novelist and playwright Frances Sheridan, had been produced twice by Garrick in the 1760s. One might reasonably have expected that these legacies from his mother and Garrick would have caused him to take women playwrights on as part of the ethos of Drury Lane. But his record where women playwrights are concerned is mixed. Hannah Cowley's well-publicized anger with him in her preface to *Albina* may have had a warning effect on a number of other women: Elizabeth Inchbald avoided him almost entirely; as did Frances Brooke and Sophia Lee. Boaden speculated about why Sheridan had never solicited Mrs. Inchbald to write for Drury Lane:

> The truth was, that Sheridan really did not wish for any striking talent there to dispute his sovereignty; and, as to his deputy Mr. Kemble, he never scrupled to declare his opinion that we had plays enough, and far beyond all modern competition . . . besides, we naturally prefer a plan in which we are the leading instrument ourselves.[1]

The surprising twist to Burney's story is that contrary to his normal pattern, Sheridan actively solicited her to write drama for Drury Lane. But his efforts, instead of continuing Garrick's tradition of hospitality to women playwrights, instead precipitated a crisis. Sheridan's inability to perform the role of literary father meant that mentoring, as a form of access for women, was in jeopardy.

The other issue which Burney's story raises is the issue of rehearsals. Rehearsals were one of the essential means by which a playwright learned the craft and made crucial last-minute revisions. To quote the manager and playwright George Colman the Younger:

> It is well known, to those conversant with the business of the stage, that no perfect judgement can be formed of the length of a play, apparent to the spectator, until the private repetitions among the actors have reduced the business into something like *lucidus ordo* [a clear, orderly sequence]: then

133

*Plate 10*
Richard Brinsley Sheridan
1751–1816
Occupations: Theatre Manager, Playwright, Poet, Politician

Sheridan's private feelings about women working in the theatre were equivocal at best, making him a complicated choice as the heir to Garrick's empire at Drury Lane. In 1775, he received word from his father-in-law Thomas Linley that one of Linley's daughters, Polly, had been approached by Garrick to join Drury Lane as an actress. Sheridan erupted. "No Gentleman of Character and Fortune ever yet took a Wife from behind the Scenes of a Theatre . . . You will say that Polly is to be in a different Light – is to have Particular Countenance, Protection etc. This is what Mr. G [Garrick] has promised to hundreds – . . . The Reputation and Progress of a young Actress once engaged is entirely in the Power of a Manager – and if she refuses to comply with his Choice or re[c]ommendation in her Business She may as well throw up the Profession at once. – and G. [Garrick] has damn'd and sunk numbers whom he had first cajoled, and fo[u]nd afterwards not servilely manageable . . . Sincerely interested for the welfare of all your Children, I have the same Feelings for the *Honour* of your Daughters as of my own Sisters – their present situation – or any public situation – is not *without* Hazard –."
(Quoted from *The Letters of Richard Brinsley Sheridan*, Cecil Price (ed.), Oxford at the Clarendon Press, 1966, vol. 3, p. 293 ff.)

*Plate 11*
Frances Burney
1752–1840
Occupations: Novelist, Playwright

When Frances Burney was growing up in London, David Garrick was a frequent and favorite guest. He used to show up unannounced early in the morning, sometimes in costume, just for the fun of setting the household on its ear. He also provided occasional seats for the family to see plays at Drury Lane. Frances Burney saw a lot of theatre as a young woman growing up in London, and reported her reactions to various productions in her journal. In 1773, when she was twenty-one years old, she wrote: "We had yesterday the – I know not whether to say pain or pleasure, – of seeing Mr. Garrick in the part of Lear. He was exquisitely Great – every idea which I had formed of his talents, although I have ever idolized him, was exceeded. – I am sorry that this play is Acted with Cibber's Alterations, as every Line of his, is immediately to be distinguished from Shakespeare, – who, with all his imperfections, is too superiour to any other Dramatick Writer, for them to bear so near a comparison: & to my Ears, every Line of Cibber's, is feeble & paltry." Burney was mistaken about Cibber; the adaptation she objected to, as Frances Brooke and others had done before her, was Nahum Tate's. (Quoted from *The Early Journals and Letters of Fanny Burney, 1768–1773*, ed. Lars Troide, McGill-Queen's University Press, Kingston and Montreal, 1988, vol. 1, p. 242.)

comes the time for the judicious author to take up his pruning-knife . . .[2]

Mrs. Inchbald's experience has shown how essential watching plays, both in rehearsals and during the run, could be. But it is important that in this history of women playwrights we do not take rehearsals for granted. The women we have looked at to this point, particularly Cowley, Inchbald, Lee, and Brooke, had their own connections to the theatre world, and for them, attending rehearsals and performances raised no particular difficulties. But rehearsals seem to have constituted an area of trouble for a number of other women. In Burney's case, and in Baillie's, it is clear that being present at rehearsals would have been advantageous, but both these women stayed away. There were always good practical reasons for not attending, but there was also an underlying reluctance, as if the backstage were alien territory. Backstage space was still gendered: men could tread there without penalty, but women who worked there ran very real risks of no longer being treated as "ladies," as Mrs. Inchbald had discovered at the hands of Thomas Harris.

Mrs. Clive's script, *The Rehearsal, or, Bays in Petticoats*, may offer some clues, even though it dates back to 1750. The character of the playwright, Mrs. Hazard, is about to supervise the final rehearsal for her opera. Mr. Cross, the Drury Lane prompter, is present to help run the rehearsal, but there is no sign of the manager, nor is there any indication from the conversation that he is expected. Mrs. Hazard is apparently expected to run the rehearsal by herself, backed up by the very limited authority of Mr. Cross. It soon becomes clear that she cannot be effective. The lead actress (the insolent "Mrs. Clive") has refused to show up; she is busy organizing her own benefit and can't be bothered. Without the commanding presence of the manager, Mrs. Hazard is helpless and has to put the actress's costume on herself and fill in. At one point during rehearsal, Mrs. Hazard reflects on the difficulty of trying to talk Mrs. Clive into performing the role in the first place. Witling, Mrs. Hazard's friend, is curious: "And what did you say to her, pray?" Mrs. Hazard: "Say to her! why do you think I wou'd venture to expostulate with her? – No, I desir'd Mr. *Garrick* wou'd take her in hand; so he order'd her [to take] the Part of the Mad-woman directly."[3] In the end, Mrs. Hazard's efforts are all for nothing; in a rage at her condescending friends and uncooperative cast, she leaves the theatre in the midst of rehearsal, swearing never to write another play.

In actual eighteenth-century theatre practice, the job of rehearsing a new play was usually divided between the manager (or acting manager, as in the case of Kemble), and the playwright. The playwright might be very actively involved, but the authority for final decisions usually rested with the manager. All a manager had to do, as Sarah Gardner had discovered, was to covertly signal the actors that they had his tacit permission to sabotage the play and she was lost. Most cases were not that extreme. In Mrs. Hazard's case, the absence of the manager at rehearsal is signal enough. She is not being overtly sabotaged, but neither is she receiving full support. Without that support, a woman playwright was a vulnerable figure backstage. In Mrs. Hazard's case, there is a symbolic demotion to the lesser status of actress. Even in the act of interpreting her own script, her agency and authority still came from the manager. Even if we take into account the fact that women playwrights found more general acceptance in the post-Garrick era, this reluctance about participating in rehearsals still lingers.[4] Male playwrights in rehearsals carried with them the authority that came with being male in the culture. As this chapter will show, Richard Cumberland's reports about rehearsals are full of incident, but he manages the cast and the revisions with the kind of deftness that comes with authority and confidence, even though the manager, in this case Sheridan, has failed to turn up. But Sheridan's failure to turn up for the rehearsal of a woman playwright might have created a different message and a different dynamic. In the absence of the manager, the woman playwright did not carry with her his vested authority. And since Sheridan was habitually late or absent from the rehearsals of new plays, Drury Lane was now risky ground for women.

Burney's story begins in 1778 with the anonymous publication of her first novel, *Evelina*. Even her father, the respected musician and music historian Charles Burney, did not know about this immensely successful novel until it had been in print for six months. Burney must have had good reasons for secrecy; at age fifteen, she had burned the manuscript of her first completed work of fiction and some early plays and journals. She may have known that unless she published *Evelina* anonymously, it might not be published at all.

137

Among *Evelina*'s most outspoken admirers was Hester Thrale (later Piozzi). Thrale's home at Streatham was a gathering place for a number of prominent literary figures, including Dr. Samuel Johnson and the playwrights Arthur Murphy and Richard Cumberland. Thrale herself was an important if unofficial catalyst for contemporary literary opinion. Burney's novel was read and discussed by this circle of friends, and in a diary entry dated 3 August 1778, she reported with great excitement to her sister that Mrs. Thrale had written a letter to Dr. Burney (dated 22 July 1778), which spoke in glowing terms of *Evelina* and further remarked: "I cannot tell what might not be expected from Evelina, was she to try her genius at Comedy."[5] In a letter to her father dated 25 July from Chessington, where she was visiting her close friend and mentor, Samuel Crisp, Burney herself weighs the possibility of "insinuating the plot into the boxes" (all theatrical terminology) and refers to herself, as she was to do several times later, as "Miss Bayes," [*sic*] which was a comic way of calling herself "Miss Playwright."[6] The idea of writing a comedy seeded itself early on, as a direct consequence of her success with *Evelina* and Mrs. Thrale's support.

Six months later, in January of 1779, Frances Burney met Richard Brinsley Sheridan at the home of mutual friends. Sheridan by this time had been the manager of Drury Lane for three years, and had already acquired a reputation for brilliance as a playwright but unreliable behavior as a businessman and manager.[7] In her account of this meeting, Sheridan takes on the magnitude of a legend, and she presents herself as a kind of humble onlooker. In fact, in age and reputation, there were striking similarities between the two. At the time he was twenty-eight years old to Burney's twenty-seven, and they were both celebrities in literary circles, Sheridan because of *School for Scandal* which had premiered in 1777, and Burney because of the publication of *Evelina* in 1778. She reported in her journal:

> Mr. Sheridan has a very fine figure, and good though I don't think a handsome face. He is tall and very upright, and his appearance and address are at once manly and fashionable, without the smallest tincture of foppery or modish graces. In short, I like him vastly, and think him every way worthy of his beautiful companion [his wife, Elizabeth Linley]. And let me tell you what I know will give you as much pleasure as it

gave me – that by all I could observe in the course of the evening, and we stayed very late, they are extremely happy in each other: he evidently adores her, and she as evidently idolises him. The world has by no means done him justice.[8]

There are rumors of marital discord implicit in her comments which she attempts to put to rest.[9]

Upon seeing Burney and her father at this gathering, Sheridan seated himself between them, and turning to Dr. Burney asked permission to be introduced to her. "Why, it will be a very formidable thing to her to be introduced to you," demurred Dr. Burney, as if such a meeting might be too much for his daughter, and Sheridan acceded, saying, "Well then, by and by." A little later, however, Sheridan decided to bypass Dr. Burney altogether. According to Frances Burney's diary, he "waived the ceremony" and introduced himself directly. He began by praising *Evelina* and asked: "But I hope, Miss Burney, you don't intend to throw away your pen?" "You should take care, sir, what you say," she replied, "for you know not what weight it may have."[10] Later Sheridan took Burney's father aside a second time and formally repeated his opinion that

I should write for the stage, and his desire to see my play. . . . And now, my dear Susy [Burney addresses her sister Susanna], if I should attempt the stage, I think I may be fairly acquitted of presumption, and however I may fail, that I was strongly pressed by Mrs. Thrale, and by Mr. Sheridan, the most successful and powerful of all dramatic living authors, will abundantly excuse my temerity.[11]

Burney's report of this encounter reveals an assumption about women becoming playwrights that is already familiar: that they risked public exposure in a way that was distinct from that of writers in other genres. But it is 1779, and the fact that she entertains the idea seriously gives some indication of just how much things had changed. Was she game enough to endure the public scrutiny associated with becoming a playwright? She was, but she wanted Sheridan's benediction first.

Frances Burney's diary entry about this first meeting with Sheridan also reveals the way key figures of authority in her life began to usurp her right to make her own decision about playwriting. These influences were conspicuously absent when

Burney was struggling through the writing and publication of *Evelina* two years before. Her brother Charles had assisted her by spiriting her anonymous manuscript off to a publishing house, but artistically she was completely on her own. Her decision to publish *Evelina* anonymously was probably not based just on maidenly authorial modesty but also on a shrewd instinct for circumventing interference. The irony of her situation was that because she was now famous, she had unimagined opportunities, but that quiet space in which to work was irrevocably lost.

The invitation to become a playwright, because it took place subsequent to the publication of *Evelina*, turned playwriting itself into contested territory. Burney's name was now a valuable commodity. Sheridan's claims to that talent were staked against other claims, notably those of Burney's father. Dr. Burney's initial refusal to introduce Sheridan to his daughter suggests that a polite but firm struggle was taking place. One wonders if things would have turned out differently had Sheridan approached Frances Burney privately, or if Mrs. Thrale's letter had not alerted her father to the possibility of a play. Unfortunately, the fact that Burney had completed and published *Evelina* without her father's permission or knowledge had undermined his role as paternal guardian. As a consequence, any venture into playwriting was now loaded, more so than it might have been otherwise.[12] Playwriting became a means by which both Dr. Burney and Frances Burney's mentor Samuel Crisp (whom she called "Daddy" in all her letters), could begin to reposition her as daughter, invoking all the duty and obedience which that role had historically demanded. Dr. Burney must have felt a powerful need to reassert his control if he was willing to foil the hopes and expectations not just of his daughter and Sheridan, but also of his friend, patron, and sometime employer, the powerful and well-connected Mrs. Thrale.

Whatever his stated reasons, Dr. Burney, together with Samuel Crisp, ruthlessly suppressed Frances Burney's first effort at playwriting, a full-length comedy entitled *The Witlings*, which she completed during the summer of 1779, and which was read aloud by assembled family and friends in August of that year. Until recently, it was a commonplace of literary history that this suppression was all for the best, that Burney's plays would have been an embarrassment to an otherwise distinguished career in letters. Margaret Doody's biography of Frances Burney challenges that assumption and offers this assessment:

> *The Witlings* is an unpretentious but intelligent comedy which truly accomodates female knowledge and experience . . . The presentation of the milliners is in itself new, and the presentation of them neither as angels of virtue nor demons of hypocrisy and frivolity but rather as working women – persons, albeit comic persons, in their own right – seems an impressive piece of understated liberalism . . . We see that the author advocates self-dependence – and independence for women – but there are real doubts about the possibilities of achieving this . . . Burney found in drift, inconsequentiality, and anticlimax dramatic principles that can work without falsehood. Her little play is more expressive of the real state of the drama and of society in her time (in expressive hesitation, fatigued boredom with old modes, repetition without certain form) than many grander pieces by well-known playwrights of the time.[13]

The suppression of the text was accomplished simply by Dr. Burney's notifying Frances that under no circumstances was she to go forward with plans for production. Crisp brought up the rear by intimating that *The Witlings* bore a disturbing resemblance to Molière's *Les Femmes savantes* (a play which Burney herself claimed she had never read). Dr. Burney said he was concerned that her play might offend. Frances Burney's shock and dismay at their decision cannot be doubted. In what Doody calls "an epistle of miserable obedience," Burney wrote to her father "I most solemnly declare, that upon your account any disgrace would mortify and afflict me more than upon my own; for whatever appears with your knowledge, will be naturally supposed to have met with your approbation."[14]

Sheridan's inability in 1779 to assert his claim over that of Burney's biological father marks an important shift in this history of women in playwriting because it marks the end of an era in which the manager and the father were seen to be more or less co-extensive. In an important strategic move, Garrick had set himself up as the father substitute. But in January of 1779, as Garrick lay dying and Sheridan was in the middle of his second season as the manager of Drury Lane, it was no longer possible to imagine these two fathers, the literary and the biological, as a fused presence. Sheridan, because of youth, temperament and an already compromised reputation where his marriage was concerned, was in no position to sustain this delicate illusion. So father and manager separated, each into their separate corners of the ring, and each making their separate and implicitly competitive claims on the daughter. Garrick's genius had been to turn this complex social icon of "the father" to his own advantage, and bypass the confrontation entirely.[15] Dr. Burney, a one-time composer and personal friend of Garrick's, would have been keenly sensitive to the change in management style. There was no immediate issue of Frances's moral or physical safety; it was an issue of whether or not Sheridan could provide the *perception* of someone identified with paternal authority in the way that Garrick could. Evidently, he could not.

Even if Sheridan's personal reputation had been immaculate, which it was not, his attitude towards women playwrights was ambivalent. In January of 1778, Sheridan wrote David Garrick a remarkable letter regarding a piece of poetry that had been commissioned either by Garrick himself or by an unnamed third party. The occasion for this poetry apparently had something to do with "the characters of women."[16] Sheridan wrote Garrick as follows:

> I have been *about finishing* the Verses which were to have follow'd you to Althorp every day since you left Town . . . such as it is, the Poem shall salute your return . . . I mean to be vastly civil to Female Talent of all sort[s], and even to the affectation of it where the Person is very handsome ( – for the Grace of Venus which passes all understanding, atones for an abundance of Frailty – ) and my Bards shall be *very easily* recompensed.[17]

This jaunty assurance to Garrick appears to have been made in response to a prior query from Garrick, to the effect of 'what exactly is your poem going to say about women?' Sheridan evidently does not refer to women *playwrights* when he talks about "female talent," since he makes reference to Bards (in contradistinction to *female* talent) later in the same sentence. His comments combine an effortless mastery of language with sentiments that are perhaps a professional woman's worst anxiety: that her talents have been praised (or damned) according to her physical appearance or her sexual availability. In retrospect, it is suprising that Sheridan would have addressed Garrick with this kind of boys-will-be-boys backslapping familiarity; one can only assume that he was riding the crest of recent triumphs and had failed to take note of Garrick's careful management of women playwrights. Garrick's own letters are frequently salty, and even sometimes cruel, but they never indulge in this kind of crude chauvinism.

Sheridan's conflicting sentiments, in spite of his fervid pursuit of Frances Burney's prospective play, continued to reveal themselves. In the spring of 1779, just months after his first encounter with Burney, he wrote the following lines as an epilogue to Hannah More's *The Fatal Falsehood*, which had just opened at Drury Lane:

What motley cares Corilla's mind perplex,
While maids and metaphors conspire to vex!
In studious deshabille behold her sit,
A letter'd gossip, and a housewife wit:
At once invoking, though for diff'rent views,
Her gods, her cook, her milliner, and muse:
Round her strew'd room, a frippery chaos lies,
A chequer'd wreck of notable and wise.
Bills, books, caps, couplets, combs, a vary'd mass,
Oppress the toilet and obscure the glass;
Unfinish'd here an epigram is laid,
And there a mantua-maker's bill unpaid.
Three newborn plays, foretaste the town's applause,
There dormant patterns pine for future gauze.
A moral essay now is all her care,
A satire next, and then a bill of fare.
A scene she now projects, and now a dish,
Here's act the first, and here – "remove with fish."
Now, while this eye in a fine frenzy rolls,
That soberly casts up a bill for coals,
Black pins and daggers in one leaf she sticks,
And tear and thread, and bowls and thimbles mix.[18]

This time the message is public and unmistakeable: that a woman with pretensions to being a playwright makes an ass of herself and would be better off sticking to domestic duties like sewing and paying bills. This epilogue caused quite a controversy in the London papers and brought down on Sheridan's head considerable negative publicity.[19] One wonders if Dr. Burney saw or heard about this controversy; it may have been one factor among several in his decision two months later to suppress *The Witlings*.

Sheridan was regarded with anxiety and suspicion by many of the playwrights who had come up through the ranks under Garrick. Richard Cumberland, for example, characterized Sheridan as unreliable and undisciplined. In a letter to Garrick as early as December 1777, he wrote:

> Your successor in management [Sheridan] is not a representative of your polite attention to authors on such occasions, for he came in yawning at the fifth act, with no other apology than having sate up two nights running. It gave me not the least offence, as I put it all to habit[s] of dissipation and indolence; but I fear his office will suffer for want to due attention, and the present drop [in attendance] upon the theatre justifies my apprehensions.[20]

Cumberland's circumspect tone in this letter is not characteristic of the women playwrights. Hannah More and Hannah Cowley regarded Sheridan with frank hostility and were convinced that he was antagonistic to their efforts. To what extent these sentiments were influenced by old and fierce loyalties to Garrick is difficult to gauge, but it is interesting how negative reactions to Sheridan tended to break down along gendered lines: the male playwrights endured him as a frustrating liability; the women saw him as a personal enemy. Hannah More, in a fit of irritation, wrote Garrick in October of 1778:

> Few things could vex me more than that that little bard should get into the winter management (if that can be called management which appears to me all anarchy and wild uproar; but at this distance I cannot pretend to judge): should he get in, it would be the greatest mortification to me ever to have any transactions with him; and I am very sure he would do all in his power to crush any attempts of mine.[21]

In a similar vein, Hannah Cowley wrote her patroness Lady Harrowby on 31 October 1777:

> That Mr. Sheridan is my Enemy from principle, I have too much reason to believe – for he not only last year did all in

his power to crush *The Runaway* [her first success, produced under Garrick in 1776], but this year, when Mr. Henderson [a top-ranked comic actor] is very desirous of performing George Hargrave [lead male character in *The Runaway*] (which he avows to be his favorite character) and that he has been requested to do it, by some persons of rank who saw him in it frequently at Bath – he is not allow'd to appear in it; doubtless, because it would give the Comedy a new run, and its unfortunate Author, new reputation.[22]

It is always difficult with Sheridan to distinguish between sloppy management and covert sabotage. In point of fact, during the 1780s and 1790s, Drury Lane actually produced about the same number of women playwrights that had been produced under Garrick, and in a shorter span of time. But virtually every single production failed, most in a single night,[23] and in the end, these repeated failures probably undermined the idea of the woman playwright as professional. The women themselves consistently attribute malicious intentions to Sheridan's behavior. Even in the free-for-all open-market atmosphere of the post-Garrick era, Drury Lane stands out as a theatre of last resort for women playwrights. Sheridan's pursuit of Frances Burney's play has to be carefully contextualized: Burney's celebrity status would have made her a very attractive box-office prospect for any of the theatres. His interest in her was undoubtedly and understandably connected to enhancing his management profile at Drury Lane. But it would be a mistake to attribute to Sheridan the same impulses where female playwrights are concerned that drove his predecessor. Sheridan thought the theatre a deplorable place for any respectable woman. His campaign to solicit Burney's work consequently has a peculiar double edge.

*The Witlings* was never produced. Sheridan continued to make intermittent overtures, and for a time it appeared that both Dr. Burney and Crisp were nervously reconsidering. But by this time, Frances Burney had "so much more fear than hope, and anxiety than pleasure," that she decided to let the matter die.[24] There is one final letter from Crisp to Frances Burney that deserves attention:

My great scruple all along has been the consideration of the great stake you are playing for, how much you have to lose, and how unequal your delicate and tender frame of mind would be to sustain the shock of a failure of success, should that be the case. You can't easily imagine how much it goes against me to say anything that looks like discouragement to a spirit already too diffident and apprehensive. Nothing but so rooted a regard for my Fannikin, and her peace and happiness, as I feel at this instant, could ever have prevailed on me to have used that freedom with her.[25]

In this letter Crisp reveals how he has overidentified with his "Fannikin," and how he had probably substituted his own bitterness over the failure of his play *Virginia* at Drury Lane almost thirty years before.[26] He is without critical distance, unable to distinguish between his own sensitivities and those of the young woman to whom he speaks. Frances Burney and her career become an extension of his own failures and anxieties. His role as male and as mentor perhaps make it impossible for him to claim those feelings for himself, so he has to attribute them to her.

Frances Burney, as an artist and as a person, was not in focus for either her father or Crisp. She was a means by which they constructed themselves, as father, as strength-giver, as mentor, and protector. Sheridan functioned as a catalyst in this equation, giving both men an opportunity to re-assert their claims after the awkward fact of her literary coup without their help or protection. It would be many years before Frances Burney was to understand the damage her father and Crisp had inflicted, and to find her own way forward.

Burney's first production did not take place until fifteen years later, at Drury Lane in March of 1795. It had one dreadful opening night, was hissed off the stage, and closed for good. The tragedy, entitled *Edwy and Elgiva*, had been written by Burney during a grim period at court as a lady-in-waiting to Queen Charlotte (from about 1790–1794). The failure of *Edwy and Elgiva*, despite the presence of John Philip Kemble and Sarah Siddons in the title roles, has been attributed to her inexperience and incompetence as a playwright.[27] In fact, the failure was not all hers. It was occasioned by gross theatrical mismanagement, Burney's illness during the pre-production period, and her failure to engage fully the production and rehearsal process. However, to judge from her letters, the experience appears to have left Burney inexplicably exhilarated. Far from convincing her of the truth of her father's judgement fifteen years before, or of Crisp's warning that her "delicate and tender frame of mind" was unequal to the shock of failure, the experience with *Edwy and Elgiva* knocked something loose in her thinking. She did not read this failure as a sign that she should stay out of theatre. She read it as a sign that if she were going to continue as a playwright, she would have to take more control.

The production Burney witnessed that night of 21 March 1795 was inexcusably bad. Whether the incoherence was due to the script or the production was difficult to judge, because in fact not very much of the original script got heard. One of the lead actors, John Palmer, had failed to memorize his lines and made them up as he went along. The prompter could be heard throughout the show, feeding the actors their lines. After the production closed, Burney began sorting out responsibility for the play's failure. In a letter to her friend Mrs. Waddington, she wrote:

> It was not written with any idea of the stage, and my illness and weakness, and constant absorbment, at the time of its preparation occasioned it to appear with so many undramatic effects, from my inexperience of theatrical requisites and demands, that when I saw it, I myself perceived a thousand things I wished to change. The performers too were cruelly imperfect, and made blunders I blush to have pass for mine, – added to what belong to me. The most important character after the hero and heroine had but two lines of his part by heart! [Aldhelm, played by John Palmer.] He made all the rest at random, and such nonsense as put all the other actors out as much as himself; so that a more wretched performance, except Mrs. Siddons, Mr. Kemble, and Mr. Bensley, could not be exhibited in a barn. All of this concurred to make it very desirable to withdraw the piece for alterations, which I have done. And now you have the whole history –[28]

On 13 May 1795 she wrote her father, Dr. Burney, to quell his anxious sympathy and lay out her plans for the future:

> I am not at all without thoughts of a future revise of *Edwy and Elgiva*, for which I formed a plan on the first night, from

what occurred by the repr[esen]tation: but then – I want Mr. Palmer to be so obliging as to leave the Stage! – though everybody agrees he would not dare, after what has already passed, play the same part a second time. And let me own to you, when you commend my "bearing so well a theatrical drubbing," I am by no means enabled to boast I bear it with conviction of my utter failure. The piece was certainly not heard, and therefore not really judged.[29]

The reports in the newspapers vividly describe the extent to which management and acting had gone afoul. One paper speculated that there had been intentional sabotage. "The acting," reported the *Morning Advertiser*,

> was disgraceful to the Company, and shamefully injurious to the Author. Surely there was no intention to affect the piece by such proceedings – it may, however, be shrewdly suspected . . . if the Piece was accepted, it should have been played. There is no palliation for imperfect study [line memorization] in a Theatre of the Metropolis.[30]

The *Morning Herald* described

> Elgiva's dying scene, when a passing stranger, in a fine tragic tone, says, "Let us carry her to the other side of the hedge." This hedge, which is supposed to be remotely situated from any dwelling [Burney's script specifies "A forest"], nevertheless proved to be a very accommodating retreat; for, in a few minutes after, the wounded lady is brought from behind it on an elegant couch, and, after dying in the presence of her husband, is carried off and placed once more "on the other side of the hedge." The laughter which this scene occasioned, although supported by the dying words of Mrs. Siddons, was inconceivable.[31]

The couch, which had materialized in the middle of a wilderness, had never been a part of the original script and made Burney's dialogue ridiculous.[32] If it was a necessity for practical reasons (Mrs. Siddons's increasing bulk, for instance), it should have been either justified with additional dialogue, or replaced with something more suitable to a remote rustic setting.

The reviewer for *The Oracle, Public Advertiser* (23 March 1795) was so disgusted by the mishandling of the play that he also speculated that there had been malicious intent. He was particularly outraged about John Palmer's performance, and his review underscores Burney's own observations. He wrote that he found no way to account for the fact that

> any Actor can dare stand before the MANAGER [Sheridan's appointed acting manager, John Philip Kemble], who engages his services, and receive EVERY WORD of his PRINCIPAL SCENE from the *mouth* of the Prompter! . . . Duty demands not his CENSURE [of the play] but [censure of] his PERFORMANCE.[33]

Burney's play had been caught in a cross-fire between Sheridan and his company.[34] There had been rumblings within the company from the earliest days of Sheridan's management in 1776. In 1788, Sheridan had appointed his lead male actor, John Philip Kemble, as his deputy, to use Boaden's term (the actual title was 'acting manager'). Sheridan was preoccupied with national politics and spent most of his time tending to his office as Member of Parliament. There was an improvement in Drury Lane's fortunes after the Kemble appointment, but not enough to sustain the theatre financially through a huge rebuilding project during the 1793–1794 season during which the size of the house ballooned up to 3,611 (Drury Lane had seated 650 under Garrick). The debt load attending this building project was enormous (estimated at about £70,000), and Sheridan juggled the theatre's finances by not paying his actors.[35] As Mrs. Siddons, Kemble's sister and the lead actress at Drury Lane, wrote:

> I am, as you may observe, acting again; but how much difficulty to get my money! Sheridan is certainly the greatest phenomenon that Nature has produced for centuries. Our theatre is going on, to the astonishment of everybody. Very few of the actors are paid, and all are vowing to withdraw themselves; yet still we go on.[36]

There were additional complications. In 1793, Kemble attempted to refurbish the Drury Lane company with new performers by discharging some of the old ones.[37] The *Thespian Magazine* elaborated briefly on the rumored firings: "John Palmer and near forty others."[38] But Palmer was still engaged two years later in 1795, so these dischargings must not have taken place.

Kemble was trapped, managing and performing with a company of unpaid actors, many of whom had reason to believe that he wanted them replaced. To make matters worse, in January of 1795, just two months before Burney's opening, Kemble himself was accused of attempted rape by one of the actresses in the Drury Lane Company, Maria Theresa DeCamp. The situation was complicated by the fact that Kemble's own wife, the former Priscilla Brereton, was also a member of this acting company, and that Kemble's brother Charles wanted to marry DeCamp. Kemble eventually made a public apology, but the incident can have done nothing to enhance his already precarious position within the company, not to mention his unofficial reputation among prospective women playwrights.[39]

The failure of Burney's play takes on new complexity in this context. Palmer's audacious refusal to learn his lines must be read as a deliberate and hostile confrontation over unpaid salaries. In a management dispute that had no institutionalized procedure for grievance and redress, he was acting as an unofficial labor representative. His failure to learn lines was a form of work stoppage. One can only imagine Kemble's impotent rage, since he too was struggling to collect his own salary and that of his sister and wife, and probably felt himself as much a victim of Sheridan's mismanagement as Palmer did.

However, as Burney herself pointed out, some of the responsibility for the failure of *Edwy and Elgiva* must accrue to the playwright. One development in particular provides perspective. About three months after Burney's play closed, she heard through her father that Richard Cumberland had come forward with an offer to help her revise *Edwy and Elgiva* in the event of another production.[40] In writing to Burney's father to make the offer, Cumberland let something else slip. In a letter dated 10 June 1795, Burney reported to her brother: "I have had an extraordinary message from Mr. Cumberland: – *that he knew the play would fail, by what he gathered from the players before performance* . . ." [my italics].[41] He doesn't say that the actors *planned* to make the play fail; he implies that the actors felt that it didn't have a chance to begin with. Why did Cumberland have access to information that should have been Burney's, information that might have enabled her either to take the play in hand and rework it, or to withdraw it until such time as she was able to give it her full attention?

Cumberland made an ironclad practice of attending the rehearsals of his new plays, and in doing so, became privy to a good deal of inside information, both about his productions and about other people's. In attending rehearsals for his *The Wheel of Fortune*, which opened a month before *Edwy and Elgiva*, he must have heard the actors talking disparagingly about Burney's script. They were already familiar with her script because it had been read aloud to them in the green room in early January.

By contrast, Frances Burney never attended a single rehearsal for *Edwy and Elgiva*, so she was out of the loop of backstage theatre gossip. Also she had no way to observe actors reacting to her script. There was no early-warning system in place, and consequently no opportunity for substantive revisions prior to opening. Moreover, there was no one in place willing or competent to oversee rehearsals on her behalf, the way Garrick had done for so many playwrights during his tenure. Certainly Sheridan had never made it a priority to oversee readings and rehearsals, and Kemble, whose job it was to do so in Sheridan's absence, was having his own difficulties maintaining control of the company.

Burney's absence from rehearsals was costly. A playwright who was effectively involved in rehearsals could make the difference between success and failure on opening night. Richard Cumberland's experience in 1778 with his play, *The Battle of Hastings*, will provide the counter-example. A series of letters from Cumberland to David Garrick have survived, which were written during the rehearsal period, just prior to opening. Garrick, now retired, continued to function as an advisor to a number of playwrights who felt abandoned by Sheridan's laissez-faire style of management.

On 4 January 1778 Cumberland wrote Garrick: "Thank you for your advice . . . without some prudence and patience I should never have got the ladies [actresses] cordially into their business [their roles]."[42] Shortly afterward he wrote:

I owed the correction to Miss Younge's [one of the actresses] protest against the simile of the *lightning* . . . In the close of the fifth act, out of fifty-three lines which followed after the death of Matilda, twenty-nine only remain, so that all things are now settled . . . We are advertised for next week, viz. Saturday. My women will be very good, and are in high good-humour with their parts. I am interceding with Mr. King to speak my prologue.[43]

Later the same day he commented:

> Mr. Smith made good my apprehensions, and refused taking any part in my tragedy but that of Edgar [Edgar had already been assigned to Henderson]. He was disposed to take this step with some small accompaniments of asperity, but as I wished not to give him offence, so I laboured hard to prevent his taking any, and we parted, as I hope, in perfect friendship and good understanding. Mr. Bensley plays *Harold*; Mr. Palmer, *Edwin*; Mr. Brereton, *Waltheof*, and Mr. Aickin, *Northumberland*: Miss Younge is *Matilda* and Mrs. Yates, *Edwina*. So stand my forces.

And shortly thereafter:

> I have this morning, my dear friend, rehearsed the "Battle," and a brave battle we made. Madam Yates rehearsed without book her whole part [that is, her lines were memorized]; all was harmony, zeal and good will: nothing lagged or hobbled in the whole; and the new corrections (especially the *finale* to the fourth act) were applauded. The fifth act, which was long, is now very brilliant, and I am well contented to take my trial.[44]

It does not require extensive backstage theatre experience to see that Cumberland's involvement in the rehearsals for his play had a decisive impact on casting, cast morale, and the overall momentum and coherence of the production. It also appears that Cumberland made revisions on the script, not only according to Garrick's suggestions but sometimes according to those of the actors. By the time he says "I am well content to take my trial," he actually has a fairly seasoned script on his hands. He has taken the opportunity to refine the script in the context of actual production, and can now face an opening night with confidence. *The Battle of Hastings* was in fact received with "uncommon applause"[45] and became a regular part of the theatre repertoire.

By contrast, Burney neither saw nor heard any part of her play until the actual night of the opening. This was in part a function of illness: certainly the seriousness of her condition after her son's birth in December of 1794 cannot be overstated. But rehearsals, of which there were only ten, actually began in earnest on 4 March, by which time she was well on the way to recovery. However, she never went to London to look in, nor is there any record that she even inquired through Charles. It is possible that, as a writer of novels, she underestimated the importance of being present at rehearsals. But it is also possible that she was protecting herself from caring too much by keeping her distance, or to use Burney's own word, staying "indifferent."

Burney's detachment was complicated by the fact that from the earliest part of the production period (January of 1795), she was protected from knowing anything about the production by her brother Charles. Here it becomes difficult to separate cause from effect. Her illness, Charles's protective impulses, and her own withdrawal are all integrally connected. Typically, a woman playwright who wanted to avoid rehearsals delegated the responsibility of attending to a male emissary. In Burney's case that person was her brother Charles. Charles made initial contact with Kemble about the script in the fall of 1794, and followed up in January of 1795 by conducting a reading of the play to the assembled actors in the green room. Charles himself read the play aloud to them from beginning to end since he had only one copy. Readings were a key moment in the rehearsal process because they gave the author an early indication of how the play might be received, not only by the actors, but by extension, the public.

Charles presented himself at the Drury Lane green room on 5 January 1795 with script in hand. The event was recorded without comment by the Drury Lane prompter, William Powell.[46] But when Charles came to visit his sister, on 9 or 10 January, he reported to her that the reading of the play hadn't taken place yet, that "he was *the next morning* to read the Piece in the Green Room" [my italics].[47] This small white lie made it possible for Charles to avoid telling Burney the unpleasant truth: the reading had been a disaster. Somehow, probably through Sarah Siddons, news of the reading was leaked to Hester Piozzi, who noted in her diary that Charles: "when reading the Play in the Green Room before the exhibition – the Actors dropt silently off, one by one and left him *all alone.*"[48]

Out of an understandable determination to minimize Burney's anxieties following childbirth, Charles failed to sound the alarm after this reading. He didn't tell her that the script gave every early indication of failure, that the actors had gotten up and walked out of the green room and left him there, alone and foolish; that they were antipathetic to her script, and that without strong managerial intervention, the play did not have a chance. In an effort to protect her health and her peace of mind, Charles left her exposed to an infinitely more damaging public defeat. His loyalty and affection for his sister are not at issue here, but his protection of her and his control over her script took away from Burney the chance to take charge of her own production, if only to cancel it until further notice.

In the end, ironically, it was Burney herself who proved most resilient after the production had failed. Her father and Charles both agonized over the reviews, while Burney, for the first time, took charge, if not of the production's rehearsals, then certainly of its aftermath. According to Sarah Siddons, she met with Kemble the day after the play opened (22 March) and without acrimony or finger-pointing, withdrew the script.[49] Eventually she decided to abandon it entirely and work on another. Without flinching from her responsibility for the failure, or conversely taking on more responsibility than was really hers, she moved briskly through closing the book on *Edwy and Elgiva* and on to other writing projects.[50]

I want to return for a moment to that night of 21 March 1795, when Burney sat in a box at Drury Lane with her husband, Monsieur d'Arblay, her brother Charles, and her sister, Susanna Phillips, and watched her play for the first time. It occurs to me that in addition to embarrassment and exasperation, something else must have been going on inside her head. In her letter to Mrs. Waddington, she wrote: "I myself perceived a thousand things I wished to change," and to her father she wrote: "I formed a plan on the first night [for a revision], from what occurred by the repr[esen]tation."[51] In other words, even in the moment of defeat, Burney was revising in her head, making mental notes of things that needed changing with an eye to some future production. She doesn't speak in terms of failure, but in terms of revision, of a second production. I imagine her making up a list of things in her head as she watched, just the kind of list she would have made at a rehearsal if she'd been to one, everything from the outrage of Palmer not having learned his lines, and Mrs. Siddons being hoisted about on an upholstered divan in the middle of a wilderness, to her own sense of where characters were underdeveloped and where scenes were running too long. In other words, I think what Burney saw was that the play had material roots. It had failed, not because her playwriting was mysteriously and hopelessly deficient, as her father and Crisp had pronounced years before, but because of concrete mistakes and cast misconduct. Some of the mistakes were hers, and some were management's. But that was very different from thinking, as she had been led to believe, that for her, *trying to write plays was a mistake*. I wonder if this production, because it was so poorly managed and performed, didn't lift from her some of the burden of judgement and failure that had followed her after *The Witlings*. It might account for her letters after the production closed, which, far from sounding depressed, are vital, assured, and even wickedly humorous.

In evaluating the evidence as a whole, one has the sense that this production woke Burney from a trance of indifference. It put her back in charge. It demonstrated that good playwriting was not the province of some indefinable mystique; it was a concrete process of trial and error. It necessitated being present at rehearsals, and fixing things that didn't work. This production allowed her to admit to herself at last that she cared passionately about writing plays. Most importantly, it showed her that she could survive and go on even if a play failed, because the failure reflected on nobody. The failures, like the successes, were her own.

Three years later, in 1798, Burney completed another play, entitled *Love and Fashion*, and headed directly into production. There was a different energy about this entire undertaking. Her play this time was a comedy, and she chose to work with Thomas Harris at Covent Garden, perhaps because it released her from a Drury Lane legacy that included her father's and Crisp's past associations with Garrick.[52] Although her father raised querulous objections to this production, citing her failure with *Edwy and Elgiva*, Burney sailed past him without even engaging in the debate. The transactions leading up to *Love and Fashion* reflect a new sense of Burney's involvement and command. Charles worked with her on this show as he had on *Edwy and Elgiva*, but Burney herself was more actively involved throughout.

In October of 1799, Charles reported to his sister that Harris had read "the fable" (*Love and Fashion*) and was interested in putting it into production the following spring. Harris's notes for Burney included a list of suggested revisions which Charles passed on to her with the comment "But Mr. H must see you – & state his objections to some parts . . . when you are at my house, I will contrive the meeting between you & H . . ."[53] Then abruptly, the correspondence becomes quite cryptic. On 31 December 1799, Burney wrote Charles: "I conclude you had not an instant to see about the Furniture I mentioned to you. I shall now wish you to arrange my meeting with the upholsterer[54] upon my going to Town [London] . . . I can see the Upholsterer, Mr. H from or at Beaumont Street, without any revelations."[55] She concludes: "Try to see H & state what I wrote last, in case he has no more to say, or wants more previous consideration what to urge."

Burney's letters to Charles, after he had made the initial contact with Harris, had to be coded. The "Upholsterer" is Thomas Harris, and the "Furniture" is her play. By meeting the Upholsterer at the home of her sister Esther in Beaumont Street, she prevents the possibility of "revelations," that is, of her ever-vigilant father finding out what she is up to, either by seeing her with Harris or by meddling in her private correspondence to Charles. These letters document a covert plan by Burney, now forty-seven years old, to circumvent her father and to begin dealing with her theatre manager face to face. Her decision to meet with Harris was a significant change of strategy because it got rid of the middle-man, of half-delivered messages and the protection that had proven so costly to both *Edwy and Elgiva* and *The Witlings*. It was certainly Charles who initiated the negotiations with Harris, but in the letters that follow, Burney started taking over for herself.

In the end, tragedy intervened. Her sister Susanna's death on 6 January 1800 had a devastating effect on the whole Burney family.[56] Her father became increasingly anxious and distressed, especially after "Fanny" Burney's name was leaked to the newspapers on 29 January, probably by Harris himself. On 2 February she withdrew the play from further consideration. Between 1800 and 1802 she wrote two more comedies, *A Busy Day* and *The Woman-Hater*, but they were not produced. In 1802, Burney and her son followed her husband to France, where she was to stay for ten years. By the time she returned, she was sixty years old, and the impulse to write and produce plays had left her.

It is tempting to catalog Burney's story among those of the many women writers whose work was suppressed and for whom access to a profession was ultimately denied. But I take from her story something very powerful and instructive which may lend another perspective. In a letter to her father on 11 February 1800, in which she informed him that *Love and Fashion* was not to be produced after all, for the first time she also spoke to him of her anger with him:

> This release [the cancellation of *Love and Fashion*] gives me present repose which indeed I much wanted – for to combat your – to me – unaccountable but most afflicting displeasure, in the midst of my own panics & disturbance, would have been ample punishment to me, had I been guilty of a crime in doing what I have all my life been urged to, & all my life intended, writing a Comedy. Your goodness, your kindness, your regard for my fame, I know have caused both your trepidation, which doomed me to *certain* failure; & your displeasure that I ran, what you thought, a wanton risk. But it is *not* wanton, my dearest Father. My imagination is not at my own controll or I would always have continued in the walk you approuved. The combinations for another long work did not occur to me. Incidents & effects for a Dramma did. I thought the field more than open – inviting to me. The chance held out golden dreams.[57]

This letter was a long-overdue statement of what Dr. Burney's anxious, controlling interference had cost his daughter. Her use of words like "combat," "wanton risk," and "doomed" has the sound of someone who is no longer interested in sparing his feelings, or in propping up certain fictions for the sake of maintaining the relationship on an even keel. It was a moment for telling the truth, whether it hurt the old man's feelings or not.

For women of this period in the arts, the province of art and imagination, and the province of being female in a culture constituted on the notion of male authority and female obedience, were in profound and irreconcilable conflict. In her letter to her father, Burney goes to the heart of that conflict when she says, with utter simplicity, that her imagination is not under her own control. She did not mean that someone else controlled her imagination. She meant that she could not control it, even to please her father.

Women artists like Burney were blocked, not just by the usual obstacles to successful production, but by a lifetime of habitual deference. The "protections" put in place by family and by culture were simply strategies for control. Playwriting, which left a woman open to reactions and demands from managers, actors, and family, forced her into a confrontation with her own cultural conditioning. She either had to relinquish that conditioning or relinquish her work. In this letter to her father, Burney goes to the source of her own conditioning and with great courage and simplicity refuses to cooperate any longer.

Oddly, what is most moving to me about Burney's letter is its restraint. This is not the voice of an enraged adolescent but of an adult woman whose love and anger are in balance. Her letter confirms for me the importance of restructuring relationships of the heart, rather than destroying them, so that there is energy enough left over for writing the next play.

# 7

# JOANNA BAILLIE *VS.* THE TERMITES BELLICOSUS

About the turn of the nineteenth century, Garrick's ethos of gallantry toward women playwrights began to break down. Frances Plowden's opera (yet another *Virginia*), which played for only one night at Drury Lane in 1801, was hissed off the stage by an unruly audience. It was later revealed that there had been a cabal organized by Michael Kelly, a singer and composer of operas at Drury Lane, whose "opposition to the claims of all musical candidates for fame at Drury Lane except his own" was well known.[1] There had been no organized public demonstration against a woman playwright since Richard Cumberland's attack on Charlotte Lennox's *The Sister* in 1769. The Kelly incident sparked an indignant pamphlet in Plowden's defense, but there were no serious repercussions for Kelly. Garrick's injunction to the public in 1777 to "protect" rather than "hurt" women playwrights had lost its potency, at least among members of the theatre profession. The Plowden incident was closely followed by another in 1802, in which Mary Berry's play, *Fashionable Friends*, was summarily hissed off the Drury Lane stage for "loose principles."[2] Change was in the air.

In 1798, an anonymous book entitled *A Series of Plays* was published. There were three plays in the *Series*, two tragedies, entitled *De Monfort* and *Basil*, and one comedy, *The Tryal*.[3] There was also a lengthy "Introductory Discourse" which contained some of the most comprehensive criticism of current drama that anyone had read for some time. The author did not mince words: "in presenting to us those views of great characters, and of the human mind in difficult and trying situations which peculiarly belong to tragedy . . . even of those who may be considered as respectable dramatic poets, have very much

*Plate 12*
John Philip Kemble
1757–1823
Occupations: Actor, Theatre Manager

One of Kemble's lifelong friends, since their earliest days as actors in a provincial company, was Elizabeth Inchbald. In 1784, after four years of unremitting effort to interest theatre managers in her work, Mrs. Inchbald's play *The Mogul Tale* was finally produced. Kemble wrote her from Liverpool to congratulate her. The letter is puzzling because in spite of coming on the heels of Kemble's first year of major success in London, he sounds wistful, both about his own failed attempts at writing and something less definable, a sense of his own limitations: "The Truth is my health declines every day – You know me, I believe, well enough to feel for me when I say that with all my ambition I am afraid I shall live and die a common Fellow – your regular and continent life gives you the appearance of many healthful years, and your uncommon Talents, having now forc'd themselves into notice, will crown you with growing Reputation – If I could write I wou'd – I cannot – so you must receive Esteem instead of Flattery, and Sincerity for jest, when I swear there is no woman I more truly admire, nor any man whose abilities I more highly value." There was some talk of Kemble and Inchbald marrying, but they never did. It is interesting in retrospect to consider how Mrs. Inchbald would have been viewed professionally if she had become "Mrs. John Philip Kemble." (Quoted from a manuscript letter dated 17 July 1784, in the Forster Collection, Ms. 48 G 4/16, courtesy of the Board of Trustees, the Victoria and Albert Museum.)

*Plate 13*
Joanna Baillie
1762–1851
Occupation: Playwright, Poet

In 1803, with the launching of the influential *Edinburgh Review*, a campaign against Baillie's work began which lasted for well over a decade. The critic, who was carving out a national reputation as one of the "great guns of taste," was Lord Francis Jeffrey, who by coincidence had a background very similar to Baillie's: born in Glasgow and educated in Scotland. In 1812, on the publication of her third and final volume of *A Series of Plays*, he wrote: "Miss Baillie, we think, has set the example of plays as poor in incident and character, and as sluggish in their pace, as any that languish on the Continental stage, without their grandeur, their elegance, or their interest; and, at the same time, as low and as irregular in their diction as our own early tragedies, – and certainly without their spirit, grace, or animation." Baillie once commented privately to a good friend: "John Any-Body would have stood higher with the critics than Joanna Baillie." (Quoted from the *Edinburgh Review*, February 1812, vol. 19, pp. 265–266, and from a letter written by Baillie to Sir Walter Scott ca. 1825, Ms. 3903, f. 131, by kind permission of the Trustees of the National Library of Scotland.)

failed."[4] This writer was also pointedly critical of contemporary comedy, and felt that as a genre it had failed in its responsibility to *instruct*.

> In what I have called Witty Comedy, everything is light, playful, and easy. Strong, decided condemnation of vice is too weighty and material to dance upon the surface of that stream, whose shallow currents sparkle in perpetual sunbeams, and cast up their bubbles to the light.[5]

The writer had a plan for the three plays in the book: they were an experiment to see if some new approach to comedy and tragedy couldn't be devised, one which put an emphasis not on plot contrivance but on human nature, the way passions took root in people and shaped the course of human action. The writer made a strong case for nuanced, contradictory, detailed character development rather than the broad and convenient stereotypes that currently prevailed: "Our desire to know what men are in the closet as well as on the field . . . is very imperfectly gratified by real history."[6] Drama, this writer believed, could make up the difference. The voice of this critic and playwright was educated, declarative, and confident.

The writer also demonstrated an unusual sensitivity to gender as an issue for dramatists, and argued in favor of letting women be central characters in tragedy, that they intrinsically had the intellectual and moral capacity for filling the role of tragic "hero." Within a longer footnote, there was this observation:

> I believe there is no man that ever lived, who has behaved in a certain manner on a certain occasion, who has not had amongst women some corresponding spirit, who, on the like occasion, and every way similarly circumstanced, would have behaved in the like manner.[7]

The *Series of Plays* lay dormant for about a year after its initial publication. Then, in 1799, the book suddenly took hold in literary circles and began to generate a lot of discussion. There was talk of a possible production at Drury Lane. But the author still remained anonymous. Mary Berry, who took a lively interest in affairs literary and theatrical, wrote her friend Mrs. Cholmley in March, 1799:

> Do you remember my speaking to you in high terms of a series of plays upon the passions of the human mind, which

had been sent to me last winter by the author? I talked to everybody else in the same terms of them at the time [1798], anxiously enquiring for the author; but nobody knew them, nobody cared for them, nobody would listen to me; and at last I unwillingly held my tongue . . . This winter, the first question on everybody's lips is, "Have you read the series of plays?" Everybody talks in the raptures (I always thought they deserved) of the tragedies and of the introduction as of a new and admirable piece of criticism. But, whoever the author is, they still persist in preserving a strict incognito, for which I honour their honest pride, which scorns to be indebted to ANY name for the success of such a work, and, with the patient sense of real merit, has quietly waited a whole twelvemonth for the impression it has at last made on an obdurate public. The author . . . still refuses to come forward even to receive emolument; says the piece is before the public, that the Theatre may do what they please with it, only desires the simplicity of the plot may not be infringed upon. Neither fame nor a thousand pounds therefore have much effect upon this said author's mind, whoever he or she may be. I say she, because and only because no man could or would draw such noble, such dignified representations of the female mind as the Countess Albini and Jane de Mount-fort [sic]. They often make us clever, captivating, heroic, but never *rationally superior* . . . [my italics][8]

*De Monfort* went into production at Drury Lane in April of 1800, but the identity of the author remained a mystery, and speculation mounted. Rumors circulated that it was Sir Walter Scott, and then John Philip Kemble, but nobody knew for sure. The play opened on 29 April, and although public demonstrations of approval after the epilogue were strong, the private reactions of people who saw it were equivocal. Elizabeth Inchbald wrote to a close friend:

I sat in the same box with Mrs. Hughes on the first night of 'De Montford' [sic]. That fine play, supported by the most appropriate acting of Kemble and Siddons, is both dull and highly improbable in the representation . . . its very charm in the reading militates against its power in the acting.[9]

Inchbald's response is echoed in this reaction from Jane Linley (the younger sister of Richard Brinsley Sheridan's first wife

Elizabeth), who also attended opening night and wrote to her fiancé, who was discreetly seated in another section of the house:

> If I rightly understood your action at the conclusion of the Play my Charles, it signified Your approval of it, & did you see me second the Applause you gave it? indeed I liked the representation of it better than I thought I should, for Kemble & Mrs. Siddons conceived their characters very finely but still Charles, you must allow the subject [hatred] to be a very unpleasing one, & therefore I don't think it will ever become a popular Play altho' the language is infinitely superior to any which has been produced for some time.[10]

On 30 April, the day after opening night, the author's name was at last revealed. One paper announced that a "Miss Baillie, daughter of the Physician of that name, is the supposed Author of the Play of *De Monfort*." That information was corrected on 1 May (Dr. Matthew Baillie was in fact her brother), and this time the paper commented "Miss Bailey [*sic*] is a lady of a very fine genius, and promises to be a literary ornament to her country."[11] Shortly after opening night, the winds of fortune began to shift. Receipts dropped from £308 on opening night to £273 on 30 April, £239 on 2 May, £212 on 3 May, and £166 on 9 May, the closing night. There was a brief improvement on Mrs. Siddons's benefit night (5 May) when receipts went up to £296, but the house charge was £207, leaving only about £90 for Mrs. Siddons to take home. As Dutton put it, "she was honoured with a fashionable, but not a numerous house."[12] For another actor this turnout might have been respectable, but for Mrs. Siddons, it was dismal. The play ran for eleven nights and finally closed for good.

Hester Piozzi, who seems to have watched Joanna Baillie's career with more than passing interest (Piozzi herself had toyed with the idea of writing drama), is one of the few commentators to name gender as a central issue in this narrative. She wrote of the *Series of Plays* in her Commonplace Book:

> I remember a knot of Literary Characters met at Miss Lees' House [Sophia, Harriet and Anna of Belvedere House; see Chapter 4] in Bath, deciding – contrary to my own judgement – that a learned man must have been the author; and I, chiefly to put the Company in a good humor, maintained

it was a woman. Merely, said I, because both the heroines are Dames Passées [women a little over the hill], and a man has no notion of mentioning a female after she is five and twenty. What a goose Joanna must have been to reveal her sex and name! Spite and malice have pursued her ever since . . . She is a Zebra devoured by African Ants – the Termites Bellicosus.[13]

Unfortunately for us Piozzi doesn't name the termites or what they did. But her observations are useful because she characterizes Baillie as having been *devoured* by spite and malice. Her image suggests that the restraints in place during the post-Garrick years were gone. Rather than the intermittent sniping experienced by women twenty years before, it was now open season. The description of Baillie as an undefended carcass to be feasted upon is adjacent to the observations about her gender. Piozzi characterizes Baillie as an exotic striped animal, one that cannot defend itself except by running. If it is injured and prone, it becomes vulnerable. The predators in this case are not large animals, but warlike little insects. Piozzi suggests that Baillie has been brought down by injury, and is now getting feasted upon. Years later Mrs. Piozzi reflected in a letter to a friend:

I well remember when her plays upon the "Passions" first came out, with a metaphysical preface. All the world wondered and stared at me, who pronounced them the work of a woman, although the remark was made every day and everywhere that it was a masculine performance. No sooner, however, did an unknown girl own the work, than the value so fell, her booksellers complained they could not get themselves paid for what they did, nor did their merits ever again swell the throat of public applause. So fares it with *nous autres*, who expose ourselves to the shifts of malice or the breath of caprice.[14]

Far from activating a certain protective impulse in the public, the discovery that the author of *Plays on the Passions* was a woman apparently damaged both the sale of her book and the box-office receipts.

Certainly not everyone felt negatively. Baillie's work seems to have activated a certain sense of recognition and excitement among a number of women. People like Hester Piozzi, Mary

Berry, and Sarah Siddons were quick to sense that something about the way Baillie constructed women on the stage was different. Piozzi commented privately to a friend about Baillie's work: "I felt it was a woman's writing; no man makes female characters respectable – no man of the present day I mean, they only make them lovely."[15] Shortly after *De Monfort* closed in May 1800, Mrs. Siddons visited Joanna Baillie and asked her to write more plays. Or, to be more precise, Siddons reportedly said to Baillie, "Make me some more Jane De Monforts!"[16] It is the first instance I have come across in which an actress approached a woman playwright and proposed this kind of artistic collaboration. Mrs. Siddons apparently loved playing Jane De Monfort; even after the production at Drury Lane closed, she continued to do solo readings from her own condensed version of the play for fund-raisers and private gatherings, at least through 1802.[17]

In the spring of 1801, perhaps in response to Mrs. Siddons's urgings, Baillie began work on another historical tragedy based on the fall of Constantinople, which she entitled *Constantine Paleologus*. She wrote Mrs. Siddons about her ideas for the play in order to find out if she was still interested and if a place might be kept for bringing out her play the following spring at Drury Lane (which would have been the spring of 1802). Mrs. Siddons wrote back encouraging Baillie to proceed, and, as Baillie later told her friend Anne Millar, "assuring me of the friendly dispositions of herself & Mr. Kemble."[18] Baillie may have felt the need for such reassurances after the tepid reception of *De Monfort*, especially from Kemble, since in addition to being the lead tragedian at Drury Lane, he was also managing the company and all aspects of production in Sheridan's absence.

A few days later, Baillie – who was by now a friend of Mary Berry's – was told by Berry that Kemble was "very eager in the business, wishing me to begin immediately, and expressing himself very warmly."[19] Some days later Baillie was visiting at Berry's house and met Kemble, for the first and last time in her life. He reiterated his support of the play and encouraged her again to begin writing immediately. Baillie went to work for seven weeks during the summer, and then put the play down until about mid-October, when she finally felt ready to have Kemble look at it. She wrote Kemble, telling him what she had done, and asking for more time for revisions. He responded at once, saying he was very pleased and suggesting that she send him a fair copy in early December. According to plan, she sent it to him with a letter making it clear that she felt the play needed more work and that if he and Mrs. Siddons for any reason did not like the roles she had written for them, they need not present it to the Proprietor, Sheridan, at all. If this should be the case, she promised in closing, it would not discourage her from attempting to do something better for them another time. Kemble's response was as stunning as it was inexplicable. Baillie wrote her friend Anne Millar to explain:

> After all this, Mr. Kemble, about a week ago, returned my manuscript with a short stiff letter; entering into no particulars of any kind, but just saying he doubted the success of the piece, and taking no notice at all of the last part of my letter. I was very much disposed before hand to think that my play would not be accepted of, but I must confess to you that I had not the least idea of the business ending in this manner, and that I have been hurt by it. That Kemble should not like my play is not at all surprising, but that he should signify his opinion in this manner, after all that has passed between us, is to me perfectly unaccountable. It is so much so that I don't venture even to form any conjectures in regard to it. I have for a long time heard from so many different quarters that Mr. Sheridan (for you guess very right) is unfriendly to me, that I can't help giving credit to it, but in the present case it does not appear that he has had anything to do with it. How this general impression of his being unfriendly to me has prevailed I don't know; the idea of jealousy is too absurd to be thought of. How the matter really stands I shall most probably always remain ignorant of.[20]

The simple explanation of course would be the obvious one: that Kemble simply didn't like the script and didn't want to produce it. But we know from Frances Burney's experience with *Edwy and Elgiva* that in the matter of play selection, Kemble did what he was told to do by Sheridan, even when he was faced with performing in what he knew would be an embarrassing failure. Also, there is the matter of Kemble's letter to Baillie, which she reads as a categorical rejection, rather than a rejection of a specific play. The terseness of his language seems to leave no avenue open for further collaboration. Critics and historians have tended to focus on the 1800 production of *De Monfort* as the beginning of a downward spiral in Baillie's career, and certainly its lukewarm reception must have been disappointing to her. But Baillie was still game to continue work after *De Monfort*, and evidently both Kemble and Siddons were committed to continue working with her. So in that context alone, it becomes difficult to dismiss *De Monfort* as a categorical failure. It would be much more accurate to characterize it as a promising first attempt, which in fact is how Mrs. Inchbald responded to it in her remarks in 1808.[21] In fact, it was this 1801 letter from Kemble about *Constantine Paleologus* which marked the first serious defeat, because it ended a potentially fruitful collaboration, one in which Baillie and Siddons in particular stood to benefit. Siddons, even though she held a position of considerable influence, was apparently unable or unwilling to reverse the situation.

Unless new material emerges, we will probably never know for certain what transpired. However, the circumstantial evidence points strongly to Sheridan. He was the only person in authority at Drury Lane over Kemble, and Baillie's letter to Millar states that she has heard – not once, but "from many different quarters" that Sheridan is "unfriendly" to her. His reasons for being unfriendly to Baillie remain a mystery, but one possibility presents itself.[22] In her 1798 Introductory Discourse, Baillie was outspoken about the failings of contemporary comedy, and although she never mentions him by name, it would have been impossible to launch such a critique without making reference to Sheridan, who was still considered to be the foremost contemporary English playwright. My assessment of the evidence is that Sheridan would have responded to her Discourse in much the same way that Garrick had responded to Mrs. Brooke's critique of his *King Lear* many years before: by being offended not only by the substance of what was said, but most particularly by the revelation that the critic was a woman. Like Garrick, Sheridan would have made no public gesture of irritation with Baillie; in fact, he later was to extoll her work to the House of Commons. But it was well within his power to directly influence whether or not Baillie's plays got produced at Drury Lane, and perhaps at Covent Garden as well. He could have intervened by speaking quietly to Kemble and ordering him to cancel production plans for *Constantine* when he found out who had written the play. This sequence of events would explain Kemble's sudden abandonment of Baillie after all the initial encouragement. In 1800, neither Sheridan nor anyone else had known who had written *De Monfort* until the second night of the run, which might explain why that play didn't get vetoed in the first place. However, Sheridan was by no means the only problem for Baillie. Her direct contact with Drury Lane was through John Kemble, both as manager and as leading actor. It comes as something of a shock to be reminded that having Kemble and Siddons as the two leading characters in a new tragedy was no guarantee of success. In fact, within the limited scope of this study, Kemble's record as a producer and actor in new tragedies by women has been zero successes for three attempts: Burney's *Edwy and Elgiva* in 1795, Lee's *Almeyda* in 1796, and now Baillie's *De Monfort* in 1800. Kemble's acquired skills in management apparently did not include the editing and pruning of new texts. He was remarkably passive in his handling of new plays; there was nothing of the energetic give-and-take that characterized Garrick's work with playwrights. In fact, Kemble's passivity in this area made him something of a liability for first-time playwrights. His time on *De Monfort* was largely occupied with the scenic effects, which apparently were quite extraordinary, but he did not involve himself in script development at all. Dutton (of the *Dramatic Censor*), who did a careful comparison of the 1800 promptscript with the original 1798 version, pronounced finally that "Kemble's changes consisted largely in the correction of grammatical errors."[23] Baillie's script needed help of a different order: the play needed to be shortened considerably (after opening night, it was), scene sequence needed to be rethought, and some of the offstage action should probably have been staged. But Kemble was either unwilling or unable to take a new playwright in hand, and turn a rambling first effort into something crisp and stageworthy. In this all-important department of script development, he was still functioning like a conscientious actor, learning his lines and cues without questioning the piece as a whole. This reluctance, combined with the peculiar lack of warmth and candor that characterizes his relationship with Baillie, were hardly conducive to creating successful first-time collaborations.[24] Kemble's cold dismissal was more than enough to keep Baillie, a woman of "quiet retired character," away permanently.

The dramaturgical problems which resulted from the

consequent lack of productions were to be a constant source of frustration and disappointment to Baillie. In critical assessments, she was seen to be lacking in theatrical viability. Various contemporary critics and historians, including Elizabeth Inchbald, Thomas Campbell, and Genest, were impressed by Baillie's obvious skills with language but felt her dramas did not perform as well as they read.[25] Baillie imputed these difficulties to a domino effect, by which her rejection at Drury Lane had also ended her chances everwhere else:

> I have the mortification to find that, as they [my plays] are not acted in the London Theatres, they are considered as not adapted to representation; and how long this opinion may continue after I am gone, should it ever be changed, I know not.[26]

The result of this difficulty with getting produced was that she could not see her plays on their feet, and as a consequence, she could not grow. As early as 1804, in her preface to her *Miscellaneous Plays*, she wrote:

> Each of the plays contained in this volume has been, at one time or another, offered for representation to one or other of our winter theatres and been rejected. This my reader will readily believe is not done in the spirit of vanity; and I beg of him also to believe, that neither is it at all done in that of complaint . . . I must, in this case, have either appeared pusillanimously timid in shrinking from that open trial to which my contemporaries submit, or sullenly and ungraciously fastidious. The chief thing to be regretted in this failure of my attempts is, that having no opportunity of seeing any of my pieces exhibited, many faults respecting stage effect and general impression will to me remain undiscovered, and those I may hereafter write be of course unimproved.[27]

The other major issue for Baillie's career, however, was her deep distaste for rehearsals. She dreaded them. This was not just an affectation on her part, but deeply connected to her creative mechanism. She was a quiet observer, and the ways in which most playwrights were involved in rehearsals were simply beyond her capacity. Baillie's distance from production was typically coupled with complete deference to whomever she designated as her emissary. When her good friend Sir Walter Scott offered to produce *The Family Legend* for her in Edinburgh, she turned the entire production over to him. On 23 January 1809, she wrote to thank him for his interest in getting the play produced, and said "Do for me what you think right, and desire me freely at all times to do for myself what you think right, and you shall both find me thankful and docile."[28] On 21 October 1809, she wrote: "I entirely agree with you in the alterations you propose, and will set about making them forthwith . . . "[29] On 12 February 1810, in response to Scott's news of *The Family Legend*'s successful reception on opening night, she wrote him in language that evoked the chivalric code of his own novels: "What shall I say to you, my brave and burly champion, who have taken the field so zealously in my behalf, and thro' many difficulties gained for me this proud day?"[30] Two days later, in response to a letter from Scott in which he gently admonished her for not attending rehearsals, she was more forthcoming:

> You are very kind to say that when I bring out another Play in Edin[burgh] I must come down and look after it myself. Indeed, if I had been down with you now, you would not probably have gone on so well with me as you have done without me; I should, at best, only have been to you like the Child in Wordsworth's story of Old Michael "something between a hindrance & a help," for the sight of all the actors & actresses about me at a rehearsal, repeating what I have almost never had face enough to hear the reading of, even in the most private way by my own intimate friends, would have cowed my better parts entirely. If ever I go to a rehearsal in which I am at all interested, it will be when you have a Piece coming out here . . . I learnt from my friend Miss Millar that the alterations you & your friends have made in the Legend are very judicious and I (no thanks to me for it) am perfectly satisfied with it.[31]

The image of the child is a striking one; she describes herself as if she were a five-year-old getting under foot, rather than a fifty-year-old woman with publicly stated ambitions for being included in the dramatic canon. But the image reveals something important: attending a rehearsal of her own work, or even thinking about attending such a rehearsal, made this playwright feel like a child. Rather than risk that sense of diminishment, of being indulged and under foot, she hands the reins over to a man, someone who presumably will not feel like a child and will not be treated like one. She evidently feels more comfortable delegating this job out, than she does trying to do it herself.

It is important, however, not to assume that Baillie's determination to stay away from rehearsals meant that she was a kind of literary dabbler, a theatrical illiterate. In 1812 she published the third and final volume of her *A Series of Plays*.[32] In a lengthy preface entitled "To the Reader," Baillie demonstrated a level of mastery where production values and design issues were concerned that is completely at odds with the reports (which continue to this day) that she was someone who knew nothing about practical theatre. This preface reinserts Baillie into public discourse as a person with opinions of consequence, someone who cannot be dismissed lightly. Taken as a whole, her writings in the 1812 preface on lighting effects, blocking, and audibility are some of the most detailed and perceptive that we have from this period, because they reveal the way technical issues could shape audience reception and textual intent. A brief sample will give the reader a sense of her range and her acuity. She was disturbed by the unnatural angle of light created by footlights: " . . . whenever an actor, whose features are not particularly sharp and pointed, comes near to the front of the stage, every feature becomes immediately shortened and snub, and less capable of expression, unless it be of the ludicrous kind."[33] She recommended the possibility of bringing the "roof" of the stage forward, and "placing a row of lamps with reflectors along the inside of the wooden front-piece" in order to create an angle of light that made shadows on the face less grotesque. She recommended the removal of stage-boxes because they interfered with the realism of the staged event:

> The front-piece at the top, the boundary of the stage from the orchestra at the bottom; and the pilasters on each side, would then represent the frame of a great moving-picture, entirely separated and distinct, from the rest of the theatre: whereas at present, an unnatural mixture of audience and actors, of house and stage, takes place near the front of the stage, which destroys the general effect in a very great degree.[34]

She further observed that the blocking of actors was a lost art on the oversized stages of the larger houses:

> This is particularly felt in Comedy, and all plays on domestic subjects; and in those scenes also of the grand drama, where two or three persons only are produced at a time. To give figures who move upon it proper effect, there must be depth as well as width of stage; and the one must bear some proportion to the other, if we would not make every closer or more confined scene appear like a section of a long passage, in which the actors move before us, apparently in one line, like the figures of a magic lanthorn.[35]

Finally, she was keenly aware that the enlargement of the winter houses in London, dating from the 1790s, had damaged the ability of (by her reckoning) two-thirds of the audience's ability to hear the language of a play. And she is the only commentator to my knowledge who writes about the impact of these new houses on the work of the *actress*, as distinct from the *actor*: "the features and voice of a woman, being naturally more delicate than those of a man, she must suffer in proportion from the defects of a large theatre."[36]

Baillie's 1812 volume of plays met with some of the harshest criticism she had yet received in her career. Her arch-critic Francis Jeffrey of *The Edinburgh Review* (who had been spotted weeping in the audience for *The Family Legend* in Edinburgh just two years before) was scathing: "It was reserved for a writer of no ordinary talents . . . to set the example of plays as poor in incident and character, and as sluggish in their pace, as any that languish on the Continental stage."[37] His critique makes no mention whatever of Baillie's preface, partly, one suspects, because it raised a lot of unanswerable questions. To wit, how was one to reconcile the various claims of theatrical illiteracy, including Jeffrey's, with the obviously acute technical judgement that prompted the preface in the first place? These were not the apologetic ramblings of a maiden lady who becomes faint at the sound of her own dialogue being rehearsed. They were rather sternly worded admonitions about the state of the art, distinctly reminiscent of her Introductory Discourse of 1798.

There was to be one more important production of *De Monfort* at Drury Lane. In 1820, after a good deal of prompting from both Sir Walter Scott and Lord Byron (who had been a member of the Drury Lane management subcommittee in 1815, and thereby charged with breathing new life into the repertory), Edmund Kean finally read *De Monfort* and thought he saw some possibilities in it for himself.[38] He first tried out the play during a tour to the United States, but decided that the play's ending needed revising in order to show off his skill at dying onstage to better advantage.[39] Robert Elliston, the manager of Drury Lane, was delegated by Kean to visit Joanna Baillie in Hampstead where she lived (then one of the outlying suburbs of London) with Kean's requests for changes. Elliston complied, in spite of some unspecified illness (probably a hangover), and Baillie wrote a new ending, fair-copied it, and sent it back to the theatre. Her covering letter confirms that she made the required changes in a turnaround time of two days, from Elliston's visit on Saturday to her return letter with the revised manuscript on the following Monday. Elliston's visit to Hampstead is recorded by James Winston, the Drury Lane stage manager, who on 10 November wrote: "Elliston ill at home but went in Kean's carriage to Mrs. Baillie at Hampstead about *De Monfort*."[40] Baillie's subsequent letter to Kean reads as follows:

Hampstead, Monday evening

Dear Sir:

On Saturday evening I set myself to work and endeavoured to write such a conclusion to *De Monfort* as I imagined might somewhat agree with your ideas on the subject. Having laid it by for a day, I read it to myself this morning, when I thought I should be better able [to] judge of its defects, and have made out a fair copy with some alteration, which I now enclose. I shall be very happy indeed if you are satisfied with it, but *beg that you will not scruple to make any change or corrections which you may think proper* [my italics]. As to the stage directions, I have set them down to connect the subject, and not as any rule for you; you will therefore regard them no further than you entirely approve of them. How proud I am to think that any character from my pen should be represented by you, I will not attempt to express. I hope Mr. Elliston was not the worse for his visit to us on Saturday, when moving was to him so troublesome. – My Sister begs me to present her best compliments. Believe me, Dear Sir,

Your truly obliged and obedient servant, J. Baillie.
P.S. If I should have anything further to say regarding *De Monfort*, I will write it down and leave it at your house, when I pay my respects to Mrs. Kean which I hope to do before long.[41]

Evidently her changes to the ending met with Kean's approval because by Wednesday, 14 November, production planning was in full swing.[42] Winston records for that day a series of ugly and manipulative negotiations about who would play the female lead opposite Kean, the role of Jane De Monfort, which twenty years before had been Sarah Siddons's. Ultimately, a compromise was worked out: not the strongest available actress for the role, but a young woman, Mrs. Egerton, who thankfully would offer Kean no competition onstage.

The show opened two weeks later on 27 November 1821. Baillie attended opening night, and professed herself delighted with Kean's interpretation, but the reviews were mostly negative. The consensus was that Kean's requirements for revision had materially damaged the play, and that hatred in this particular version was not so much a passion as a disease, "an incipient madness."[43] Furthermore, it was the general consensus that in this new version, the character of Jane De Monfort, the diamond of the original, was lacking in force and completeness. Winston's diary entry is laconic: "*De Monfort* over twenty minutes after ten. Failed. Elliston wide [drunk]."[44]

## THE MANAGER

The line in Winston's journal that I keep coming back to is his depressing account of Elliston coming to see Baillie in *Kean's carriage*. There is something in this description which epitomizes for me the way in which the power vested in the eighteenth-century manager had unravelled. Elliston, the manager of Drury Lane, was being treated by Kean like a messenger boy. All of Joanna Baillie's negotiations around script changes were with Kean, not with Elliston. Sheridan, even as (we think) he was vetoing Joanna Baillie's *Constantine Paleologus* late in 1801, was himself being brought up on charges of mismanaging Drury Lane in front of the Lord Chancellor. His control of the theatre over the years was increasingly distributed among trustees and management subcommittee members.

This diminishment of centralized power in the theatre managers coincided with an unforeseen development in women's playwriting. Women, specifically Hannah Cowley and Elizabeth Inchbald, had moved rather rapidly from the contingency status accorded to women playwrights during the Garrick era, to professional status in the post-Garrick era. Both in terms of the sheer numbers of successful productions over a period of two decades, and in terms of their ability to earn a living, these two women were now part of the establishment. In other words, at exactly the historical moment in which the power of the manager was being redistributed, the power of these two women playwrights had become comparable to that of a man. Theatre was not an isolated example; by this time women writers had established themselves in a number of genres.

The idea of the manager as a paternal mentor figure had been a useful one because it had provided a form of ideological containment for women in playwriting. It positioned them as literary daughters to the manager as literary father. Even though it appeared to be a benevolent form of assistance, it was also a very effective device for controlling numbers, and for according such women as did receive entrée contingency status. Now the situation was reversed. There were two women playwrights with relative autonomy within the profession, and no manager to function as benevolent patron.

When Joanna Baillie's first play was first produced in 1800, an opportunity to reinstate the old order presented itself. Hannah Cowley had stepped down in 1794, and Elizabeth Inchbald was coming to the end of her playwriting career; she produced one play in 1799 and one in 1805, but her attentions were largely taken up by her activities as critic and anthologist after 1800. If, as Davidoff and Hall have asserted, liquid capital meant that new forms of control were necessary, then it became incumbent on the profession to make sure first that Baillie did not get a foothold, and second, that playwriting no longer presented itself as an option for respectable middle-class women. Sheridan apparently took care of making sure Baillie did not get a foothold; it is consistent with other incidents in our study that the strongest opposition to women playwrights came from men in the same profession. But the job of ideological containment, once handled by the manager, seems to have been dispersed into the critical community.

## CRITICISM

Critical assessments of women playwrights undergo interesting changes in the early nineteenth century. First we notice a certain restlessness in the critics themselves, as if they were tired of having to handle women carefully. In 1800 there was this slightly apologetic preamble to a review of Hannah Brand's recent publication of her *Plays and Poems*:

> It is never our wish to repress the love of literary fame, especially when we see it acting in a female's mind: but our office imposes on us the task of discrimination; and the young lady who is desirous of improving, as a writer, will not be offended if we discharge our duty.[45]

When Frances Plowden's failed opera *Virginia* was published in 1801, it was reviewed as follows:

> The preface informs us that it was composed under the pressure of misfortune; we shall therefore be glad if it meets with more favour in the closet; and *that we may throw no obstacles in the way of its success, we shall dismiss it with merely our good wishes*. [my italics][46]

In 1803, a play "by a lady" entitled *Almeda, or the Neapolitan Revenge*, was reviewed as follows: "Our deference for the author's sex leads us to say little of her performance. We are unwilling to blame, and we cannot praise it . . . We cannot advise the fair writer to persist in her attempts at the drama."[47] These reviews indicate that no comfortable compromise had been reached between the requirements imposed by deference to females, and the requirements imposed by the job of critic. In each case the reviewers mark their liberal position by stating their support of the *idea* of the woman as playwright. But they then simultaneously state or imply that the woman's work is not up to standard. Remnants of the ethos of gallantry survive, but the reviewers appear a little impatient, as if they would like to get on with business. What these reviews did was to advertise that a double standard was in operation and that women were getting kid-glove treatment. They set the stage for backlash.

The next clear sign of what was to come is in two letters written by Byron, in which he has already made an important ideological leap. In the first letter, written in 1815, he says: "Women (saving Joanna Baillie) cannot write tragedy. They haven't the experience of life for it." In a second letter, written in 1817, he comments: "When Voltaire was asked why no woman has ever written even a tolerable tragedy, 'Ah (said the Patriarch) the composition of a tragedy requires testicles.' If this be true, Lord knows what Joanna Baillie does – I suppose she borrows them."[48] Byron, both as a reflector of dominant culture and also as a catalyst in that culture, here perceives the writing of tragedy as a gendered operation. That kind of thinking was new. The tragedies written by women in the eighteenth century were greeted with all kinds of criticism, but this particular kind of thinking, which held that tragedy was out of their reach, was a strategic shift. Tragedy had been open to all comers, and Cowley, More, Brooke, Inchbald, Lee, and Burney all took their turns at writing it. Now suddenly Byron perceives tragedy to be something beyond the reach of a woman writer. The fact that Baillie is the exception to this rule only underscores the contradictory position that he has put himself in. Baillie must borrow testicles, which is to say, she must become adept at making herself male in order to keep Byron's categories intact.

In 1829, a more complete and fully articulated statement was finally forthcoming about the way writing had become gendered. Francis Jeffrey, who by now had established himself as one of the leading critical voices in literature (Byron once referred to him as "the monarch of existing criticism"),[49] wrote a critical essay in 1829 about a book of poetry by Felicia Hemans. This essay, which in fact lauds Mrs. Hemans's poetry, is very revealing about gender expectations around writing. Jeffrey begins almost as if to refute Garrick's 1777 epilogue for Hannah More's *Percy*, in which Garrick says "I'll prove, ye fair, that let us have our swing, | We can, as well as men, do any thing." Jeffrey sets Garrick straight:

> Women, we fear, cannot do everything; nor even everything they attempt. But what they can do, they do, for the most part, excellently, and much more frequently with an absolute and perfect success, than the aspirants of our rougher and more ambitious sex. They cannot, we think, represent natu-

rally the fierce and sullen passions of men, nor their coarser vices, nor even scenes of actual business or contention, nor the mixed motives, and strong and faulty characters, by which affairs of moment are usually conducted on the great theatre of the world. For much of this they are disqualified by the delicacy of their training and habits, and the still more disabling delicacy which pervades their conceptions and feelings; and from which they are excluded by their necessary inexperience of the realities they might wish to describe, by their substantial and incurable ignorance of business, of the way in which serious affairs are actually managed, and the true nature of the agents and impulses that give movement and direction to the stronger currents of ordinary life. Perhaps they are also incapable of long moral or political investigations, where many complex and indeterminate elements are to be taken into account, and a variety of opposite probabilities to be weighed before coming to a conclusion. They are generally too impatient to get at the ultimate results, to go well through with such discussions; and either stop short at some imperfect view of the truth, or turn aside to repose in the shade of some plausible error. This, however, we are persuaded arises entirely from their being seldom set on such tedious tasks. Their proper and natural business is the practical regulation of private life, in all its bearings, affections, and concerns; and the questions with which they have to deal in that most important department, though often of the utmost difficulty and nicety, involve, for the most part, but few elements; and may generally be better described as delicate than intricate; requiring for their solution rather a quick tact and fine perception than a patient or laborious examination . . . We think the poetry of Mrs. Hemans a fine exemplification of Female Poetry; and we think it has much of the perfection which we have ventured to ascribe to the happier productions of female genius.[50]

Jeffrey's commentary makes the important link between the domestic functions of women and their writing. He doesn't indulge himself in crude assertions that women should not be writing at all; on the contrary, he notes regretfully that it has not been the fashion to encourage women to write. What he does instead is to create a logical relationship between women's writing and the natural limitations of domestic life. Women's writing is seen to lose its validity and power when it moves beyond the spheres in which women serve their "proper and natural" function. Any work by a woman that presumes to guess at the machinations of public life is doomed to failure because women know nothing of this life; it is not their life. In this context, it is instructive to go back to Jeffrey's review of Baillie's plays, published in 1812. At the same time that he dismisses her as a dramatist, he lauds her accomplishments as a *poet*, and remarks in closing that he hopes she will favor her public now and then "with a little volume of . . . verses."[51]

However, what I find most arresting about Jeffrey's statement is not what he puts in, but what he leaves out. In this essay, he makes a list of fifteen women writers, working in forms ranging from the novel to letters to essays on religion and education. One of these women, Mary Russell Mitford, was among the most highly acclaimed tragedians of her day.[52] At the time this review was written, her best-known tragedy, *Rienzi*, was running in London. But she is mentioned only in the context of her fiction. Playwriting as a category of endeavor for women writers has simply dropped out.[53] Hemans herself, although not particularly successful, had had original plays produced in both London and Edinburgh. Inchbald and Cowley are not on this list, so by inference comedy as well as tragedy is now beyond serious critical consideration, even though comedy was for years the area of drama in which these two women excelled, in part because it worked within the sphere of the domestic.[54] Baillie herself, who was recognized as one of the leading women writers of her day, and with whose tragedies and comedies Jeffrey was intimately acquainted, appears nowhere in this review, no doubt because her presence would have made some discussion of playwriting inevitable.

I see a gradual development, from women "not being able to write tragedy," to women not being associated with playwriting at all. Baillie's prefaces and her plays, which she continued to publish through 1836, were to complicate and resist the prevailing narrative of harmonious domestic retreat. But they were not enough. It is important to keep in mind that Jeffrey's brand of revisionism in this first third of the nineteenth century had long-term consequences, the most important of which was that women's historical presence in playwriting was gradually being erased. I don't think his omissions in this 1829 review were accidental. I think he was declaring the category closed.

## ANONYMITY

Joanna Baillie's first volume, published in 1798, was an audacious attempt to participate in literary discourse as a combined critic and artist. Even Mrs. Inchbald's critical remarks in her anthologies do not have the same comprehensive sweep as Baillie's Introductory Discourse. But Baillie published anonymously, and, in effect, her first production was anonymous. It cannot be overstated how closely anonymity was connected to a woman's effort to take charge of in her own work and to circumvent prejudice and interference on the outside. In Baillie's case, however, there were unforeseen consequences. The book as a whole, and the Introductory Discourse in particular, unexpectedly attracted tremendous attention. All the early reviews refer to the author as "he," and clearly very few people were prepared for a work of this assertiveness and scope to have been generated by a woman.[55] Not only was her writing mistaken for that of a man; it had been noticed in such a way as to put it in the *forefront of work by men*. When her gender was revealed, it precipitated a cultural crisis. Her work revealed that the boundaries separating male and female were not as clear as they should be, or had been inaccurately drawn in the first place. The job of critics like Jeffrey, then, was to re-inscribe the lines between women's writing and men's writing, lines that had been badly blurred by Baillie's delayed declaration of authorship.[56]

Mrs. Piozzi's comments about the *termites bellicosus* now come into sharper focus. The malice and backbiting she describes may have had less to do with substantive debates about the quality of Baillie's work than with the embarrassing discovery that she was female. Her work had thrown gender assumptions into disarray, and people who were made anxious by that disarray reacted by distancing themselves from her and from her work. Their responses were visceral, unconscious, and even violent, as reactions connected to fear often are.

## OTHER WOMEN

One of the things we encounter in Baillie's history over and over is the way her work helped to identify communities of women. We note in the response of Sarah Siddons, Hester Piozzi and Mary Berry, for example, a quickening of recognition where Baillie's female characters were concerned for which there is no parallel in the work of the earlier playwrights. Baillie also seems to have created communities of women writers. A few were playwrights, but most wrote in other forms. There are testimonials to the kind of support she offered that also have no parallel in the last quarter of the eighteenth century. Baillie didn't mentor other women in the way Garrick did, for example, but she provided a quiet sense of community, confidence and direction. One example was her effort to help Felicia Hemans mount a tragedy in Edinburgh in 1823 through her friendship with Sir Walter Scott.[57] She was also a friend and supporter of Barbarina Wilmot (author of *Ina*, Drury Lane, 1819),[58] Maria Edgeworth, Lucy Aiken, Mary Berry, Harriet Martineau, and Anna Laetitia Barbauld, all of them writers. She actively solicited money for destitute "female Authors."[59] One of Baillie's protégées was a young unpublished poet named Catherine Moody (later Gore) who went on to become a novelist and probably the most accomplished and produced female playwright in London in the first half of the century. Martineau spoke for a number of women when she wrote: "For these twenty years past, I have solaced and strengthened myself with the image of Joanna Baillie, with the remembering of the invulnerable justification which she set up for intellectual superiority in women."[60] Mary Russell Mitford, when she received scathing reviews for her poetry from the *The Quarterly Review* in 1810, commented with some humor: "I have little reason to complain. If he [the reviewer] attacked Joanna Baillie, even to be abused with her is an honour."[61]

One of the legacies of Garrick's style of mentoring is documented in the anxious, competitive behavior of Cowley and More after his death. However, in the absence of a male figure to act as literary father, the competition among the literary daughters could redirect itself towards cooperative effort and mutual support, perhaps even putting the critical acclaim or dismissal of people like Jeffrey into some kind of perspective.

## REHEARSALS

I take a serious lesson from Baillie's refusal to go to her own rehearsals, and from her appointment of Kemble, Scott, and Kean as successive emissaries for those productions. Even though there was no manager to function as mentor to women playwrights, Baillie kept looking for one and appointing surrogates. These surrogates had power over her productions that she could not afford to relinquish without serious consequences to her work. Kean's deliberate dilution of Jane De Monfort is a perfect case in point. Her reluctance to go to rehearsals, for whatever reasons, is directly connected to a loss of control over the product, and until this disparity could be resolved, until women felt comfortable and engaged in rehearsals and not like children under foot, their work was in jeopardy. Baillie was shy. It is by no means uncommon in writers to prefer the quiet place of watching and listening. But it left her vulnerable in a way that she could not afford.

In appointing male emissaries, as Burney had done before her, Baillie was invoking the literary father, the all-powerful figure who could authorize, support, and manage a woman's work into production. Until this historical ghost was named as an ideological obstacle to women doing fully realized productions, their work would continue – and does continue – to be literally and figuratively in the hands of the father.

# 8

# AFTERPIECE

The histories of the seven women playwrights in this study present us with a terrible paradox. Each of them is inextricably bound to the authorizing presence of a man, be he theatre manager, father, brother, or mentor. It is he who provides access to the profession and to professional legitimacy, but it is he who also controls and contains expansion and growth, ultimately preventing women from taking a more commanding position in the field. The power to confer legitimacy is predicated on the power to take it away.

I have argued that playwriting was an intrinsically treacherous form for women because of its permeability to the appropriate and inappropriate interventions of others, beginning with the theatre manager. This permeability is potentially one of theatre's greatest strengths, because it makes possible an exchange among artists in a range of disciplines. As a play develops, it gets seasoned and shaped by the grinding demands of production on the one hand, and the playwright's vision on the other. For a woman playwright, however, the aesthetics of social conduct required her explicit compliance with male authority. Accommodation to those demands often took precedence over creative impulse, and so she was separated from her own sources and her own vision.

Nonetheless, as details of these various careers unfold, it becomes evident that the tendencies toward containment by men and the inherent difficulties of the genre met with powerful resistance from the women themselves. Frances Brooke's decision to manage the King's Theatre was a strategic attempt to establish an important power base. After initial periods of hardship and anxiety, Hannah Cowley and Elizabeth Inchbald became skilled at deflecting interference. As a group, these women were able to persuade the public that they had a rightful place in the profession. By the mid-1790s, although antagonistic currents survived – many from within the profession itself – women's presence in playwriting had a modest momentum and stability for the first time in over a hundred years.

In a similar vein, it has been the common wisdom that women of this period shrank from theatre because the form itself forced them into a public space that was antithetical to their social conditioning and innate delicacy. Here too, the remaining documents tell a very different story. The women in this study, including Joanna Baillie, were eager for public exposure, and, under attack, proved able and shrewd advocates of their own work. In fact, this shrinking from the public gaze usually appears as part of a carefully constructed *public persona*, as in Hannah More's and Hannah Cowley's letters in the newspaper, or in Sophia Lee's published preface. Common wisdom notwithstanding, the papers of these women playwrights reflect ambition, tenacity, and resilience.

And yet, history also teaches us that tenacity and skill were not enough to sustain a place in the profession. Garrick's patronage was based on a narcissism that was not only his personal trademark, but mirrored the prevailing ethos of male centrality. Women playwrights were useful because their presence publicly demonstrated the generosity and benevolence of male patronage. As they developed their own momentum and achieved professional status, however, the need for patronage began to atrophy. Ironically, as self-authorized artists, women no longer served any useful purpose. The narcissism of the original contract began to reassert itself, and this period of momentum and expansion for women in the late eighteenth century was reduced to a trickle in the early nineteenth. Women had made a temporary impact on the profession, but they had not achieved control of the means by which their plays were produced.

By 1829, the notions of female authorship on the one hand, and playwriting on the other, had been forcibly separated in critical discourse, and the history of eighteenth-century women in playwriting was in the process of being erased. Consequently, there was a subtle but important shift in public perception. Rather than constituting a small but integral part of the playwriting landscape, as they had done in the late eighteenth century, women playwrights in London once again were perceived to be a rarity, isolated and exposed. The normative expectations around gender had shifted; what had been "genius" in the eighteenth century was now a little unseemly.

And so we turn to the present. What do these histories teach us about the situation for women playwrights today? It is baffling and disconcerting to discover that in spite of substantial changes in the social conditions governing women's lives, their collective presence in playwriting continues to be fragmentary and thin. The figures are consistent: productions of plays by women hover at about ten percent or less of the total in London, New York, and in American regional theatres (see Figures 4–8). These figures are particularly galling when one considers that during one season in the late seventeenth century, plays by women or plays based on works by women constituted fully *one third* of the

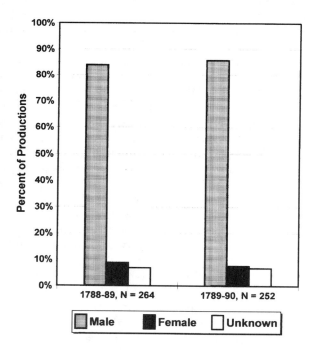

*Figure 4* Percentages of productions by male and female playwrights in London during the 1788–1789 and 1789–1790 seasons. Anonymous playwrights are listed as "unknown." Figures based on *The London Stage*

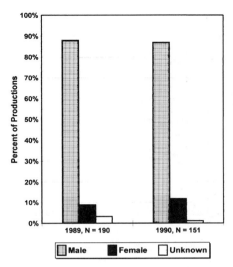

*Figure 5* Percentages of productions by male and female playwrights in London's West End during the calendar years 1988 and 1989. Figures based on *British Theatre Yearbook, London: West End*, ed. David Lemon, London, Christopher Helm, 1989 and 1990

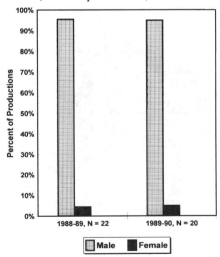

*Figure 6* Percentages of productions by male and female playwrights in Broadway theatres in New York City, for the 1988–1989 and 1989–1990 seasons. Based on *Theatre World*, ed. John Willis, vols. 45 and 46, New York, Crown Publishers, 1989 and 1990

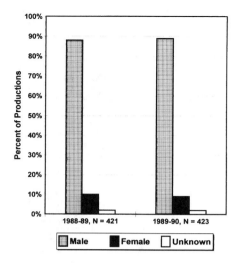

*Figure 7* Percentages of productions by male and female playwrights in United States regional theatres for the 1988–1989 and 1989–1990 seasons. Based on *TCG Theatre Directory*, New York, Theatre Communications Group, 1989 and 1990

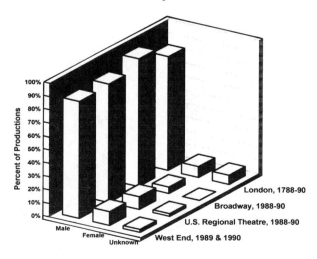

*Figure 8* Season figures of productions of works by male and female playwrights in London (eighteenth century and twentieth century), New York (twentieth century), and United States regional theatres (twentieth century)

188

available offerings. [1] After the initial decline in the early eighteenth century, the numbers have levelled out at seven to ten percent for the past two hundred years, as if an unofficial quota had been imposed. How can this be, when so much else on the landscape has changed?

Facing the figures head on, we know that contemporary women playwrights, like their earlier counterparts, enter the field with only a fragmentary history and an uncertain trajectory. There is some momentum, but the number of women firmly established in the field is still small. There is no secure and ongoing presence, and tokenism is a subtle but persistent undercurrent. The consequence of having an embattled history in a profession is that one enters it tentatively, always the newcomer, always carrying the double burden of proving not only one's personal talent, but also the worth of the group one *represents*. And to whom must this proof be offered? In the vast majority of cases, the power to authorize and legitimize is still owned by men. The resulting dynamic invokes an ominous repetition of the patterns of compliance that pervaded the personal and professional lives of women in the eighteenth century. Garrick, that great genial permission-giver, continues to cast a long shadow.

As I sift through the materials of this book, I come back again and again to Frances Burney's letter to her father, to the way it names certain patterns of obedience and defeat. I no longer find it surprising that Burney was forty-seven years old when she finally called him to account for his deadly masquerade of protection: it takes a long time to make the transition from attendant daughter to self-authorized woman. For me, Burney's letter marks that quiet, incandescent moment in which the woman writer becomes steel, and she finally understands that she can write to or even about this father without writing *for* him.

Art and the authority of experience are inextricable from one another. There can be no middle man, no buffer, no mannerly middle ground. Women cannot afford to write for someone else, and most particularly they cannot afford to write for this father. His investment, even where there is love, may lie elsewhere. Until a woman can name her experience of life without fear of annihilation, her work will always be a conflicted gesture of compliance.

189

But history also warns me that the authority of the self may not be enough. There also has to be a sense of identity as a community. For the most part, these eighteenth-century women worked in isolation from one another, as if on separate ice floes. And, what is even more insidious, history has erased not only their presence as individuals but also their collective impact on the profession. I try to imagine what it might mean for contemporary women playwrights to have a sense of community that extends not only outward to colleagues, but also back through history to the women who shaped the profession two hundred and three hundred years ago.

This book has been my own effort to find out who these remarkable women were, and to see if there was a coherent shape to their history. I am convinced there was. I know with certainty that women moved rapidly into the top ranks of a profession which offered them a brief foothold, and then all but closed its doors to them. I also know that subsequent to that closure, they began to vanish from the historical record. Having resurrected part of that record, I now discover that the value of these women is not just in how remarkable they were individually, even as I acknowledge that fact, but in how they collectively constitute a fabric of continuity and a tradition of resilience. That is the real legacy: an ongoing community of working women in the arts who lean, with increasing confidence, on a tradition of women artists before them.

In bringing these lives to the surface, I want to encourage contemporary women playwrights to move forward, not only with full confidence in their gifts, but with a heightened sense of their own legitimacy. However, that sense has to be tempered by the deeper understanding that historically, *playwriting without control over production has provided women with only contingent membership in the profession.* In order to break the patterns of the past, it will not be enough for women to write marvellous plays. They must develop foolproof strategies for producing them. In this way, they may be able to transform the future of their profession in ways we have yet to imagine.

*In the middle of an open field, a small troupe of women make their way slowly across a terrain of overgrown brush and scattered boulders. They speak quietly among themselves. At the edge of the field they come to a stone wall. The woman in front moves to one side and offers her hand to the others as, one by one, they climb over, managing their skirts with difficulty. Finally only the first woman is left. She stands for a time without moving. Then, bunching her skirt over one arm, she turns and begins to climb. Poised on top of the wall, she extends her arms for balance. In that instant, her skirt catches the wind and snaps open like a sail.*

# NOTES

## 1 GETTING INTO THE ACT

1 For the actual wording, see Judith Milhous, *Thomas Betterton and the Management of Lincoln's Inn Fields, 1695–1708*, Carbondale, Southern Illinois University Press, 1979, p. 6.

2 The term "middle class" will have very specific meaning for economic historians. It usually refers quite specifically to those who prospered (beginning in about 1760) as a consequence of the Industrial Revolution. I am using it more generically to designate those people of modest to moderate incomes whose earnings fall in between recipients of inherited wealth at one end of the spectrum, and subsistence wages (or less) at the other. To be more specific, the fathers of the playwrights in this study were all either self-employed or wage-earners: a bookseller (Cowley), rectors (Brooke and Baillie), a musician and music teacher (Burney), an actor (Lee), a schoolmaster (More), and a farmer (Inchbald). Leonore Davidoff and Catherine Hall use the term throughout their study, *Family Fortunes: Men and Women of the English Middle Class, 1780–1850*, Chicago, University of Chicago Press, 1987.

3 All three of these activities were offered as a part of the normal curriculum at Sophia Lee's school for girls in Bath, called Belvedere, founded in 1780. See *The Memoirs of Susan Sibbald (1783–1812)*, ed. Francis Paget Hett, New York, Minton Balch, 1926, pp. 44–45.

4 Ciji Ware has written a meticulously researched novel based on the lives of several late eighteenth-century women playwrights entitled *Wicked Company*, New York, Bantam, 1992.

5 I have included in this figure women living and dead, for a total of twenty-seven, including actresses writing their own benefit pieces: Abington, Baillie, Behn, Brooke, Burney (d'Arblay), Craven (Anspach), Centlivre, Cowley, Cuthbertson, DeCamp, Gardner, Griffith, Haywood, Hooke, Inchbald, Lee (Harriet), Lee (Sophia), Lennox, More, Parsons, Rainsford, Richardson, Robinson, Sheridan (Frances), Smith, Starke, Wallace. If I subtract deceased

playwrights and count only living women playwrights for this period, the figure drops to twenty-three (Haywood, Sheridan, Behn and Centlivre drop out), and these seven cases constitute about one-third. These figures would shift again, depending on whether I counted *produced* plays by women playwrights, again if I counted *productions* of women's plays from season to season, and yet again if I counted actual nights of performance. Because Inchbald and Cowley led the field in terms of numbers of plays, and because they also were extremely popular and were revived year in and year out, this sampling of seven playwrights actually keys us in to most of the theatrical activity for women during the period. Listings were taken from *The London Stage*, ed. Charles Beecher Hogan, Carbondale, Southern Illinois University Press, 1968. See also Judith Phillips Stanton, "'This New-Found Path Attempting': Women Dramatists in England, 1660–1800," in *Curtain Calls*, ed. Marianne Schofield and Cecilia Macheski, Athens, Ohio University Press, 1991, pp. 325–354.

6 From a paper entitled "Rewriting the Restoration of the English Stage: Patronage and Protest" which was read at the February 1988 meeting of the West Coast Eighteenth Century Studies conference at Long Beach, California by Deborah Payne.

7 *The Excursion*, Frances Brooke, London, Printed for T. Cadell in the Strand, 1777, Book V, chapter viii, p. 33.

8 From "To the Artist" by Elizabeth Inchbald, *The Artist*, 1, no. 14, 13 June 1807, p. 16.

9 Paula Backscheider's introduction to *The Plays of Elizabeth Inchbald*, vol. 1, New York, Garland Publishing, 1980, is extremely useful in this regard especially pages xxx and xiv.

10 See "The Purchase of Tickets" and "Keeping Places," in Charles Beecher Hogan's critical introduction to *The London Stage, 1776–1800*, pp. xxiv–xxxiii.

11 Managers during most of the eighteenth century at the main London houses were male, with the exception of a period of several years in the early 1770s during which Mary Anne Yates and Frances Brooke co-managed the King's Opera House, although the legal documents connected to this house are usually signed by the respective husband and brother-in-law of the two women. The only other women involved in theatre management in London are Ann Bracegirdle and Elizabeth Barry during the late seventeenth and early eighteenth century. For a more complete listing of female managers working in provincial English theatres throughout the eighteenth and nineteenth centuries, see Tracy C. Davis, *Actresses as Working Women*, London and New York, Routledge, 1991, pp. 50–52.

12 One interesting exception to this rule is Frances Burney's *Edwy and Elgiva*, although Burney had the advantage of a reputation as a novelist. See Chapter 6.

13 See Backscheider, op. cit., note 8, pp. xxxvii–xxxviii. She writes that in the early part of the final quarter century, only three new

plays a season was the norm; later the number went up to five or six. A "winter" season ran from September through June. For numbers of new plays during the Restoration, see Milhous, op. cit., p. 97 ff.

14 Two key collections of primary documents relating to women's conduct and education in the eighteenth century are *Women in the Eighteenth Century: Constructions of Femininity*, ed. Vivien Jones, London and New York, Routledge, 1990; and Bridget Hill, *Eighteenth Century Women: An Anthology*, London, George Allen & Unwin, 1984.

15 See Nancy Cotton, *Women Playwrights in England c. 1363–1750*, Lewisburg, Bucknell University Press, 1980, p. 123; and John Wilson Bowyer, *The Celebrated Mrs. Centlivre*, Durham, Duke University Press, 1952, pp. 8–9.

16 Jones, op. cit., p. 101.

17 John Homer Caskey, *The Life and Works of Edward Moore*, New Haven, Yale University Press, 1927, p. 8.

18 Richard Cumberland, *Memoirs of Richard Cumberland* (first published in 1856), reissued by Benjamin Blom, 1969, p. 22.

19 See Frederick Link's introduction to *The Plays of Hannah Cowley*, New York, Garland, 1979, vol. 1, p. vii.

20 "It's important to realize that the absence of formal prohibitions against committing art does not preclude the presence of powerful, informal ones." See Joanna Russ, *How to Suppress Women's Writing*, Austin, University of Texas Press, 1983, p. 6.

21 Thomas Gisborne, M.A., *An Enquiry into the Duties of the Female Sex*, London, Cadell & Davies, 1797, p. 2.

22 Ibid., pp. 10–11.

23 Ibid., pp. 12–13.

24 Miriam Rossiter Small, *Charlotte Ramsay Lennox: An Eighteenth Century Lady of Letters*, New Haven, Yale University Press, 1935, pp. 42–43.

25 Gisborne, op. cit., pp. 172–175.

26 *The Deportment of a Married Life*, written by the Honorable E— S—. a few years since to a Young Lady, Her Relation, Then Lately Married, 2nd edn, London, Mr. Hodges, 1798.

27 Ibid., pp. 17, 222, and 225.

28 *Feme covert* was the legal term for a married woman, as distinct from *feme sole*, an unmarried woman. Coverture was the condition or state of a married woman.

29 Susan Staves, *Married Women's Separate Property in England, 1660–1833*, Cambridge and London, Harvard University Press, 1990, p. 229.

30 See Bridget Hill, op. cit., chapters entitled "Women Without Husbands," "Women and Agriculture," "Women in Industry and Other Occupations," and "Female Domestic Servants."

31 "'My Want of Skill': Apologias of British Women Poets, 1660–1800," by Rebecca Gould Gibson, in Frederick M. Keener and Susan E. Lorsch (eds), *Eighteenth-Century Women and the Arts*, New York, Greenwood Press, 1988, p. 79 ff.

32 "Statistical Profile of Women Writing in English from 1660 to 1800" by Judith Phillips Stanton, ibid., p. 247 ff. Stanton's figures correspond closely to my own findings in Bath, which actually pinpoint the rise of productions of plays by women to 1779. See Chapter 4.

33 Delarivière Manley, *Memoirs of the Life of Mrs. Manley*, London, Printed for E. Curl in Fleet Street, 1717, p. 14.

34 Milhous, op. cit., p. 192.

35 Ibid., p. 98.

36 See for example Maureen Mulvihill's analysis of Katherine Philips's career as a playwright. Among other things, Mulvihill shows how complicated for Philips any kind of public recognition was, and how she manipulated it in order to stay within assigned cultural boundaries. "A Feminist Link in the Old Boys' Network: The Cosseting of Katherine Philips," in *Curtain Calls*, op. cit., p. 71 ff.

37 Sara Heller Mendelson, *The Mental World of Stuart Women*, Amherst, University of Massachusetts Press, 1987, p. 190.

38 Maureen Duffy, *The Passionate Shepherdess: Aphra Behn 1640–89*, London, Jonathan Cape, 1977, p. 117.

39 Ibid., p. 287.

40 See Mendelson, op. cit., pp. 187 and 191–192 for a discussion of what constituted culturally approved behavior for women.

41 See Jeremy Collier, *A Short View of the Profaneness and Immorality of the English Stage*, 1698, reprinted Hildesheim, Georg Olms Verlag, 1969.

42 Colley Cibber (1671–1757) managed Drury Lane from 1710– 1740. George Colman the Elder once commented that Cibber "delighted in crushing SINGING BIRDS," by which he apparently meant that Cibber took pleasure in shortening the careers of fledgling playwrights. Quoted by Wally Oulton in *The History of the Theatres of London*, London, Martin and Bain, 1796, vol. 1, p. 162.

43 See his letter to Frances Cadogan in *The Letters of David Garrick*, ed. David M. Little and George M. Kahrl, Cambridge, Mass., Belknap Press at Harvard University, 1963, 3: 1172, no. 1109.

44 See Elizabeth Kowaleski-Wallace, "Milton's Daughters: The Education of Eighteenth Century Writers," *Feminist Studies* 12, no. 2, Summer 1986, p. 275 ff.

45 Ibid., p. 288.

46 The private letters of Frances Brooke and Frances Sheridan in particular give evidence of a consciously critical perspective on Garrick. See Frances Sheridan's letter to Mrs. Victor, dated 1743, four years before Garrick becomes manager at Drury Lane, in which she outlines her objections to how he has critiqued a comedy of hers: "I have the utmost deference for Mr. Garrick's opinion; I think extremely well of his wit, and still better of his discernment in judging what will, or will not succeed with the public; and for his abilities in his own profession [acting], you

know how highly I rate them: yet notwithstanding all this, and that I live too at present in a Roman Catholic country [France], I allow not infallibility to mortal man." *The Private Correspondence of David Garrick*, ed. James Boaden, London, Henry Colburn and Richard Bentley, 1832, vol. 1, pp. 16–17.

47 See Murphy's furious allegations with regard to Garrick in his preface to *Alzuma* (originally produced and published in 1773), currently published in *The Plays of Arthur Murphy*, ed. Richard B. Schwartz, New York, Garland, 1979, vol. 1, n.p.

48 Other scholars will differ from me here. There has been important research on both Elizabeth Griffith and Hannah Cowley by Melinda Finberg, and on Pix, Manley and Trotter by Kendall in her article "Finding the Good Parts: Sexuality in Women's Tragedies in the Time of Queen Anne," in *Curtain Calls*, op. cit., p. 165 ff. See also Kendall's introduction to *Love and Thunder: Plays by Women in the Age of Queen Anne*, London, Methuen, 1988. Kendall points to the eroticism among women that appears in some of their plays, and how theatre history has managed to erase or ignore this important intervention. Paula Backscheider's *Spectacular Politics* also makes a very persuasive argument that the plays, both in the seventeenth and eighteenth centuries, were disrupting hegemonic notions of womanhood (Baltimore, Johns Hopkins University Press, 1993).

49 Fredric Jameson, *The Political Unconscious*, Ithaca, NY, Cornell University Press, 1981, p. 85.

50 *The Times*, also by Elizabeth Griffith, was produced at Drury Lane in 1779 after his retirement.

51 Frances Sheridan (1724–1766) was the mother of Richard Brinsley Sheridan and wife to the well-known theatre manager, Thomas Sheridan. Celisia was the daughter of David Mallet (1705?–1765) a poet and playwright, who collaborated with Arne on operas and wrote a tragedy that was revived by Garrick and performed by him in 1759.

52 *The London Stage* only takes us as far as 1800, so Allardyce Nicoll's handlists are our best source. See Nicoll, *A History of English Drama 1660–1900*, Cambridge, The University Press, 1952, vols. IV and V. Caroline Boaden began producing in 1825, and Mary Russell Mitford wrote a series of tragedies for both the major and minor theatres between 1823 and 1835. Women who followed them include Catherine Grace Gore, whose very substantial career begins in 1831, and Elizabeth Planché, who starts producing in 1833. Anna Maria Hall produced five plays between 1837 and 1845 (at the "minor" theatres). Planché was married to James Robinson Planché, the theatre manager and antiquarian, and Boaden was the daughter of James Boaden, himself a critic and a theatre historian. Only Gore, Mitford, and Hall appear to have entered the profession from the outside.

53 Quoted by kind permission of the Trustees of the National Library of Scotland, MS 9236, letter dated 30 January 1817 to Anne Millar.

54 See *Edmund Kean* by Raymund FitzSimons, London, Hamish Hamilton, 1976, p. 124 ff.
55 Quoted by kind permission of the Glasgow University Library, MS 519/11. Letter to the actor George Bartley, dated 31 March 1819.
56 Glasgow University Library, ibid.
57 Davidoff and Hall, op. cit., p. 13.
58 Ibid., p. 58.
59 Catherine Hall, *White, Male and Middle Class*, Oxford, Polity Press, 1992, pp. 110–111.
60 Ibid., p. 111.
61 Ibid., "The Shop and the Family," pp. 108–121.
62 Davidoff and Hall, op. cit., p. 451.
63 For a very thorough discussion, see Jane Rendall's *The Origins of Modern Feminism 1780–1860*, New York, Schocken Books, 1984.
64 See Katherine B. Clinton, "Femme et Philosophe: The Enlightenment Origins of Feminism," *Eighteenth Century Studies* 8, Spring, 1975, pp. 296–297.
65 Rendall, op. cit., p. 33.
66 Ibid., p. 66.
67 Mrs. Inchbald's surviving diaries are held by the Folger Shakespeare Library, Washington D.C.
68 Quoted from Michelene Wandor's *Carry On, Understudies: Theatre and Sexual Politics*, London and New York, Routledge & Kegan Paul, 1986, p. 128, and cited by Lynda Hart in *Making a Spectacle: Feminist Essays on Contemporary Women's Theatre*, ed. Lynda Hart, Ann Arbor, University of Michigan Press, 1989, p. 1.
69 *The Early Journals and Letters of Fanny Burney*, (1768–1773), ed. Lars Troide, Kingston and Montreal, McGill-Queen's University Press, 1988, vol. 1, p. 2.

## 2 FRANCES BROOKE

1 Brooke attempted to get *Virginia* produced both at Drury Lane and at Covent Garden, but by 1756 it had been turned down by both David Garrick and John Rich, the respective managers. It is not exactly clear when her *Virginia* was actually written, but the published version held by Columbia University, entitled *Virginia, A Tragedy with Odes, Pastorals and Translations* (London, A. Millar for the author) is dated 1756, which suggests that she waited to publish in London until all chances of producing it there were disappointed. I have found reference to a 1754 Dublin edition but have been unable to locate it. Readers of the play will vary in their responses: the play struggles with the conventions of poetic tragedy, but the power of the scenes between Virginia and a woman friend are striking, as is the relative flatness of the male characters. The play is weighted heavily in favor of its female characters, especially Virginia herself, and it's interesting to speculate whether or not this influenced Garrick's decision to finally reject it. James Boaden, a

contemporary theatre historian, believed that Garrick's choices of plays tended to avoid those scripts in which a female character predominated. See James Boaden, *Memoirs of the Life of John Philip Kemble*, Philadelphia, Robert H. Small, 1825, p. 479.

2 *Virginia, a Tragedy,* As it is acted at the Theatre-Royal in Drury-Lane by His Majesty's Servants, London, Printed for J. and R. Tonson, and S. Draper, 1754.

3 *Appius, a Tragedy,* As it is acted at the Theatre-Royal in Covent-Garden London, Printed for A. Millar, and D. Wilson and T. Durham, 1755. Moncrieff's name also appears as "Moncrief."

4 David M. Little and George M. Kahrl (eds), *The Letters of David Garrick*, 3 vols, Cambridge, Mass., The Belknap Press at Harvard University, 1963, vol. 1, p. 208. Letter is tentatively dated 1754 by Little and Kahrl based on the internal references to Moncrieff and his subsequent production.

5 The production opened Thursday, 6 March 1755.

6 *The Old Maid by Mary Singleton, Spinster,* London, A. Millar in the Strand, 1764: "A New Edition, Revised and Corrected by the Editor." Bound copies of the original 1755–1756 editions are held by the British Library. See Lorraine McMullen's biography on Frances Brooke, *An Odd Attempt in a Woman,* for details on the discrepancies between the 1755–1756 editions, and the 1764 revised edition.

7 Spranger Barry (1717?–1777) was a gifted six-foot Irish actor whose relationship with Garrick was a long and sometimes stormy one. He was considered to be Garrick's first rival in a number of roles in addition to *Lear.* A woman commented as follows on their respective performances as Romeo: "Had I been Juliet to Garrick's Romeo, – so ardent and impassioned was he, I should have expected he would have *come up* to me in the balcony; but had I been Juliet to Barry's Romeo, – so tender, so eloquent, and so seductive was he, I should certainly have *gone down* to him!" See Philip H. Highfill, Jr., Kalman H. Burnim, and Edward A. Langhans (eds), *A Biographical Dictionary of Actors, Actresses, Musicians, Dancers, Managers, and Other Stage Personnel in London, 1660–1800,* Carbondale, Southern Illinois University Press, 1973–, vol. 2, p. 330.

8 See pp. 149–150 of the 1764 revised edition of *The Old Maid.* These revised issues still had the original date on the first page (this one is for Saturday, 13 March 1756). The odd syntax of this final sentence suggests that something may have slipped out from the earlier edition, unless the ambiguous reference to "he" means David Garrick, i.e., "which in my opinion Garrick does."

9 Nahum Tate altered King Lear for the stage in 1681 on the advice of a friend, omitting the Fool, inventing a love affair between Cordelia and Edgar, and restoring the happy ending that characterized the original legend.

10 Quoted in "Garrick's Production of King Lear: A Study in the

Temper of the Eighteenth Century Mind" by George Winchester Stone, *Studies in Philology* 45, 1948, p. 93.

11 See Garrick's very warm letter to Foote in 1773, Little and Kahrl, op. cit., vol. 2, pp. 889–890. However, Garrick's feelings must have been mixed. See Little and Kahrl, op. cit., vol. 3, p. 1198, for a letter to Countess Spencer dated 1777, in which Garrick describes Foote as someone with "much wit and no feeling; sacrificed friends and foes to a joke, and so has died very little regretted, even by his nearest acquaintance."

12 Stone, op. cit., pp. 93–94.

13 See "Mrs. Frances Brooke: Dramatic Critic" by Gwendolyn B. Needham, *Theatre Notebook* 15, no. 2, Winter 1960–1961, pp. 47–52.

14 It is of interest that Garrick's subsequent correspondence with Madame Riccoboni began in 1765, just one year after *The Old Maid* had been revised and reissued. Mrs. Brooke was probably capitalizing on the success of her own novel, *The History of Lady Julia Mandeville*, which had come out the year before, in 1763.

15 *The Feminist Companion to Literature in English* cites *Les Lettres de Juliette Catesby* as having been published in 1757; Lorraine McMullen and James C. Nicholls dates the novel's publication at 1759. See *Madame Riccoboni's Letter to David Hume, David Garrick, and Sir Robert Liston, 1764–1783*, ed. James. C. Nicholls, *Studies on Voltaire and the Eighteenth Century*, vol. 149, Oxford, Voltaire Foundation, 1976, p. 15.

16 *L'Année littéraire* 5, 17 August 1764, pp. 172–202.

17 Cited in Lorraine McMullen's *An Odd Attempt in a Woman*, Vancouver, University of British Columbia Press, 1983.

18 Nicholls, op. cit., pp. 45–46. Translations throughout are by Audrey Bibby Donkin.

19 Ibid., pp. 47–48.

20 By 1792, the *History of Lady Julia Mandeville* had gone through ten editions.

21 I am unable to discover whether or not Garrick actually stood to profit from these transactions financially; if, for example, by commissioning a translation himself, he was receiving some form of remuneration from the person receiving the commission. Betty Rizzo states that Garrick routinely edited manuscripts for a fee. See "Depressa Resurgam," in *Curtain Calls*, Athens, Ohio University Press, 1991, p. 121.

22 Nicholls, op. cit., p. 51.

23 Ibid., p. 49: "Pour ce libraire maudit, très maudit, mille et mille fois maudit! . . . The devil take him." ["As for this wretched bookseller, a thousand, thousand times wretched! . . . The devil take him."]

24 Ibid., p. 51.

25 Little and Kahrl, op. cit., vol. 2, pp. 778–779.

26 *Monthly Review*, 47, July 1772, p. 13. I am indebted to Little and Kahrl for unearthing this information.

27 Nicholls, op. cit., p. 19.

28 Quoted by permission of the Houghton Library, Harvard University, MS ENG 1310, p. 23. Letter dated 6 April, n.y. McMullen dates it to *c*. 1772 from internal evidence.

29 Quoted by permission of the Houghton Library, Harvard University, MS. ENG 1310, p. 11. n.d. McMullen dates it to 1772.

30 *The Private Correspondence of David Garrick*, ed. James Boaden, vol. 2, London, Henry Colburn and Richard Bentley, 1832, pp. 167–168. Letter is dated 13 July; from the address (Glanville Street) McMullen has dated it to 1772 or 1773 at the latest, rather than 1776, which was Boaden's best guess although he did not bracket it as such.

31 This correspondence can be found in Boaden, *Correspondence*, op. cit., vol. 1, p. 331, and in Little and Kahrl, op. cit., vol. 3, p. 1163.

32 *The Siege of Sinope* by Mrs. Brooke, T. Cadell, 1781. A printed version and a manuscript version are held by the Huntington Library San Marino, California; the manuscript notes that request for permission to perform was made by Harris on 24 January 1781. The printed version also includes a preface with this comment about Mr. Harris: "to Mr. Harris, my obligations are great . . . his candour and politeness have removed the dragons which have been supposed to guard the avenues to the theatre, and which have too long deterred many of our greatest writers from taking this road to the Temple of Fame" (p. iii). See Chapter 4.

33 *Rosina, A Comic Opera in Two Acts*, London, T. Cadell, 1783. The manuscript copy show that Harris's request for permission to perform was made on 27 December 1782.

34 See *The London Stage, A Critical Introduction* by Charles Beecher Hogan, Carbondale, Southern Illinois University Press, 1968, p. clxxii. Hogan cited play titles but not names of the playwrights when he assembled statistics for the top-grossing plays and afterpieces of the last quarter of the century, so it is impossible to tell whether the plays were written by men or women unless each title is looked up. Women playwrights show up in almost every category.

35 *Marian, A Comic Opera in Two Acts*. Performed at the Theatre-Royal, Covent-Garden. By Mrs. Brookes [*sic*], London, T. N. Longman and O. Rees, 1800. This may be a second edition, although it is not so noted.

36 *The Excursion* by Mrs. Brooke, London, T. Cadell, 1777. Actual date of publication was 10 July 1777. This book originally appeared in two volumes.

37 Ibid., Book V, p. 27.

38 Ibid., Book V, p. 28.

39 Ibid., Book V, pp. 38–39.

40 See Little and Kahrl, op. cit, p. 1172 (to Frances Cadogan, dated 17 July 1777), and p. 1173 (to Dr. Charles Burney, dated 20 July), and also Boaden, *Correspondence*, op. cit., vol. 2, pp. 239–240 for Cadogan's reply, and another reply from Henrietta Pye dated 21 July. Nicholls includes letters from Madame Riccoboni, who sprang

to Garrick's defense on the same subject, tentatively dated 9 November 1777, in Nicholls, op. cit., pp. 420–423.

# 3 THE PAPER WAR OF HANNAH COWLEY AND HANNAH MORE

1 M. G. Jones, *Hannah More*, Cambridge, Cambridge University Press, 1952, p. 52.

2 See Penina Glazer and Miriam Slater's *Unequal Colleagues: the Entrance of Women into the Professions, 1890–1940*, New Brunswick, Rutgers University Press, 1987, for a fuller discussion of professional access for women through male mentors.

3 See Elizabeth Kowaleski-Wallace's "Milton's Daughters: The Education of Eighteenth Century Women Writers" for a discussion of the complexities of literary mentoring for middle-class women in the eighteenth century. *Feminist Studies* 12, no. 2, Summer 1986, pp. 275–293.

4 Lest the parallels to *Lear* appear to be purely literary, it is interesting to recollect that Lear was one of Garrick's most successful roles, and one with which he was personally identified, both by his public and by other actors. Leigh Woods describes an actress who knelt backstage to recieve Garrick's benediction *in character as Lear*. See Leigh Woods, *Garrick Claims the Stage*, Westport, CT, Greenwood Press, 1984, p. 42.

5 See Harry William Pedicord, *The Theatrical Public in the Time of Garrick*, Carbondale, Southern Illinois University Press, 1954, pp. 198–237.

6 Dorothy Celisia, *Almida*, London, T. Becket & Co., 1771, n.p.

7 David M. Little and George M. Kahrl (eds), *The Letters of David Garrick*, 3 vols, Cambridge, Mass., Belknap Press at Harvard University, 1963, vol. 2, pp. 582–583.

8 Ibid., vol. 2, pp. 630–631.

9 Ibid., vol. 2, p. 583.

10 This and all subsequent quotations from Cowley's *The Runaway* are taken from MS LA 402, 1776, Larpent Collection, Huntington Library, San Marino, California.

11 Letter to David Garrick from Hannah Cowley, n.d. MS y. c. 646 (1), the Folger Shakespeare Library, Washington D.C.

12 Little and Kahrl, op. cit., vol. 3, p. 1126.

13 Ibid., vol. 3, p. 1172.

14 *King Lear*, Act I, Scene 1, line 68.

15 I would include male playwrights here; see for example Thomas Harris's opportunistic handling of the playwright Thomas Holcroft, in Cecil Price's essay "Thomas Harris and the Covent Garden Theatre," in *The Eighteenth Century English Stage*, ed. Kenneth Richards and Peter Thomson, London, Methuen, 1971.

16 Hannah Cowley, *Albina, Countess Raimond*, was first printed (with the accusatory preface intact) in 1779. A later edition, printed for

George Cawthorne in 1797, omitted her angry preface but alluded to it as follows: "In prefaces to the first edition of this play, Mrs. Cowley charges the Managers of Drury-lane and Covent-garden theatres with unfair practices while it was in their hands. In this she is not singular. Similar charges have been made by other authors; but, probably, they originated more in their own fancy than in the conduct of the Managers." This quotation is taken from the 1779 first edition, p. v. All subsequent quotations from the *Albina* preface are taken from this edition.

17  Cowley, *Albina*, op. cit., p. ix.
18  William Roberts, *Memoirs of the Life and Correspondence of Mrs. Hannah More*, 2 vols, London, R. B. Seeley and Burnside, 1834, vol. 1, p. 163.
19  *Morning Post*, 9 September 1779.
20  Ibid.
21  Colman the Younger, *The Female Dramatist*, MS LA 598, 1782, Larpent Collection, Huntington Library, San Marino, California.
22  *The Gazetteer*, 18 May 1779.
23  *St. James Chronicle* 8 May 1779.
24  Charles Dibdin, *A Complete History of the Stage*, London, printed by Charles Dibdin, n.d., vol. 5, pp. 303–304.
25  *Morning Chronicle*, 7 May 1779.
26  *St. James Chronicle*, 5–7August 1779.
27  Ibid., 12–14 August 1779.
28  Ibid., 14–17 August 1779.
29  Cowley, *Albina*, op. cit., p. i.
30  Ibid.
31  Ibid., p. vii..
32  For example, see Garrick's letter to More ("My dearest of Hannahs"), Little and Kahrl, op. cit., vol. 3, pp. 1233 and 1254.
33  Cowley, *Albina*, op. cit., p. vi.
34  George Winchester Stone and George M. Kahrl, *David Garrick: A Critical Biography*, Carbondale, Southern Illinois University Press, 1979, p. 434.
35  James Boaden (ed.), *The Private Correspondence of David Garrick*, 2 vols, London, Henry Colburn and Richard Bentley, 1832, vol. 2, p. 315.
36  Little and Kahrl, op. cit., vol. 2, p. 535.
37  Roberts, op. cit., p. 72.
38  Little and Kahrl, op. cit., vol. 3, p. 1166, and Boaden, op. cit., vol. 2, p. 223.
39  Little and Kahrl, op. cit., vol. 3, p. 1165.
40  Boaden, op. cit., vol. 2, pp. 224–225.
41  Cowley, *Albina*, op. cit., p. vii.
42  Ibid.
43  Dibdin, op. cit., pp. 303–304.

## 4 SOPHIA LEE

1 She ventured back into the theatre with a tragedy called *Almeyda* in 1796, but without success, even though Kemble and Mrs. Siddons took on the leading roles. She made one last attempt in 1805, and reports differ as to whether the play (*The Assignation*) survived beyond a first night. Lee's sister Harriet wrote and produced a play called *The New Peerage* at Drury Lane in 1787 which struggled through nine nights but was afterwards not revived.

2 Sophia Lee, *The Chapter of Accidents*, London, T. Cadell, 1782, pp. i–iv. The language of the 1782 fourth edition of the preface is identical to that of the 1780 first edition.

3 See Chapter 3 above.

4 *The Plays of Hannah Cowley*, ed. Frederick Link, 2 vols, New York and London, Garland Publishing, 1979, vol. 1, preface to *The Runaway*. This is a facsimile version of the original, published in London, J. Dodsley, 1776.

5 Catherine Clive, *The Rehearsal, or, Bays in Petticoats*, London, R. Dodsley, 1753, p. 6.

6 Cumberland, Boaden, Murphy, Mallet, Moore, Thompson, Reynolds, Colman the Younger, Bickerstaffe, Holcroft, Home, and Jephson.

7 *The Plays of Richard Cumberland*, ed. Roberta F. S. Borkat, New York and London, Garland, 1982, vol. 2, *The Choleric Man*, p. vii.

8 *The Plays of James Boaden*, ed. Steven Cohan, New York and London, Garland, 1980, preface to *The Cambro-Britons*, pp. v–vi.

9 Sophia Lee's *The Chapter of Accidents* was even imputed at one point to her father, but Genest jovially rebuts the charge, saying that John Lee's efforts to write plays had been so disastrous as to make any such claim poppycock. See *Some Account of the English Stage*, ed. John Genest, 1832, reprinted New York, Burt Franklin, 1965, vol. 6, p. 166. See also Joanna Russ, *How to Suppress Women's Writing*, Austin, University of Texas Press, 1983. In a chapter entitled "Denial of Agency" (pp. 20–24), Russ outlines some of the ways in which successful work by women routinely gets called into question as having been ghostwritten by an unnamed male in the background. It seems to me charges of plagiarism are partly based on the same impulse.

10 Dr. Doran, in his extra-illustrated volume at the Harvard Theatre Collection, calls her "petulant Sophia Lee," David Erskine Baker's *Biographia Dramatica*, London, Longman, Hurst, Rees, Orme and Brown, 1812 (reprinted by AMS Press, New York, 1966) refers to her as "irascible," and Wally Oulton deplores her lack of judgement in striking back at Harris in his *History of the Theatres of London*, 3 vols, London, C. Chapple, 1818, vol. 2, p. 95.

11 Genest, op. cit., vol. 6, p. 381.

12 Quoted by Miriam Rossiter Small, in *Charlotte Ramsay Lennox, An Eighteenth Century Lady of Letters*, New Haven, Yale University Press, 1935, p. 175.

13 Genest, op. cit., vol. 6, pp. 426–428.
14 Ibid., p. 590. See Paula Backscheider's very useful discussion of what exactly Kemble's alterations did to neutralize the impact of the original, in *Spectacular Politics*, Baltimore, Johns Hopkins University Press, 1993, pp. 98–99.
15 Sophia Lee, *The Life of a Lover: In a Series of Letters*, Printed for G. & J. Robinson, 1804.
16 Audrey Bibby Donkin translated and abstracted Diderot's lengthy original for me.
17 One exception to this rule is Hannah More's patronage of Ann Yearsley of Bristol, but this relationship ended in conflict. See Elizabeth Kowaleski-Wallace's *Their Fathers' Daughters*, New York and Oxford, Oxford University Press, 1991.
18 Richard Brinsley Peake, *Memoirs of the Colman Family*, 2 vols, London, 1841, vol. 2, pp. 44–45. Letter is dated 21 February 1780.
19 Hannah Cowley, *Albina, Countess Raimond*, London, J. Dodsley, 1779, p. ii.
20 *Diary and Letters of Madame D'Arblay*, ed. Austin Dobson, 6 vols, London and New York, Macmillan, 1904, vol. 1, pp. 207–208.
21 *The Autobiography, Letters and Literary Remains of Hester Piozzi*, ed. A. Hayward, Boston, Ticknor and Fields, 1861, p. 436.
22 See John Taylor, *Records of My Life*, New York, J. & J. Harper, 1833, p. 224, and James Boaden, *Memoirs of Mrs. Inchbald*, 2 vols, London, Richard Bentley, 1833, vol. 2, pp. 16–17.
23 Clementina Black, *The Linleys of Bath*, New York, Minton Balch, 1926, pp. 33–34.
24 Harris's mistress was the actress Jane Lessingham, whose relationship with him dates from at least 1767. When she died in 1783, she left her estate to Harris in trust for three sons, Thomas, Charles and Edwin, who were probably her children by Harris. Harris had a daughter who died at 15 in 1802, and at least two other sons, Henry, who eventually took over the management of Covent Garden after Harris's death in 1820, and George. These children were born after Lessingham's death, but no record survives of Harris having married anyone in the interim. Colman's mistress was a Miss Sarah Ford, an actress and formerly the mistress of the actor Mossop; her daughter by Mossop became part of the Colman household and an infant performer at Drury Lane in 1761. George Colman the younger was born to Ford and Colman in 1762; in 1768 Colman eventually married Ford, but she died shortly thereafter in 1771. Colman's will, when he died in 1794, left a considerable sum to a Sophia Croker, who was one of several consecutive mistresses after Ford's death. George Colman the Younger, having made a bad early marriage, lived openly with the actress Maria Gibbs from 1795. They are reported to have had one child, and to have married in 1809, but there is no substantiation to the reports of marriage. See Philip. H. Highfill Jr., Kalman H. Burnim and Edward A. Langhans, *A Biographical Dictionary of Actors, Actresses, Musicians, Dancers, Managers, and Other Stage Personnel in London,*

*1660–1800*, Carbondale, Southern Illinois University Press, 1973–, vol. 3, pp. 404–428.

25 Cowley, op. cit., *Albina*, p. vii.

26 *The Plays of Eliza Haywood*, ed. Valerie C. Rudolph, New York, Garland, 1983, *Frederick, Duke of Brunswick-Lunenburgh*, preface, n.p.

27 Clive, op. cit., p. 38.

28 Advertisement cited appeared on 14 December 1780 in the *Bath Chronicle and Weekly Gazette*.

29 Genest, op. cit., vol. 6, p. 83.

30 Ibid., p. 474.

31 David M. Little and George M. Kahrl (eds), *The Letters of David Garrick*, 3 vols, Cambridge, Mass.,The Belknap Press at Harvard University, 1963, vol. 3, p. 1166.

32 Elizabeth Griffith, *The Times: A Comedy*, London, Fielding and Walker, 1780, n.p.

33 Elizabeth Griffith, *The School for Rakes*, London, T. Becket and P. A. DeHondt, 1769, n.p.

34 F. Grice and A. Clarke, "Mrs. Sarah Gardner," *Theatre Notebook*, vol. 7, October 1952–July 1953, p. 80.

35 A brief survey of the *London Stage* index shows Harris having produced three plays by Brooke, eight plays by Cowley, two plays by More, and ten plays by Inchbald. Colman's record (one by Sophia Lee, six by Inchbald, one by Cowley, one by Gardner, and one by Elizabeth Craven) is difficult to compare, since he stepped down from managment in 1789 due to mental illness, many years before Harris. But the record does indicate considerable activity by both men.

36 *The Siege of Sinope* by Mrs. Brooke, London, T. Cadell, 1781, preface, p. iii.

37 "Dragon" was also the name of Garrick's pet dog, to whom Hannah More had written a poem.

38 Harris and Sheridan purchased King's Opera, which had been under the co-management of Frances Brooke and Mary Ann Yates until its sale in 1778. In 1779, James Brooke (Frances's brother-in-law) and the Yateses obtained a judgement against Harris and Sheridan, presumably for lack of prompt payment, and Harris, who saw the writing on the wall, promptly relinquished his share of King's to Sheridan, leaving Sheridan as sole proprietor. See "Thomas Harris and the Covent Garden Theatre" by Cecil Price, in *The Eighteenth Century English Stage*, ed. Kenneth Richards and Peter Thomson, London, Methuen, 1971, p. 113.

39 Grice and Clarke, op. cit., pp. 76–81. For a feminist analysis of this material, see Isobel Grundy, "Sarah Gardner: 'Such Trumpery' or 'A Lustre to Her Sex'?" in *Tulsa Studies in Women's Literature*, vol. 7, number 1, Spring 1988, p. 7 ff.

40 Highfill, Burnim and Langhans, op. cit., vol. 3, p. 423.

41 *The Penguin Dictionary of Economics*, 4th edn, Harmondsworth, Penguin, 1987, p. 299. The dictionary also comments that long periods of price stability intermittently get disrupted by keen price compe-

tition. "The suppliers' behavior is in reaction to their rivals, or what they think their rivals are about to do. Their failure to react as 'perfect competitors' (i.e. undercutting each other in price to get a larger market share) brings about lower output and higher prices. Or, they can collude and act as a monopoly, but this usually ends with one firm cheating on their bargain."

42 James Boaden, *Memoirs of the Life of John Philip Kemble*, Philadelphia, Robert H. Small, 1825, p. 479.

43 See Betty Rizzo's "Depressa Resurgam," in *Curtain Calls*, ed. Mary Anne Schofield and Cecilia Macheski, Athens, Ohio University Press, 1991, p. 120 ff.

44 *The Intimate Letters of Hester Piozzi and Penelope Pennington, 1788–1822*, ed. Oswald Knapp, London, John Lane, 1914, p. 173.

45 See Arnold Hare, *The Theatre Royal Bath: A Calendar of Performances at the Orchard Street Theatre, 1750–1805*, Kingsmead Press, Bath, 1977, p. xii. I am indebted to Arnold Hare and his associates for their painstaking work in assembling this calendar; additionally there was an index at the back by title of play and years performed which made it possible to scan the entire list and transform it into a database with relative ease. The second step was in tagging each playwright according to whether they were contemporary or deceased. My cutoff date here was 1750; playwrights who were alive and actively producing and writing after 1750 were tagged as "contemporary." Playwrights producing and writing prior to 1750 (Susanna Centlivre) were tagged "deceased." There was a small percentage of plays by anonymous playwrights and if authorship could not be confirmed, these were dropped from the database without any significant change in results. Total number of playwrights under consideration, discounting the anonymous ones, was 181. Total number of productions (as distinct from individual performances) was 4,453.

46 Charles Beecher Hogan, *The London Stage, 1776–1800: A Critical Introduction*, Carbondale and Edwardsville, Southern Illinois University Press, 1968, pp. clxxi–clxxiii.

47 Judith Phillips Stanton's figures show a very similar increase around 1779 for productions by women in London, although her figures for that graph (Figure 1) only go as far as 1790. "This New-Found Path Attempting," in Schofield, op. cit., p. 328.

48 Quoted by Rebecca Gould Gibson in "Apologias of British Women Poets," *Eighteenth Century Women in the Arts*, ed. Frederick M. Keener and Susan Lorsch, New York, Greenwood Press, 1988, p. 81.

49 Small, op. cit., p. 36. Letter is dated 25 October 1768.

50 Cowley, *The Runaway*, op. cit., n.p.

51 Peake, op. cit., vol. 2, pp. 99–100.

52 Elizabeth Inchbald, *The Plays of Elizabeth Inchbald*, Paula Backscheider (ed.), New York, Garland Publishing, 1980, n.p. This prologue to *Every One Has His Fault* was written by the Reverend Mr. Nares.

53 *The Rehearsal, or, Bays in Petticoats*, was produced at Drury Lane as Mrs. Clive's benefit in 1750. Shirley Strum Kenny comments about

this play: "Its interest was short-lived because it parodied specific people in the playhouse and it was not a great and lasting piece of theatrical satire." However, in 1750, we can find no woman playwright being produced in London, so her comment, as far as Mrs. Hazard is concerned, cannot be substantiated, at least in London. *The Performers and their Plays*, ed. Shirley Strum Kenny, New York, Garland, 1982, p. xxviii.

54 This incident is reported in Small, op. cit., pp. 37–38 and 54.

55 Prologue to *Percy, A Tragedy*, by Hannah More, 3rd edn, London, Cadell, 1780. Opening night was 10 December 1777 at Covent Garden.

56 Little and Kahrl, op. cit., vol. 3, p. 1010.

## 5 ADVANTAGE, MRS. INCHBALD

1 Colman (the Elder) and Harris had co-managed Covent Garden up to 1774, when Colman finally quit. That business relationship had been fraught with difficulties.

2 All but two of Mrs. Inchbald's plays were produced either at Covent Garden or at the Haymarket; only twice did her good friend John Philip Kemble prevail on her to be produced at Drury Lane where he was associated, in 1791 (*Hue and Cry*) and 1794 (*The Wedding Day*). Two of her plays, *The Massacre* and *A Case of Conscience* were never produced. In the case of *The Massacre*, the contents (which treated the French Revolution) were considered politically incendiary. *A Case of Conscience* fell through the cracks in 1800 when the actors for whom it was written, Kemble and his sister Mrs. Siddons, withdrew temporarily from Drury Lane over a dispute with Sheridan. Mrs. Inchbald herself seems to have avoided Sheridan assiduously.

3 See Chapter 4 for a few details of Gardner's efforts to reposition herself. Later in the early nineteenth century, Maria Theresa Kemble (née DeCamp), wife of Charles Kemble and actress at Drury Lane, wrote several comedies which also blurred the line demarcating amateur status. *The Day After the Wedding*, for example, was written for her husband's benefit in 1808, but continued in the repertory for several years after.

4 In 1788, on 6 May, for example, she describes watching the audience watch her play *Animal Magnetism*: "I behind at *Animal Magnetism* – very good House." But the term "I behind" occurs often in earlier diaries, well before she was produced. The Folger Shakespeare Library, Washington D.C., M.a. 153.

5 All quotations from the diaries are courtesy of the Folger Shakespeare Library, Washington D.C., M.a. 153.

6 Quoted by James Boaden in his *Memoirs of Mrs. Inchbald*, 2 vols, London, Richard Bentley, New Burlington Street, 1833, vol. 1, p. 185. The original letter is housed at the Victoria and Albert

Museum, in the Forster Collection, although it has been mistakenly ascribed to George Colman the Younger.

7 Boaden, op. cit., vol. 1, p. 183.

8 Ibid., p. 185.

9 Ibid., pp. 185–186.

10 See above, Chapter 3.

11 See *The London Stage*, ed. Charles Beecher Hogan, Carbondale, Southern Illinois University Press, 1968–, part 5, vol. 2, 1783–1792, pp. 712–717.

12 Reproduced by permission of the Huntington Library, San Marino, California, MS LA 490.

13 Boaden, op. cit., vol. 1, p. 186. This diary has not survived; Boaden had access to all her papers before they were dispersed during the nineteenth and twentieth centuries. Boaden's report reads: "As an actress in it, she was present at the reading of her own farce, and, under her mask, highly pleased by its reception in the greenroom." At this reading, Inchbald was still masquerading as actress; even her fellow performers did not know she had written the play. The incident is typical of the way she solicited unedited reactions to her work. See also *The Plays of Elizabeth Inchbald*, ed. Paula Backscheider, 2 vols, New York, Garland, 1980, vol. 1, p. xii. Backscheider interprets the "mask" to be literal.

14 See L. W. Conolly, *The Censorship of English Drama*, San Marino, California, The Huntington Library, 1976.

15 This story is related in Boaden, but with certain inaccuracies which get picked up both by Roger Manvell (*Elizabeth Inchbald*, Lanham, Md., University Press of America, 1987) and Backscheider, op. cit. Boaden lists Mrs. Inchbald as appearing in the character of "Selima." No such character exists, either in the manuscript or in the subsequent printed versions. The manuscript lists a eunuch named "Selim" which may have generated the error. Boaden perhaps got his information from an inaccurate newspaper account. The playbills in *London Stage* list Mrs. Inchbald as playing "Irene" from its opening in 1784 through to her final appearance on any stage in September 1789, in the same role at the Haymarket. "Irene" is a character name in the 1784 manuscript, but not in the 1788 printed version, which suggests that the printed version was an unauthorized one.

16 Boaden, op. cit., vol. 1, p. 237.

17 Ibid. This letter also survives in the Forster Collection, Victoria and Albert Museum, but is mistakenly ascribed to George Colman the Younger.

18 Boaden's description of how she handled *Appearance is Against Them* is instructive. See Boaden, op. cit., vol. 1, p. 224.

19 This letter, which is in the Forster collection of the Victoria and Albert, is dated 27 December 1788, and is mistakenly ascribed to George Colman the Younger.

20 Boaden, op. cit., vol. 1, p. 255.

21 Ibid., p. 193. Francis Twiss was a brother-in-law to Mrs. Inchbald's lifelong friend John Philip Kemble.

22 Ibid., p. 209.

23 There is an ironic footnote to this story: *I'll Tell You What* was a script that Colman had rejected when Mrs. Inchbald had submitted it under a female pseudonym several years before. Subsequent to her success with *The Mogul Tale*, she required him to look at it again. This time he saw possibilities in it that he had not noticed previously.

24 John Taylor, *Records of My Life*, New York, J. & J. Harper, 1833, p. 224.

25 As late as 1790, there is a letter from Harris to Mrs. Inchbald which suggests that the flame was not entirely quenched. See Boaden, op. cit., vol. 2, pp. 16–17.

26 Ibid., vol. 1, p. 163.

27 The additional £5.36 may have been overdue interest on some other payment, because Boaden reports the sale at £50 even. British Museum, The Covent Garden Ledgers, EG 2289.

28 Ibid., EG 2297.

29 Ibid., EG 2298.

30 Ibid., EG 2303. It is on the basis of this play and *Wise Man of the East* that Inchbald's reputation for being a high-priced playwright is based. In fact, these were two financial victories in a field of numerous draws and defeats, especially where Harris was concerned.

31 See St. Vincent Troubridge's *The Benefit System in British Theatre*, London, Society for Theatre Research, 1967.

32 Boaden, op. cit., vol. 1, pp. 238–239.

33 This does not include her performance in the pantomimes, which she loathed and was later able to avoid.

34 Her salary was up from £2 to £3 a week. The payments can be verified in the Covent Garden Ledgers, EG 2287.

35 Boaden, op. cit., vol. 1, p. 260.

36 The earliest letter which survives from Harris to Inchbald clearly registers her distaste from the beginning for informal verbal contracts. The letter, although it is not a contract, confirms her employment with him in the Covent Garden acting company. Dated 9 August 1780, held at the Folger Shakespeare Library, Washington D.C., W.a. 169.

37 There is one conspicuous exception: Hannah More mentored Ann Yearsley (Lactilla), a dairy worker in Bristol. Yearsley's poetry and one play circulated with some success. However, Yearsley was unwilling to have More control her earnings from these publications, and she and More parted in anger. See Donna Landry's essay, entitled "The Resignation of Mary Collier: Some Problems in Feminist Literary History" in *The New Eighteenth Century*, ed. Felicity Nussbaum and Laura Brown, New York and London, Methuen, 1987, pp. 99–120.

38 The Folger Shakespeare Library, Washington D.C., M.a. 151.

39 Quoted by Richard Brinsley Peake, *Memoirs of the Colman Family*, 2 vols, London, n.p., 1841, vol. 2, pp. 315–323. Even Peake humorously admits that Colman the Younger got the worst of this argument (p. 319).

40 See Philip H. Highfill Jr., Kalman H. Burnim and Edward A. Langhans, *A Biographical Dictionary*, Carbondale, Southern Illinois University Press, 1973–, vol. 8, p. 78 ff.

41 Carolyn Heilbrun, *Writing a Woman's Life*, London and New York, W. W. Norton, 1988, pp. 11–31.

42 The Folger Shakespeare Library, Washington D.C., M.a. 150.

43 Boaden, op. cit., vol. 1, p. 225.

## 6 FRANCES BURNEY AND THE PROTECTION RACKET

1 James Boaden, *Memoirs of Mrs. Inchbald*, 2 vols, London, Richard Bentley, 1833, vol. 1, pp. 305–306.

2 Richard Brinsley Peake, *Memoirs of the Colman Family*, 2 vols, London, n.p., 1841, vol. 2, pp. 237–238.

3 Catherine Clive, *The Rehearsal, or, Bays in Petticoats*, London, R. Dodsley, 1753, p. 15.

4 In this context it is interesting to note that Elizabeth Inchbald's first meetings about Hannah Cowley's *The Belle's Stratagem* in 1780 were not with Mrs. Cowley, but with Thomas Cowley, her husband, who evidently was sent to explain Mrs. Inchbald's role to her. The Folger Shakespeare Library, Washington D.C., M.a. 150.

5 Mrs. Thrale used "Evelina" instead of "Fanny" as if to suggest a congruence between Fanny and her ingenuous but determined heroine. *Diary and Letters of Madame d'Arblay*, ed. Austin Dobson, 6 vols, London and New York, Macmillan, 1904, vol. 1, pp. 176 ff.

6 Dobson, op. cit., vol. 1, p. 260. She is of course indirectly referring to the character of the playwright, Bayes (the spellings differ), in Buckingham's 1671 satire on heroic tragedy, *The Rehearsal*. Burney had actually seen *The Rehearsal* at Drury Lane in 1772 with Garrick as Bayes, which, because Garrick was himself a playwright of no small reputation, adds a certain interesting layer to her choice of the name. I don't know if she saw or had read Mrs. Clive's satire *The Rehearsal, or, Bays in Petticoats*.

7 This unreliability grew to serious proportions: Sheridan came in for public reprimand by the Lord Chancellor in 1801 for his mismanagement of Drury Lane. The proceedings were reported in "Law Report," *The Times*, 28 December 1801. See *The Journals and Letters of Fanny Burney*, ed. Joyce Hemlow, 12 vols, Oxford, Clarendon Press, 1977, vol. 5, pp. 105–106 for Burney's reaction to the news.

8 Dobson, op. cit., vol. 1, p. 190.

9 The first recorded incident of infidelity that I have been able to verify dates to considerably later, in June 1789, when in her

journal, Sheridan's sister Betsy revealed her embarrassment and upset over her brother's affair with Lady Duncannon (Henrietta Frances, 1761–1821), who was the second child of Garrick's intimate friend Georgiana Countess Spencer: "Opposite to us Lady Duncannon as a *Soeur Grise* casting many tender looks across the table which to my great joy did not seem much attended to." See *Betsy Sheridan's Journal*, ed. William LeFanu, London, Eyre & Spottiswoode, 1960, p. 168. Later that same June, Sheridan was caught with Lady Duncannon, and her husband, Viscount Duncannon, subsequently began divorce proceedings. See *The Letters of Richard Brinsley Sheridan*, ed. Cecil Price, 3 vols, Oxford, Clarendon Press, 1966, vol. 1, pp. 207–208, note 3.

10  Dobson, op. cit., vol. 1, p. 192.

11  Ibid., p. 196.

12  There is a very interesting and puzzling discrepancy between the reports of how Frances Burney's father found out about the authorship of *Evelina*. One report is in Burney's handwriting in her Early Journal (MS. 658) in the Berg Collection of the New York Public Library (and is quoted by Elizabeth Kowaleski-Wallace in her essay "Milton's Daughters" in *Feminist Studies*, vol. 12, no. 2, Summer 1986, p. 275.) It describes a tearful and very dramatic moment in which Dr. Burney "discovers" that the author of the novel is Fanny, and folds his daughter into his arms, almost in a gesture of forgiveness. *The Diaries and Letters* (v.1, ed. Dobson) however, relate a different sequence of events, in which it is Burney's sister Charlotte who breaks the news to Dr. Burney in Frances's absence. I am at present unable to reconcile the two accounts, but the first one suggests an attempt on Burney's part to rewrite the actual sequence of events in such a way that allows for a fantasy of reconciliation to get played out. She may have intuited certain feelings in her father that made this scene of forgiveness necessary.

13  See Margaret Doody, *Frances Burney: A Life in the Works*, Cambridge, Cambridge University Press, 1988, pp. 90–91. In an effort to see for myself what Burney's play was like, I arranged for a staged reading in the summer of 1993 at a theatre history workshop for the Women's Pre-Conference of the Association for Theatre in Higher Education. I distributed a transcription from the Berg manuscript of the opening scene of Act V, in which a group of milliners sit around a table working, talking and eating, and the heroine, Cecilia, enters the room, woebegone because she has been abandoned by her fiancé. It is an awkward moment because the milliners are not insensitive to Cecilia's difficulties, but they also want to be paid for the work they have done on her trousseau. The counterpoint in the scene is Bob, the young son of one of the milliners, who keeps reaching vainly for something to eat and is repeatedly slapped down by his domineering mother. The scene astonished us. It was a joy to perform: it timed out beautifully, it created deliciously controlled comic moments, and it also made a very pointed and thought-provoking contrast between women who

have some control over their livelihoods (the milliners), and women who don't (Cecilia). As a whole we were startled by Burney's evident and very early command of the form, although when I reflect that she had been seeing plays at Drury Lane all her young life, and had especially followed Garrick, who was a family friend, I should not be surprised. Burney comments very astutely in one of her journals about a play that she has seen (*The Masque of Alfred*) on 16 October 1777: "It is a charming Drama to *Read*, but I think it acts very badly." See *The Early Journals and Letters of Fanny Burney*, ed. Lars E. Troide, Montreal and Kingston, McGill-Queen's University Press, vol. 1, p. 312. She evidently knew the difference.

14 Dobson, op. cit., vol. 1, p. 208.

15 Doody comments precisely to the point: "Asking a young lady to write a play seems almost like making a proposal of marriage, necessitating a formal application to the paternal parent. For a well-bred and marriageable young lady to write for the stage was unusual, so daring as almost to rank with sexual activity – it needed sanctions, the approval of the masculine guardian, to make it licit." Doody, op cit., p. 72.

16 Price, op. cit., vol. 1, p. 122. Like Price, I am unable to find a corresponding event anywhere in *The London Stage*, so it is likely that this was a private event of some kind. See also *Letters of David Garrick and Georgiana Countess Spencer, 1759–1779*, ed. Earl Spencer and Christopher Dobson, Cambridge: Printed for Presentation to Members of The Roxburghe Club, 1960, p. 81.

17 Price, op. cit., vol. 1, pp. 121–122. The italics are Sheridan's. Price dates the letter to 10 January 1778 from internal references to the production of Cumberland's *Battle of Hastings*, which opened on 24 January 1778.

18 Quoted from John Watkins, LLD, *Memoirs of the Public and Private Life of the Right Honourable Richard B. Sheridan*, London, printed for Henry Colburn, 1817, vol. 1, p. 242.

19 See Chapter 3 above.

20 *The Private Correspondence of David Garrick*, ed. James Boaden, London, Henry Colburn, 1835, vol. 2, p. 285.

21 Ibid., vol. 2, p. 314. Boaden dates this letter to October 1778, but he is sometimes unreliable. The dating of this one is suspect because by 1778 Sheridan was already "in" and had been in place as manager of Drury Lane since Garrick's retirement in 1776.

22 Quoted from the Harrowby Mss Vol. VII, f 155–6, held by the Harrowby Manuscript Trust at Sandon Hall, Stafford courtesy of Michael Bosson, Archivist, and the kind permission of the Earl of Harrowby.

23 Under Sheridan, Drury Lane during this period produced Mary Robinson (1777–1778), Elizabeth Richardson (1778–1779), Elizabeth Craven (1779–1780), Harriet Horncastle Hook (1783–1784), Harriet Lee (1787–1788), Catherine Cuthbertson (1792–1793), Frances Burney D'Arblay (1794–1795), Sophia Lee (1795–1796),

Maria Theresa DeCamp (1798–1799), and Frances Plowden (1800–1801).

24 Dobson, op. cit., vol. 1, pp. 316–317.

25 Ibid., p. 321.

26 A small irony here: Samuel Crisp's *Virginia* was one of the two versions that got produced in 1754. Crisp's was produced by Garrick at Drury Lane, over Frances Brooke's play of the same name, which was turned down. Crisp's tragedy failed, and it left him permanently embittered about the theatre and Garrick. Brooke, as we know, continued to write, and eventually became an acquaintance of Frances Burney's.

27 See Hemlow, op. cit., vol. 4, p. 395. In a footnote to a letter dated 11 February 1800, the editor comments: ". . . her first comedy 'The Witlings' had been prudently suppressed by CB [her father Charles Burney] and Mr. Crisp because of its daring satire on the blue-stockings." Casual dismissals of this kind are endemic in women's writing and should be carefully weighed.

28 Dobson, op. cit, vol. 5, p. 251. Letter dated 15 April 1795.

29 Ibid., p. 257.

30 *Morning Advertiser*, 23 March 1795.

31 *Morning Herald*, 23 March 1795. Also quoted in *The London Stage*, vol. 3, part 5, pp. 1738–1739.

32 Fanny Burney, *Edwy and Elgiva*, ed. Miriam Benkovitz, Hamden, CT, Shoe String Press, 1957, p. 69.

33 See also Hemlow, op. cit., vol. 3, p. 101.

34 Sheridan himself got caught in the cross-fire, not once but many times. To take one example: the month before Burney's fatal night, on 17 Feburary 1795, the actors staged a similar sabotage of Sheridan's own *School for Scandal*. The prompter William Powell reported: "In mainpiece (*School for Scandal*) the playbill retains Barrymore as Careless, in consequence of which Dignum did the part and sang Sedgwick's song, *who came in time to the Theatre* [Powell's own italics, as if to sardonically indicate a change in routine], but begged to be excused going on from the violent pain he was in, occasioned by a swelling upon his finger. Dignum not in time to be discovered at Lady Sneerwell's rout, but came on after the Scene opened. Fisher, one of the waiters in the above Scene, was absent. Caulfield absent from the scene with Charles and Kelly Jr. not being in time to be discovered with the rest, walked on after the Scene opened." (*The London Stage*, vol. 3, part 5, p. 1729.) It hardly needs stating that this report of late and missing actors indicates a complete breakdown of theatre professionalism and actor morale. In addition, Joe Keller has suggested to me that in the absence of dependable salaries, the prospect of having to learn lines for a new play like Burney's was particularly onerous for the actors, and created great resentment.

35 In addition to heavy theatre debt, Sheridan was also carrying heavy personal debt: *A Biographical Dictionary* reports that in February of 1795, Sheridan had purchased a new house for £4,000 for his

impending second marriage. There were allegations that Sheridan was borrowing money from his own theatre treasury for personal use (see also Drury Lane financial records held by the Folger Shakespeare Library, Washington D.C.).

36 Thomas Campbell, *Life of Mrs. Siddons*, 1839, reprinted Benjamin Blom, New York, 1972, p. 273. This letter is dated 9 November 1796, the year that Kemble finally quit his job of acting manager in disgust, although he continued as a member of the acting company.

37 Price, op. cit., vol. 2, p. 271: Sheridan wrote Charles Fox on 27 December [1793?] that he was reluctant to force Kemble to take on a protégé of Fox's at a time "when he is discharging old Performers on that account and refusing so many other applications."

38 Ibid., p. 271, note 2.

39 The Harvard Theatre Collection holds two notes, one which looks to be in Kemble's hand and which is dated 28 January 1795, and reads: "Madam: As I have never been so fortunate as to find you at home, when I have called at your house to Express my sincere regret for the disquiet I have been the occasion of to you, I beg leave to do it in this Letter; and, at the same time, to assure you, that I shall always Endeavour, by the most respectfull means, to Prove my high opinion of your exemplary Conduct, in every relation of Life. I am, Madam, yr most Obed't & most humble servant, J. P. Kemble." A second note, not in his hand, is dated 27 January 1795, and reads: "I, John Philip Kemble, of the Theatre Royal Drury Lane, do adopt this method of publicly apologizing to Miss DeCamp, for the very improper and unjustifiable behavior I was lately guilty of toward her; which I do further declare her Conduct & Character had in no instance authorized, but on the contrary, I do know and believe both to be irreproachable." Herschel Baker reports on the incident briefly in his biography of Kemble, Boaden's biography of Kemble is at elaborate pains to omit it, and in the information on Kemble included in *A Biographical Dictionary* there is the additional information that after these apologies Kemble then prevented DeCamp from marrying his brother Charles for five years. See also, Hester Piozzi's comments in *Thraliana*, ed. Katharine Balderston, 2 vols, Oxford, Clarendon Press, 1942, vol. 2, pp. 910–911.

40 Burney must have been immediately suspicious. Cumberland's behavior toward other playwrights was notoriously spiteful and malicious. He and Burney had a history that went back to 1779, when he had pointedly ignored her at Mrs. Thrale's, apparently because he found out she had written a play. Burney described him as "burning with ill will," and "not only wish[es] me ill, but [wants to] do me every ill office hereafter in his power." (Dobson, op. cit., vol. 1, pp. 286 and 292). With cheerful malice, she neglected to tell Cumberland that her play wasn't coming out after all, and let him stew.

41 Hemlow, op. cit., vol. 3, p. 109. Letter is dated 10 June 1795.

42 Boaden, op. cit., vol. 2, p. 283.
43 Ibid., pp. 284–285.
44 Ibid., p. 286.
45 *London Stage*, vol. 1, part 5, p. 143.
46 Powell's note for 5 January: "High Life Below Stairs rehearsed at 11, Edwy & Elgiva read at 12." See *The London Stage*, vol. 3, part 5, p. 1717.
47 Then Burney states that she "was in doubt of the play's actual acceptance until 3 weeks after my confinement, when I had a visit from my Brother *who told me he was the next Morning to read the Piece in the Green Room*" [my italics]. Hemlow, op. cit., vol. 2, p. 98, letter dated 15 April 1795. Burney's confinement began 18 December which puts Charles's visit to her with the news of the play's acceptance at roughly 9 January. That date is corroborated by two other letters, one of which is dated 9 January, and states that she is still waiting to hear from Sheridan. The second letter, dated 12 January, makes it clear that she has just heard the news of Sheridan's acceptance, and accordingly is making arrangements to get the manuscript copied. The discrepancy lies in Charles's announcement to his sister that in addition to the play's having been accepted, "he was *the next Morning* [presumably 10 or 11 January] to read the piece in the Green Room."
48 Mrs. Piozzi's entry is begun 17 March, but spills over into the weeks that follow. See Piozzi, op. cit., vol. 2, p. 916.
49 See "The Letters of Sarah and William Siddons to Hester Lynch Piozzi in the John Rylands Library," ed. Kalman A. Burnim, *Bulletin of the John Rylands Library*, Autumn 1963, p. 66, letter no. 13: "Oh there never was so wretched a thing as Mrs. D'arblaye's [*sic*] Tragedy. Even your friend Dr. Delap's was inferior in point of laughable circumstances. She was at the representation in Spite of all I coud [*sic*] Say of the ill effects so much agitation as She must necessarily feel woud [*sic*] have upon an invalid for she has been extremely ill it seem Since her lying in. In truth it needed no discernment to See how it would go, and I was grievd that a woman of So much merit must be So much mortified. The Audience were quite angelic and only laughed where it was impossible to avoid it . . . Her brother negotiated the whole business. I never saw herself, but she went to my brothers the next day and nobly Said, She had been decievd [*sic*] by her friends, that She Saw it was a very bad thing, and withdrew it immediately. That was done like a woman of an exalted Spirit, and has wonderfully raisd her in the opinion of all those who know the circumstances."
50 She published *Camilla*, her third novel, in 1796, and received £1,000 for the copyright.
51 Dobson, op. cit., vol. 5, p. 257.
52 This change of theatre and management also suggests that Sheridan probably never paid Burney what she was owed for *Edwy and Elgiva*. The William Salt Library holds a note dated 15 October 1795, which is signed by "Dr." Charles Burney (an appelation used

by her brother as well as her father) and which states: "Dr. Charles Burney presents his complt's to Mr. Sheridan and begs leave to remind him, that the business of Edwy & Elgiva still remains unsettled. – If Mr. Sheridan will have the goodness to appoint any day and hour that may suit his numerous engagements, Dr. Charles Burney will not fail to have the honour of waiting on him." Sheridan had probably promised a flat sum of money to Burney in compensation for the use of her play, instead of the usual author's benefits. If this was the case, then he would have owed that sum whether or not her play succeeded. Quoted from the Sheridan Manuscripts by permission of the Trustees of the William Salt Library, SMS. 343.

53 The letter, dated 30 October 1799, was sent to Burney by Charles, and in it he reports that Harris has read the play and likes it and offers her a production date in March of 1800. "But Mr. H must see you – & state his objections to some parts – These are his notes." Some particulars follow from Harris about revisions for the script. "Turn over these matters in your mind," wrote Charles, "settle when you can come to Greenwich: and let me have the Fable again one week previous to that time: for H to refresh his memory – and when you are at my house, I will contrive the meeting between you & H who is surprised, that you never turned your thoughts to this kind of writing before: as you appear to have really a genius for it! – There now!" From the Berg Collection, New York Public Library, Scrapbook: Fanny Burney & Family, 1653–1890, section 62.

54 In a letter to Esther Burney (Hemlow, op. cit., vol. 4, p. 361) dated 19 November 1799, Burney makes sly references to "the upholsterer" and to "low tradespeople." Burney referred to her husband very occasionally as "the upholsterer" when they were in the process of furnishing Camilla Cottage, and that reference has to be kept distinct. On Joseph Donohue's suggestion I checked Arthur Murphy's play, *The Upholsterer*, but the main character in this play, an obsessive reader of newspapers, more closely resembles Burney's father than Thomas Harris.

55 Hemlow, op. cit., vol. 4, p. 377.

56 Susanna Phillips died as a consequence of abuse and neglect on the part of her husband, Molesworth Phillips, who transported his family to Ireland and then failed to intervene on her behalf when her health began to fail, or to notify her family. She died in the arms of her brother Charles, en route to London. Her father, and tragically Frances Burney herself, had been instrumental in convincing Susanna not to leave her husband at a time when it probably would have saved her life.

57 Hemlow, op. cit., vol. 4, p. 395.

## 7 JOANNA BAILLIE *VS.* THE TERMITES BELLICOSUS

1 There are two articles in *The Monthly Review* that cast light on this incident: one is a review of Mrs. Plowden's published opera (1801, vol. 36, p. 97), and the other, on the succeeding pages, is a summary of a pamphlet by R. Houlton in which he charges Kelly with having organized the cabal and with running a system of "private influence."

2 *The Feminist Companion to Literature in English*, ed. Virginia Blain, Isobel Grundy and Patricia Clements, New Haven, Yale University Press, 1990, p. 88.

3 1798 was a propitious year in literature: *The Lyrical Ballads* were also published, also anonymously, and also called for reforms, but in poetry. Donald Reisman comments that Baillie's 1798 work "prepared the way for Wordsworth's comments in his Prefaces to Lyrical Ballads." See the facsimile edition of Baillie's 1798 original, entitled *Joanna Baillie: A Series of Plays*, 3 vols, ed. Donald H. Reisman, New York and London, Garland, 1977, vol. 1, p. vii.

4 Joanna Baillie, *The Complete Poetical Works of Joanna Baillie*, Philadelphia, Carey & Lea, 1832, p. 16. This is the first American edition, complete in one volume, and reprints the original prefaces and introductions with a few added footnotes.

5 Ibid., p. 20.

6 Ibid., p. 13.

7 Ibid., p. 17. See also Reisman, op. cit., vol. 1, p. 36.

8 Mary Berry, *Extracts of the Journals and Correspondence*, ed. Theresa Lewis, London, Longmans, Green, 1865, vol. 2, pp. 89–90. I have combined two letters here, written within about ten days of each other.

9 James Boaden, *Memoirs of Mrs. Inchbald*, 2 vols, London, Richard Bentley, 1833, vol. 2, p. 34. Letter to Mrs. Phillips.

10 Clementina Black, *The Linleys of Bath*, London, Martin Secker, 1911, pp. 295–296.

11 Margaret S. Carhart, *The Life and Work of Joanna Baillie*, 1923, reprinted Hamden, CT, Archon Books, 1970, pp. 111–112.

12 Thomas Dutton, *The Dramatic Censor*, London, 1800–1801, vol. 2, p. 139.

13 *The Intimate Letters of Hester Piozzi and Penelope Pennington 1788–1821*, ed. Oswald Knapp, London, John Lane, 1914, p. 173. Mrs. Piozzi was reading the recent travel accounts of people like Browne and Mungo Park, who had just come back from Africa, which may account for her use of zebras and termites in her description.

14 *The Autobiography, Letters, and Literary Remains of Hester Piozzi*, ed. A. Hayward, Boston, Ticknor & Fields, 1861, p. 436. The letter is to Sir James Fellowes, and is dated 28 March 1819.

15 Quoted in Knapp, op. cit., p. 192. Letter to Penelope Pennington dated 16 May 1800.

16 Carhart, op. cit., p. 119. This was reported in the biographical

preface to the second edition of Joanna Baillie's collected works published in London, 1853.

17  A manuscript of *De Montfort* [*sic*] in Campbell's autograph, dated 29 March 1802, with notations and cuts in Mrs. Siddons's handwriting, survives at the Huntington Library, San Marino, California (LA 1287). This apparently was the copy she used for giving solo readings of the play.

18  Quoted by kind permission of the Trustees of the National Library of Scotland, MS 9236, letter to Anne Millar at Millheugh, dated 25 December 1801.

19  Ibid.

20  Ibid.

21  *The British Theatre: A Collection of Plays with Biographical and Critical Remarks by Mrs. Inchbald* (25 vols), London, Printed for Longman, Hurst, Rees and Orme, Paternoster Row, 1808.

22  I have even weighed the possibility that Sheridan might have taken offense at Joanna Baillie's politics or even her brother's, but Baillie's brother, Dr. Matthew Baillie, was routinely in attendance on the King, so it seems unlikely, given Sheridan's long standing as a Tory, that this would have been the case.

23  Dutton, op. cit., vol. 2, p. 160.

24  On the occasion of Kemble's death, she wrote a friend: ". . . during his life I always considered him as being rather unfriendly to me. Perhaps it was my own fault. He was so proud and I may have done something to offend him. I think I once unwittingly did so." National Library of Scotland, MS 3896, letter dated 2 April 1823.

25  Genest simply said of *De Monfort* that "she should have consulted with some person who was conversant with the stage." See John Genest, *Some Account of the English Stage*, New York, Burt Franklin, vol. 8, p. 333. Mrs. Inchbald wrote in 1808 in her remarks to *The British Theatre*: "This drama, of original and very peculiar formation, plainly denotes that the authoress has studied theatrical productions as a reader more than as a spectator, and it may be necessary to remind her – that Shakespeare gained his knowledge of the effect produced from plays upon an audience, and profited, through such attainment, by his constant attendance on dramatic representations, even with the assiduity of a performer." Campbell's comment was "If Joanna Baillie had known the stage practically, she would never have attached the importance she does to the development of single passions in single tragedies; and she would have invented more stirring incidents to justify the passion of her characters." Thomas Campbell, *Life of Mrs. Siddons*, 1839, reprinted New York, Benjamin Blom, 1972, p. 301. On p. 302 Campbell also quotes Kean, who allegedly remarked that "though a fine poem, it [*De Monfort*] would never be an acting play."

26  National Library of Scotland, MS 3880, letter dated 9 July 1811.

27  Joanna Baillie, *Miscellaneous Plays*, ed. Donald H. Reisman, 1804, reprinted New York, Garland, 1977, pp. viii–ix.

28  National Library of Scotland, MS 3878.

29 Ibid., MS 3878.

30 Ibid., MS 3879.

31 Ibid., MS 3879, letter dated 12 February 1810. The exact lines from Wordsworth's "Michael" read as follows:

He [the five-year-old shepherd boy] as a watchman oftentimes
was placed

At gate or gap, to stem or turn the flock;

And, to his office prematurely called,

There stood the urchin, as you will divine,

Something between a hindrance and a help;

And for this cause not always, I believe

Receiving from his Father hire [payment] of praise

Though nought was left undone which staff or voice

Or looks, or threatening gestures, could perform.

32 Volume III in *A Series of Plays* included *Orra*, *The Dream*, *The Siege*, and *The Beacon*.

33 Baillie, *The Complete Poetical Works*, p. 339.

34 Ibid., p. 339.

35 Ibid., p. 337.

36 Ibid., p. 337.

37 *The Edinburgh Review*, February 1812, vol. 19, pp. 265–266. Shortly after the review came out, Baillie wrote Sir Walter Scott in a state of apparent dejection: "Think you there is spirit at all in me now to write Plays of any kind, after all that our great Northern Critic [Jeffrey] hath said of the deplorable dullness & want of interest in those I have already written? I must try what I can do, even under this great gloom of his discountenance . . . it will do me, I doubt not, considerable mischief as far as the present circulation of the work is concerned." National Library of Scotland, MS 3882, letter dated 27 May 1812.

38 The new version of *De Monfort* commissioned by Kean from Baillie appears not to have survived. The last mention I have found of it is in the F. W. Hawkins biography, *The Life of Edmund Kean*, London, Tinsley Brothers, 1869, on page 177, in which Hawkins himself claims to have personal possession of the 1821 revised manuscript. Where the manuscript went after Hawkins's death I have been unable to discover.

39 Baillie actually had initiated some of these changes prior to her talks with Kean. On 7 December 1815 she writes to an unnamed correspondent: "Did I not tell you in a former letter that I have altered *De Monfort* and made the ending more dramatic by killing De Mon. on the stage? and I really think it a great improvement, and Mr. Lamb and Lord Byron (both of the Drury Lane subcommittee) I am told think so too." (National Library of Scotland, MS 3886.) These changes may have been preparatory to Byron's efforts to interest Kean in performing the play.

40 *Drury Lane Journal: Selections from James Winston's Diaries, 1819–1827*, ed. Alfred L. Nelson and Gilbert B. Cross, London, Society for

Theatre Research, 1974, p. 39. Winston's entry is dated 10 November 1821.

41 This letter to Kean survives in the Camden Local Studies and Archive Centre, London Borough of Camden, and is reprinted by their kind permission. The letter is undated, but with the evidence of Winston's notes, and the subsequent rehearsals and production dates, we can be certain Baillie wrote it on Monday, 12 November 1821.

42 Winston, op. cit., entry dated Wednesday, 14 November 1821.

43 *Theatrical Examiner*, no. 459, 2 December 1821, pp. 760–761.

44 Winston, op. cit., p. 40. Entry dated 27 November 1821.

45 *The Monthly Review*, 1800, vol. 32, p. 377.

46 *The Monthly Review*, 1801, vol. 39, p. 97.

47 *The Monthly Review*, 1803, vol. 40, p. 99.

48 *Byron's Letters and Journals*, ed. Leslie A. Marchand, Cambridge, Mass., Harvard University Press, 1982 vol. 4, p. 290, and vol. 5, p. 203.

49 Lord Byron's reference is in a letter dated 30 March 1814 to Lady Melbourne. See Marchand, ibid., vol. 4, p. 87.

50 Francis Jeffrey, *Essays on English Poets and Poetry from the Edinburgh Review*, London, George Routledge & Sons, n.d., pp. 573–576.

51 *The Edinburgh Review*, 1812, p. 290.

52 Jeffrey also mentions Maria Edgeworth and Elizabeth Craven. Craven was produced professionally three times in London, but there is no mention of the plays written by either woman.

53 In this context, I am fascinated to discover that as early as 1808, there was a comedy produced at Covent Garden by Tobin entitled *School for Authors*. It was a satire about playwrights learning their craft; it had a good run of thirteen nights and critics reckoned it deserved even better. No one made any particular mention of the fact that all the playwrights in the play were male.

54 Jeffrey was dismissive of Joanna Baillie's comedies. On *The Election*, one of her early comedies, he wrote: "If Miss Baillie had delighted us less with some passages of her tragedies, we should, perhaps, have had more reluctance in saying that we think she ought to write no more comedies." *The Edinburgh Review*, July 1803, vol. 2, p. 278.

55 For example, see *The Monthly Review*, 1798, vol. 27, pp. 66–69: "The author of this volume [*A Series of Plays*] has more than the merit of good intention. Though his versification is sometimes rugged and inharmonious, and his style has an antientry [*sic*] of phrase which often savours of affectation, yet his characters are in general strongly discriminated and his scenes abound in beautiful passages . . . This volume is prefaced with some very sensible observations on the several provinces of the drama, which we have perused with attention and pleasure."

56 I wonder if the situation wasn't complicated still further by the fact that Baillie was single throughout her life, and therefore in full control of her property and her earnings. This too put her, as it had Mrs. Inchbald, outside of the normal controls, by which a woman's

property and legal identity were absorbed by a male at the moment of marriage.

57 This play, called *The Vespers of Palermo*, had failed at Covent Garden on 12 December 1823, and Baillie wrote on behalf of Hemans to Sir Walter Scott, who took it up to Edinburgh where it was produced again in the spring of 1824.

58 National Library of Scotland. Letter dated 2 September 1812, MS 3883.

59 Sharpe Papers of London University, the University College Library, letter dated only 6 October, but probably written in the 1820s or 1830s. In it Baillie solicits help from the Literary Fund for assistance to a woman named Hedge.

60 Quoted by Carhart, op. cit., p. 65.

61 Quoted in Watson, op. cit., pp. 82–83 from *The Quarterly Review*, November 1810.

## 8 AFTERPIECE

1 See Paula Backscheider, *Spectacular Politics*, Baltimore, Johns Hopkins University Press, 1993, p. 71. She cites the 1695–1696 season.

# BIBLIOGRAPHY

## PRIMARY DOCUMENTS

Bath Central Library, Bath
Bodleian Library, Oxford University.
British Museum, The Manuscript Reading Room, London.
Columbia University Manuscript Reading Room.
Dr. Williams's Library, London.
Folger Shakespeare Library, Washington D.C.
Hyde Collection, Four Oaks Farm, Somerville, New Jersey.
The Garrick Club, London.
Glasgow University Library, Glasgow.
Harrowby Manuscript Trust, Sandon Hall, Stafford, Staffordshire.
Harvard Theatre Collection, Cambridge, Massachusetts.
Henry W. and Albert A. Berg Collection, The New York Public Library, Astor, Lenox and Tilden Foundations.
Houghton Library, Harvard University, Cambridge, Massachusetts.
Huntington Library, Larpent Collection, San Marino, California.
John Rylands University Library, University of Manchester.
London Borough of Camden Local Studies and Archive Centre.
National Library of Scotland, Edinburgh.
National Library of Wales, Aberystwyth.
Public Record Office, London.
Princeton University Library, Manuscript Collection.
Queen's University Library, Special Collections, Kingston, Ontario.
Reading University Library, Whiteknights, Reading.
Royal Academy of Art, London.
Sharpe Papers of London University, the University College Library.
Society of Antiquaries, London.
Theatre Museum, London.
Victoria and Albert Museum, the Forster Collection, London.
William Andrews Clark Memorial Library, Los Angeles.
William Salt Library, Stafford, Staffordshire.

# JOURNALS AND NEWSPAPERS

*L'Année littéraire*
*The Artist*
*Bath Chronicle and Weekly Gazette*
*Bath and County Graphic*
*The Dramatic Censor*
*Edinburgh Review*
*Examiner*
*Gazetteer*
*Gentlemen's Magazine*
*Monthly Mirror*
*Monthly Review*
*Morning Advertiser*
*Morning Chronicle*
*Morning Herald*
*Morning Post*
*Oracle, Public Advertiser*
*Quarterly Review*
*St. James Chronicle*
*Theatrical Examiner*
*Thespian Magazine*


# CONTEMPORANEOUS WORKS

Anonymous, *A Legacy of Affection, Advice and Instruction from a Retired Governess to the Present Pupils of an Establishment for Female Education*, London, Poole and Edwards, 1827.

Baillie, Joanna, *The Complete Poetical Works of Joanna Baillie*, Philadelphia, Carey & Lea, 1832.

Baillie, Joanna, *Joanna Baillie: A Series of Plays*, 3 vols, 1798, 1802, 1812, ed. Donald H. Reisman, reprinted New York & London, Garland, 1977.

Baillie, Joanna, *Miscellaneous Plays*, 1804, ed. Donald H. Reisman, reprinted New York, Garland, 1977.

Baker, David Erskine, *Biographia Dramatica*, Dublin, T. Henshall for Whitestone, 1782.

Berry, Mary, *Extracts of the Journals and Correspondence, from the Year 1783 to 1852*, ed. Theresa Lewis, 3 vols, London, Longmans, Green, 1865.

Boaden, James, *Memoirs of the Life of John Philip Kemble*, Philadelphia, Robert H. Small, 1825.

Boaden, James, *Memoirs of Mrs. Inchbald*, 2 vols, London, Richard Bentley, 1833.

Brooke, Frances, *The Excursion*, London, T. Cadell, 1777.

Brooke, Frances, *Marian, A Comic Opera in Two Acts*, London, A. Strahan for T. N. Longman and O. Rees, 1800.

Brooke, Frances, *The Old Maid by Mary Singleton, Spinster*, revised edn, London, A. Millar, 1764.

Brooke, Frances, *Rosina, A Comic Opera in Two Acts*, London, T. Cadell, 1783.

Brooke, Frances, *The Siege of Sinope*, London, T. Cadell, 1781.

Brooke, Frances, *Virginia, A Tragedy with Odes, Pastorals and Translations*, London, A. Millar for the author, 1756.

Campbell, Thomas, *Life of Mrs. Siddons*, 1839, reprinted New York, Benjamin Blom, 1972.

Celisia, Dorothy, *Almida*, London, T. Becket, 1771.

Charke, Charlotte, *The Art of Management*, London, W. Rayner, 1735.

Clive, Catherine, *The Rehearsal, or, Bays in Petticoats*, London, R. Dodsley, 1753.

Collier, Jeremy, *A Short View of the Profaneness and Immorality of the English Stage*, 1698, reprinted Hildesheim, Georg Olms Verlag, 1969.

Cowley, Hannah, *Albina, Countess Raimond*, London, J. Dodsley, 1779.

Cowley, Hannah, *The Runaway*, London, J. Dodsley, 1776.

Cowley, Hannah, *The Works of Mrs. Cowley, Dramas and Poems in Three Volumes*, Wilkie & Robinson, 1813.

Crisp, Samuel, *Virginia, a Tragedy*, J. and R. Tonson, and S. Draper, 1754.

Cumberland, Richard, *Memoirs of Richard Cumberland*, 1856, reprinted New York, Benjamin Blom, 1969.

Dibdin, Charles, *A Complete History of the Stage*, [1800], reprinted New York, Garland, 1970.

Doran, Dr. (John), *"Their Majesties' Servants:" Annals of the English Stage from Betterton to Edmund Kean*, New York, W. J. Widdleton, 1865.

Fordyce, James, *Sermons to Young Women*, 2 vols, 4th edn, London, A. Millar and T. Cadell, 1767.

Garrick, David, *The Private Correspondence of David Garrick*, ed. James Boaden, 2 vols, London, Henry Colburn and Richard Bentley, 1832.

Genest, John (ed.), *Some Account of the English Stage*, 1832, reprinted New York, Burt Franklin, 1965.

Gisborne, Thomas, M.A., *An Enquiry into the Duties of the Female Sex*, London, Cadell & Davies, 1797.

Gregory, Dr., *A Father's Legacy to his Daughters*, London, W. Strahan and T. Cadell, 1784.

Griffith, Elizabeth, *The School for Rakes*, London, T. Becket and P. A. DeHondt, 1769.

Griffith, Elizabeth, *The Times: A Comedy*, London, Fielding and Walker, 1780.

Hawkins, F. W., *The Life of Edmund Kean*, London, Tinsley Brothers, 1869.

Inchbald, Elizabeth (ed.), *The British Theatre: A Collection of Plays with Biographical and Critical Remarks by Mrs. Inchbald*, 25 vols, London, Longman, Hurst, Rees and Orme, 1808.

Jeffrey, Francis, *Essays on English Poets and Poetry from the Edinburgh Review*, London, George Routledge & Sons, n.d.

Lee, Sophia, *The Chapter of Accidents*, London, T. Cadell in the Strand, 1782.

Lee, Sophia, *The Life of a Lover: In a Series of Letters*, London, G. and J. Robinson, 1804.

Manley, Delarivière, *Memoirs of the Life of Mrs. Manley*, London, E. Curl, 1717.

Mitford, Mary Russell, *The Works of Mary Russell Mitford*, Philadelphia, Crissy & Markley, 185?.

Moncrieff, John, *Appius, a Tragedy*, A. Millar, D. Wilson and T. Durham, 1755.

More, Hannah, *Percy, A Tragedy*, 3rd edn, London, Cadell, 1780.

More, Hannah, *The Works of Hannah More*, London, T. Cadell, 1830.

Oulton, Wally, *History of the Theatres of London*, 3 vols, London, C. Chapple, 1818.

Oulton, Wally, *The History of the Theatres of London*, London, Martin and Bain, 1796.

Peake, Richard Brinsley, *Memoirs of the Colman Family*, 2 vols, London, n.p., 1841.

Piozzi, Hester Lynch Thrale, *The Autobiography, Letters and Literary Remains of Hester Piozzi*, ed. A. Hayward, Boston, Ticknor and Fields, 1861.

Roberts, William, *Memoirs of the Life and Correspondence of Mrs. Hannah More*, 2 vols, London, R. B. Seeley and Burnside, 1834.

Robinson, Mary Darby, *Thoughts on the Condition of Women and on the Injustice of Mental Subordination*, first published under the pseudonym Anne Frances Randall, London, Longman, Rees, 1799.

S—, The Honourable E—, *The Deportment of a Married Life, written a few years since to a Young Lady, Her Relation, Then Lately Married*, 2nd edn, London, Mr. Hodges, 1798.

Saville, R. H. George Lord, *The Lady's New-Year's Gift, or, Advice to a Daughter*, 10th edn, London, D. Midwinter, 1724.

Taylor, John, *Records of My Life*, New York, J. & J. Harper, 1833.

Thompson, Henry, *The Life of Hannah More, with Notices of her Sisters*, Philadelphia, E. L. Carey & A. Hart, 1838.

Watkins, John, *Memoirs of the Public and Private Life of the Right Honourable Richard B. Sheridan*, London, printed for Henry Colburn, 1817.

Wilkinson, Tate, *The Wandering Patentee, or, A History of the Yorkshire Theatres*, York, Wilson, Spence and Mawman, 1795.

## SECONDARY WORKS

Anonymous, *The Female Wits*, introduction by Lucyle Hook, Los Angeles, Augustan Reprint Society, Publication Number 124, 1967.

Backscheider, Paula (ed.), *The Plays of Elizabeth Inchbald*, New York, Garland Publishing, 1980.

Backscheider, Paula, *Spectacular Politics*, Baltimore, Johns Hopkins University Press, 1993.

Baker, Herschel Clay, *John Philip Kemble: the Actor in his Theatre*, Cambridge, Mass., Harvard University Press, 1942.

Balderston, Katherine C. (ed.), *Thraliana: The Diary of Mrs. Hester Lynch Thrale*, 2 vols, Oxford at the Clarendon Press, 1942.

Black, Clementina, *The Linleys of Bath*, New York, Minton, Balch, 1926.

Borkat, Roberta F. S. (ed.), *The Plays of Richard Cumberland*, New York and London, Garland, 1982.

Bowyer, John Wilson, *The Celebrated Mrs. Centlivre*, Durham, NC, Duke University Press, 1952.

Burford, E. J., *Wits, Wenchers and Wantons, London's Low Life: Covent Garden in the Eighteenth Century*, London, Robert Hale, 1986.

Burney, Fanny, *A Busy Day*, ed. Tara Ghoshal Wallace, New Brunswick, NJ, Rutgers University Press, 1984.

Burney, Fanny, *Edwy and Elgiva*, ed. Miriam Benkovitz, Hamden, CT, Shoe String Press, 1957.

Burnim, Kalman A. (ed.), "The Letters of Sarah and William Siddons to Hester Lynch Piozzi in the John Rylands Library," *Bulletin of the John Rylands Library*, Autumn 1963.

Carhart, Margaret S., *The Life and Work of Joanna Baillie*, 1923, reprinted Hamden, CT, Archon Books, 1970.

Carswell, Donald, *Sir Walter: A Four-Part Study in Biography*, London, J. Murray, 1930.

Caskey, John Homer, *The Life and Works of Edward Moore*, New Haven, Yale University Press, 1927.

Cave, Richard Allen (ed.), *The Romantic Theatre*, Totowa, NJ, Barnes and Noble Books, 1987.

Clinton, Katherine B., "Femme et Philosophe: The Enlightenment Origins of Feminism," *Eighteenth Century Studies*, Spring, 1975, vol. 8.

Cohan, Steven (ed.), *The Plays of James Boaden*, New York and London, Garland, 1980.

Conolly, L. W., *The Censorship of English Drama*, San Marino, Calif., The Huntington Library, 1976.

Cotton, Nancy, *Women Playwrights in England c. 1363–1750*, Lewisburg, Bucknell University Press, 1980.

Davidoff, Leonore and Hall, Catherine, *Family Fortunes: Men and Women of the English Middle Class, 1780–1850*, Chicago, University of Chicago Press, 1987.

Davis, Tracy C., *Actresses as Working Women*, London and New York, Routledge, 1991.

Dobson, Austin (ed.), *Diary and Letters of Madame D'Arblay*, 6 vols, London and New York, Macmillan, 1904.

Donohue, Joseph, *Theatre in the Age of Kean*, Oxford, Blackwell, 1975.

Doody, Margaret, *Frances Burney: A Life in the Works*, Cambridge, Cambridge University Press, 1988.

Duffy, Maureen, *The Passionate Shepherdess: Aphra Behn 1640–89*, London, Jonathan Cape, 1977.

East, Joyce, "The Dramatic Works of Hannah Cowley," Ph.D. dissertation, University of Kansas, 1979.

East, Joyce E., "Mrs. Hannah Cowley, Playwright," *Eighteenth Century Women in the Arts*, ed. Frederick M. Keener and Susan Lorsch, New York, Greenwood Press, 1988.

Evans, Bertrand, *Gothic Drama from Walpole to Shelley*, Berkeley and Los Angeles, University of California Press, 1947.

Fitzgerald, Percy Hetherington, *The Kembles*, London, Tinsley Brothers, 1871.

FitzSimons, Raymund, *Edmund Kean*, London, Hamish Hamilton, 1976.

Gibson, Rebecca Gould, "'My Want of Skill:' Apologias of British Women Poets, 1660–1800," *Eighteenth Century Women in the Arts*, ed. Frederick M. Keener and Susan Lorsch, New York, Greenwood Press, 1988.

Glazer, Penina and Slater, Miriam, *Unequal Colleagues: the Entrance of Women into the Professions, 1890–1940*, New Brunswick, NJ, Rutgers University Press, 1987.

Gray, Charles Harold, *Theatrical Criticism in London to 1795*, New York, Columbia University Press, 1931.

Grice, F. and Clarke, A., "Mrs. Sarah Gardner," *Theatre Notebook*, October 1952–July 1953, vol. 7.

Grundy, Isobel, "Sarah Gardner: 'Such Trumpery' or 'A Lustre to Her Sex'?" *Tulsa Studies in Women's Literature*, Spring 1988, vol. 7.

Hall, Catherine, *White, Male and Middle Class*, Oxford, Polity Press, 1992.

Hare, Arnold, *The Theatre Royal Bath: A Calendar of Performances at the Orchard Street Theatre, 1750–1805*, Kingsmead Press, Bath, 1977.

Hart, Lynda (ed.), *Making a Spectacle: Feminist Essays on Contemporary Women's Theatre*, Ann Arbor, University of Michigan Press, 1989.

Heilbrun, Carolyn, *Writing a Woman's Life*, London and New York, W. W. Norton, 1988.

Hemlow, Joyce, *et al.* (eds), *The Journals and Letters of Fanny Burney*, 12 vols, Oxford, Clarendon Press, 1977.

Hett, Francis Paget (ed.), *The Memoirs of Susan Sibbald (1783–1812)*, New York, Minton Balch, 1926.

Highfill, Philip H. Jr., Burnim, Kalman A. and Langhans, Edward A., *A Biographical Dictionary of Actors, Actresses, Musicians, Dancers, Managers, and Other Stage Personnel in London, 1660–1800*, Carbondale, Southern Illinois University Press, 1973–.

Hill, Bridget, *Eighteenth Century Women: An Anthology*, London, George Allen & Unwin, 1984.

Hill, Bridget, *Women, Work and Sexual Politics in Eighteenth Century England*, London, Blackwell, 1989.

Hillebrand, Harold Newcomb, *Edmund Kean*, New York, Columbia University Press, 1933.

Hogan, Charles Beecher, *et al.*, (eds), *The London Stage*, Carbondale, Southern Illinois University Press, 1968.

Hume, Robert D. (ed.), *The London Theatre World*, Carbondale, Southern Illinois University Press, 1980.

Insch, A. G., "Joanna Baillie's *De Monfort* in Relation to Her Theory of Tragedy," *Durham University Journal*, 1962, vol. 54.

Jameson, Fredric, *The Political Unconscious*, Ithaca, NY, Cornell University Press, 1981.

228

Jones, M. G., *Hannah More*, Cambridge, Cambridge University Press, 1952.

Jones, Vivien (ed.), *Women in the Eighteenth Century: Constructions of Femininity*, London and New York, Routledge, 1990.

Keener, Frederick M. and Lorsch, Susan E. (eds), *Eighteenth-Century Women and the Arts*, New York, Greenwood Press, 1988.

Kelly, Gary, *The English Jacobin Novel: 1780–1805*, Oxford, Clarendon Press, 1976.

Kendall (ed.), *Love and Thunder: Plays by Women in the Age of Queen Anne*, London, Methuen, 1988.

Kenny, Shirley Strum (ed.), *The Performers and their Plays*, New York, Garland, 1982.

Knapp, Oswald (ed.), *The Intimate Letters of Hester Piozzi and Penelope Pennington, 1788–1822*, London, John Lane, 1914.

Korshin, Paul J., "Types of Eighteenth Century Literary Patronage," *Eighteenth Century Studies*, Summer 1974, vol. 7.

Kowaleski-Wallace, Elizabeth, "Milton's Daughters: The Education of Eighteenth Century Writers," *Feminist Studies*, Summer 1986, vol. 12.

Kowaleski-Wallace, Elizabeth, *Their Fathers' Daughters: Hannah More, Maria Edgeworth and Patriarchal Complicity*, New York and Oxford, Oxford University Press, 1991.

Lamb, Virginia, "Joanna Baillie's Plays on the Passions Viewed in Relation to her Dramatic Theories," Ph.D. dissertation, Kent State University, 1973.

Landry, Donna "The Resignation of Mary Collier: Some Problems in Feminist Literary History," *The New Eighteenth Century*, ed. Felicity Nussbaum and Laura Brown, New York and London, Methuen, 1987.

LeFanu, William (ed.), *Betsy Sheridan's Journal*, London, Eyre & Spottiswoode, 1960.

Link, Frederick (ed.), *The Plays of Hannah Cowley*, 2 vols, New York, Garland Publishing, 1979.

Little, David M. and Kahrl, George M. (eds), *The Letters of David Garrick*, Cambridge, Mass., Belknap Press at Harvard University, 1963.

Manvell, Roger, *Elizabeth Inchbald*, Lanham, Md., University Press of America, 1987.

Marchand, Leslie, *Byron: A Biography*, 2 vols, New York, Alfred A. Knopf, 1957.

Marchand, Leslie A. (ed.), *Byron's Letters and Journals*, Cambridge, Mass., Harvard University Press, 1982.

McMullen, Lorraine, *An Odd Attempt in a Woman*, Vancouver, University of British Columbia Press, 1983.

Mendelson, Sara Heller, *The Mental World of Stuart Women*, Amherst, University of Massachusetts Press, 1987.

Meynell, Alice Christiana Thompson, *The Second Person Singular, and Other Essays*, London and New York, Oxford University Press, 1922.

Milhous, Judith, *Thomas Betterton and the Management of Lincoln's Inn Fields, 1695–1708*, Carbondale, Southern Illinois University Press, 1979.

Morgan, Fidelis with Charlotte Charke, *The Well-Known Troublemaker: a Life of Charlotte Charke*, London, Faber, 1988.

Morley, Edith J. (ed.), *Henry Crabb Robinson on Books and their Writers*, London, J. M. Dent & Sons, 1938.

Nalbach, Daniel, *The King's Theatre, 1704–1867*, London, Society for Theatre Research, 1972.

Needham, Gwendolyn B., "Mrs. Frances Brooke: Dramatic Critic," *Theatre Notebook*, Winter 1960–1961, vol. 15.

Nelson, Alfred L. and Cross, Gilbert B. (eds), *Drury Lane Journal: Selections from James Winston's Diaries, 1819–1827*, London, Society for Theatre Research, 1974.

Nicholls, James C. (ed.), *Madame Riccoboni's Letters to David Hume, David Garrick, and Sir Robert Liston, 1764–1783, Studies on Voltaire and the Eighteenth Century*, vol. 149, Oxford, Voltaire Foundation, 1976.

Nicoll, Allardyce, *A History of English Drama 1660–1900*, Cambridge, The University Press, 1952.

Pearson, Jacqueline, *The Prostituted Muse: Images of Women and Women Dramatists, 1642–1737*, New York, St. Martin's Press, 1988.

Pedicord, Harry William, *The Theatrical Public in the Time of Garrick*, Carbondale, Southern Illinois University Press, 1954.

Polwhele, Elizabeth, *The Frolicks, or the Lawyer Cheated*, 1671, ed. Judith Milhous and Robert Hume, Ithaca, NY, Cornell University Press, 1977.

Price, Cecil (ed.), *The Letters of Richard Brinsley Sheridan*, 3 vols, Oxford, Clarendon Press, 1966.

Price, Cecil, "Thomas Harris and the Covent Garden Theatre," *The Eighteenth Century English Stage*, ed. Kenneth Richards and Peter Thomson, London, Methuen, 1971.

Prosky, Ida, *You Don't Need Four Women to Play Shakespeare: Bias in Contemporary American Theatre*, Jefferson, NC, McFarland, 1992.

Purinton, Marjean D., *Romantic Ideologies Unmasked: The Mentally Constructed Tyrannies in Dramas of William Wordsworth, Lord Byron, Percy Shelley, and Joanna Baillie*, Newark, NJ, University of Delaware Press, 1994.

Rendall, Jane, *The Origins of Modern Feminism 1780–1860*, New York, Schocken Books, 1984.

Rizzo, Betty, "Depressa Resurgam," *Curtain Calls*, ed. Mary Anne Schofield and Cecilia Macheski, Athens, Ohio University Press, 1991.

Robinson, Mary Darby, *Memoirs of the Late Mrs. Robinson*, written by herself, London, Cobden-Sanderson, 1930.

Rudolph, Valerie C. (ed.), *The Plays of Eliza Haywood*, New York, Garland, 1983.

Russ, Joanna, *How to Suppress Women's Writing*, Austin, University of Texas Press, 1983.

Schofield, Marianne and Macheski, Cecilia (eds), *Curtain Calls*, Athens, Ohio University Press, 1991.

Schwartz, Richard B. (ed.), *The Plays of Arthur Murphy*, 2 vols, New York, Garland, 1979.

Scott, Sir Walter, *The Letters of Sir Walter Scott,* H. J. C. Grierson (ed.), 12 vols, London, Constable, 1932–1937.

Scott, Sir Walter, *Some Unpublished Letters of Sir Walter Scott, from the Collection in the Brotherton Library,* Oxford, Basil Blackwell, 1932.

Small, Miriam Rossiter, *Charlotte Ramsay Lennox: An Eighteenth Century Lady of Letters,* New Haven, Yale University Press, 1935.

Spencer, Earl and Dobson, Christopher (eds), *Letters of David Garrick and Georgiana Countess Spencer, 1759–1779,* Cambridge: Printed for Presentation to Members of The Roxburghe Club, 1960.

Stanton, Judith Phillips, "Statistical Profile of Women Writing in English from 1660–1800," *Eighteenth Century Women and the Arts,* ed. Frederick M. Keener and Susan E. Lorsch, New York, Greenwood Press, 1988.

Stanton, Judith Phillips, "This New-Found Path Attempting," *Curtain Calls,* ed. Marianne Schofield and Cecilia Macheski, Athens, Ohio University Press, 1991.

Staves, Susan, *Married Women's Separate Property in England, 1660–1833,* Cambridge and London, Harvard University Press, 1990.

Stone, George Winchester, "Garrick's Production of King Lear: A Study in the Temper of the Eighteenth Century Mind," *Studies in Philology,* 1948, vol. 45.

Stone, George Winchester and Kahrl, George M., *David Garrick: A Critical Biography,* Carbondale, Southern Illinois University Press, 1979.

Straub, Kristina, *Divided Fictions: Fanny Burney and Feminine Strategy,* Lexington, University Press of Kentucky, 1987.

Straub, Kristina, *Sexual Suspects: Eighteenth Century Players and Sexual Ideology,* Princeton, NJ, Princeton University Press, 1992.

Troide, Lars (ed.), *The Early Journals and Letters of Fanny Burney,* (1768–1773), Kingston and Montreal, McGill-Queen's University Press, 1988.

Troubridge, St. Vincent, *The Benefit System in British Theatre,* London, Society for Theatre Research, 1967.

Tuchman, Gaye, with Nina E. Fortin, *Edging Women Out: Victorian Novelists, Publishers and Social Change,* New Haven, Yale University Press, 1989.

Wandor, Michelene, *Carry On, Understudies,* London and New York, Routledge & Kegan Paul, 1986.

Ware, Ciji, *Wicked Company,* New York, Bantam, 1992.

Watkins, Daniel, *A Materialist Critique of English Romantic Drama,* Gainesville, University of Florida Press, 1993.

Watson, Vera, *Mary Russell Mitford,* London, Evan Brothers, n.d.

Woods, Leigh, *Garrick Claims the Stage,* Westport, CT, Greenwood Press, 1984.

Zall, P. M., "The Cool World of Samuel Taylor Coleridge: The Question of Joanna Baillie," *The Wordsworth Circle,* Winter 1982, vol. 13.

# INDEX

Note: Figures in *italics* refer to illustrations.